IN THE OWNER'S CHAIR

Success Strategies
for Building
Your Small Business

Ronald W. Torrence

Prentice Hall, Englewood Cliffs, New Jersey 07632

Library of Congress Cataloging-in-Publication Data

Torrence, Ronald W.
    In the owner's chair : success strategies for building your small
business / Ronald W. Torrence.
        p.   cm.
    Includes index.
    ISBN 0-13-492216-6
    1. Small business—Management.   I. Title.
HD62.7.T67   1992
    658.02'2—dc20   91-3719
                        CIP

Editorial/production supervision
  and interior design: *Harriet Tellem*
Cover design: *Lundgren Graphics*
Prepress buyers: *Mary E. McCartney/Kelly Behr*
Manufacturing buyer: *Susan Brunke*
Acquisitions editors: *Bernard M. Goodwin/John Willig*
Editorial assistant: *Maureen Diana*

Previously published as *IN THE OWNER'S CHAIR: Proven Techniques for Taking Your Business from Zero to $10 Million.*

The publisher offers discounts on this book when ordered
in bulk quantities. For more information, write:
    Special Sales/Professional Marketing
    Prentice-Hall, Inc.
    Professional & Technical Reference Division
    Englewood Cliffs, New Jersey 07632

Printed in the United States of America
10 9 8 7 6 5 4 3 2 1

ISBN 0-13-492216-6

Prentice-Hall International (UK) Limited, *London*
Prentice-Hall of Australia Pty. Limited, *Sydney*
Prentice-Hall Canada Inc., *Toronto*
Prentice-Hall Hispanoamericana, S.A., *Mexico*
Prentice-Hall of India Private Limited, *New Delhi*
Prentice-Hall of Japan, Inc., *Tokyo*
Simon & Schuster Asia Pte. Ltd., *Singapore*
Editora Prentice-Hall do Brasil, Ltda., *Rio de Janeiro*

Dedication

To Joan
and to Kathleen, Katherine, Daniel, and Kimberly

Contents

Foreword

At the outset of the 1990s there are more competitors chasing fewer sales dollars. The explosive sales and easy profits of the 1980s are gone. The entrepreneurs who market-market-market will be the success stories of the new decade. Those who sell relentlessly, who stay in the marketplace day after day searching out the shifting sales dollar, will take business away from the competition.

Economists expect the American pie to grow slowly. If you're to be a 1990s success story, you have to get a larger piece of that pie by being better than the competition. When I wrote *In Owner's Chair* in the mid-80s, I outlined the basics to making a success of your own business—the lessons I'd learned in over fifteen years of advising business owners. These basics of success are now more important than ever.

This new edition contains the original basics plus powerful new ideas, such as the "marketing strategy umbrella" and the "financial health check"—perspectives I've gained from over twenty years of working with business owners. I invite you to "pick over" this book for ideas and tools to help you and your business grow profitably.

Best of luck in achieving success!

Preface

I have had the privilege of working with entrepreneurs for twenty years. I have known the exhilaration of being an advisor to businesses that have achieved significant success, the owners becoming multimillionaires in the process. I have witnessed the despair of failure, that abrupt, irrevocable terminating of the enterprise that ends the owner's hopes, dreams, and livelihood, at least for a while. Afterwards, most of them survive.

Sometimes we fought for survival at the brink of failure, when the assets of the corporation seemed to be flowing down the drain like water rushing down a sewer. But we bit, gnawed, and clawed our way through to life many times to find great success in the following years.

Frequently we arranged financing when previous requests had been rejected. Crucial bank loans, sometimes venture capital, were injected into the corporation to act as levers to a new era of growth and profitability.

We've hammered relentlessly to develop realistic but ambitious goals and objectives, to render a clear, powerful statement of marketing strategy, based on the drudgery of market analysis and the drudgery of weighing the pros and cons of each factor contained in the company's marketing resources. We've gained control of job costs, established budgets and profit plans to manage for greater profitability, and constructed cash management to put the owner in control of the company's life blood.

We've reorganized to get a grip on operations for companies which have blasted through several stages of growth in a year or two. We've regained control by establishing comprehensive management control programs focused on the critical variables for success. We've dealt with the psychological problems for success. We've dealt with the psychological problems of entrepreneurship, the stresses of both failure and success. Even the seemingly intractable breakdowns in communication between owner and managers can be untangled to find a new movement toward innovation and achievement.

Our report card has mixed grades. Sometimes the results were splendid across the board—marketing, profit management, cash-flow management, financing, organization, and management development. Sometimes we did well at some, not so well at others. Occasionally we couldn't get anything to stick . . . there seemed to be an incapacity to achieve improvements.

These efforts took place in retailing, wholesaling, manufacturing, construction, government contracting, state-of-the-art electronics, microbiological laboratories, computer technology, cleaning and maintenance services, a master mechanic's garage, a modeling agency, importers, exporters, printing, consulting, nonprofit organizations, you name it. Some of the businesses were start-up ventures, some a few years old, some several years old, and a couple were family companies forty years and older.

Through the success and failure, the splendid results, the partial achievements, the times it didn't stick, some constants have emerged—factors, characteristics, management moves, tools, and techniques that promote success when they are present and failure when they are absent.

I have written this book out of my experiences. My intent is to focus on what I have seen that led entrepreneurs to success in many different industries. I report on what has led other entrepreneurs to failure at the same time. This is a book about the life and death of enterprises. Those of us who have been at it for enough time know that success is truly here today and gone tomorrow. We have to get out and re-create ourselves month after month, year after year. It isn't easy, never was, never will be.

Every entrepreneur I have known, including the ones who didn't make it, had a core of skills in running their businesses. You can't go out and start a business from scratch and build it up to a hundred thousand, hundreds of thousands, millions, tens of millions of dollars, without being an exceptional person, no matter whether you ultimately fail, achieve great success, or just muddle through.

This book focuses on the core of skills most entrepreneurs bring to their companies. It addresses the gaps in their knowledge of management, issues essential to making it or not making it, along with what they have been able to do well all along. To the extent that I have succeeded, reading this book will alert business owners and those who work with them to the areas they must deal with, right away, to bring the management of their enterprises up to a high level.

In running your own business, you don't have the luxury of making many mistakes. I hope this book will help you screen your own management for those areas where you are most vulnerable to trouble. I don't propose magical or fancy solutions, but some common sense which has worked consistently for twenty years.

Acknowledgments

My thanks to George Sass, President of Sass Associates Advertising who completed the Marketing Matrix for me.

1

Realize You Are Faced with Many Unknowns

SMALL BUSINESS IS THE LAST FRONTIER

When you start a business, you enter uncharted territory. There's that moment of panic when you wonder if you've made a terrible mistake. Surely the time and money you are about to put into your venture will be lost. But stronger is the dream, or you wouldn't have chanced it in the first place. The anxiety will return again, as economic conditions change or as competition takes part of your share of the market, or as your expansion costs exceed the sales which follow. Sometimes an entrepreneur's worst fears become reality.

The entrepreneur operates in a hostile environment, where banks charge the highest rate to the smallest companies. Where government regulations favor big business and make life harder and more costly for the small. Where increasingly big business is invading the small company's market to get that extra sales dollar.

The entrepreneur has to be a marketing strategist, a good salesperson, a specialist in the products or services the business offers, a financial manager, a psychologist, a lawyer, even a bit of an economist. "Many are called but few are chosen," is particularly applicable. Fifty percent of small businesses fail within their first year. Within

1

five years, seventy-five percent are gone for one reason or another. Yet some of the most successful people in our society made it with a small business. For those with an entrepreneurial bent, there's no other way. Once you've tasted working for yourself, it's extremely difficult to go back to working for someone else. In many ways, managing your own business is America's last frontier.

What are those factors, at the heart of running a business, that make the difference between success and failure? What some owners do or don't do that enables them to make it, whether it is at the start-up, during the initial years, or when the enterprise is pushing into middle size? The purpose of this book, as I have said, is to provide some answers to that question, in terms of fundamental, day-to-day management.

Everyone Starts with the Dream

Dick Wilson sat back on his couch and looked over his three companions. Simultaneously each opened a can of beer.

"Should we do it?"

Silence answered him at first. Then Bob Green cleared his throat.

"I never thought I'd be involved in starting a business." He took a sip of beer. "I don't know. What if it doesn't work? What will we do for jobs? And I can't afford to lose the money. I don't know. I think it's a good idea. I think we can get the contract. But the risk. . . ."

Arnie Johnson thumped the table.

"We've gone through all this! It's time to decide, and I'm in. Let's do it!"

Bob shook his head, along with Blake Edwards. He obviously answered for both.

"I can't take the risk. My job and an investment, too. . . " He shook his head again. "I can't. But it's a good idea. If you guys start the company, I'll work for it. I'm willing to take that chance."

Blake nodded that he would do that, too. Dick looked to Arnie.

"Then you and I'll put up the money?"

Arnie nodded decisively. After Bob and Blake left, the two new entrepreneurs began plotting their start-up strategy.

At First—Success

The business was an instant success. Dick, as the senior member of the group and majority stockholder, negotiated a substantial, for them, federal government contract. Bob and Blake each landed less demanding jobs. Arnie concentrated on the administration of their rapidly growing enterprise. Halfway through their first year, billings were over $180,000.

Dick threw a party for employees, wives, his new friend, Jill, and friends in general. It was quality Scotch he sipped this time. He put an arm around Arnie on one side and Jill on the other. Life begins at forty-five, he thought. He looked over the packed living room, the crowd spilling into the dining room, even the kitchen, and cleared his throat to hide the emotion as he squeezed Arnie's shoulder.

"We did it! We're a success."

Arnie smiled happily.

"What's next?"

Dick squeezed Jill's shoulder.

"We're going to expand Precision Research into the big time!"

The next week Dick gave Arnie instructions for enlarging the facility. A second floor of offices had become vacant immediately above them, which Arnie was to lease and fully equip with furniture, phones, and word-processing equipment. The landlord would take care of improving the leasehold. A follow-on to the federal contract was being negotiated, as well as a substantial new contract with the city government. The staff was enthusiastic, and smaller contracts were popping constantly. Arnie was putting out several competitive bids. Dick immediately began interviews. Within three weeks he had hired the additional personnel to staff the second floor and take on the new contracts.

Then—Reality

Precision Research lived for only a year. The federal government contract was not renewed. The city contract was awarded, but it amounted to about half of the federal contract. Only two of the smaller contracts were won, leaving Precision with $90,000 in billings for the second six months, but with twice the payroll, twice the rent, twice the debt, and its cash depleted from the additional office supplies and down payments for equipment that had been made. Only severe surgery on the payroll, which left Precision with Dick and a secretary as the sole remaining staff at month eleven, prevented Dick and Arnie from losing much more than their original investment. Draws on the final stages of the city contract, which Dick performed himself, enabled him to pay off the bank loans and remaining accounts payable. Precision died owing nothing to anyone and owning nothing, except two unusual desks which couldn't be sold. Dick had them moved to his home, and then found work as a senior engineer, joining the other members of Precision who found similar jobs in research companies around the metropolitan area.

WHY SMALL BUSINESSES ARE DIFFERENT

The Owner Deals with Many Unknowns

One of the key differences between small businesses and large businesses is that so much is unknown. When Dick and his friends started Precision Research, they hoped to get a federal government contract. The chances were good, but not 100 percent certain. After that contract, they had no hard facts about what might happen. There was enthusiasm about the systems research which their assembled talents could offer to federal agencies and local governments, but there was no way they could investigate before they started the company whether an ongoing business could be maintained.

This kind of uncertainty about the market is typical for the entrepreneur, especially in starting up a new business, but also for the small company trying to grow. When Procter & Gamble brings out a new product, an extensive series of consumer panel and regional testings must be done before a commitment is made to market nationwide. No entrepreneur has the resources or the time to investigate a market so thoroughly before taking the risk. Frequently an entire company, not just a product line, must be committed without clear evidence.

It is not simply the lack of resources that precludes market research for the entrepreneur. Frequently a small company's products or services require the establishment of a new market. Procter & Gamble is usually trying to find out if a new hair spray is more appealing to consumers than already existing products. How do you test whether the Precision Research concept will sell or not? True—one could ask various government technical officers if they liked the idea, but what would their responses mean? They could say yes, but never have occasion to buy. They could say no, and then develop a need later. Dick and Arnie had to risk their investment to find out.

There's Never Enough Money

The amount of money at risk is another difference between small and large. Procter & Gamble's total product development and market testing expenditures are within a budget that the corporation can afford. If a product doesn't test out, scrap it. If a new product is marketed and becomes a disappointment, that's a cost of doing business. For Dick and Arnie, it took all they could afford just to find out whether Precision Research would work or not. Bob couldn't afford the risk at all.

This leaves the entrepreneur faced with a guess about whether the business concept will work or not. The price of finding out will probably absorb all that he or she has to spend. At the start of the race, it's impossible to pick the winners. One study of the first successful venture capital firms found that no matter how brilliant the financial analysts and economists on their staff, at the beginning they were never able to predict which companies would be the successes years in the future. Many who have made it big on venture investments did so because of one superb success, which canceled out the losses and offset the mediocre performers. To get that one hit, they had to spread their investments out over many companies. But the entrepreneur gets only one company in the portfolio. No matter how optimistic the feelings about what might happen, the future is likely to be a surprise one way or another.

This plunge of money into the unknown isn't a factor merely at the start of a business, although that is when it is most dramatic. In fact, some ventures are started up with very little capital. The commitment of substantial sums comes later, after some successful growth has expanded the company's resources. Even if a company grows to several million in sales, the steps needed to evaluate a market can be too costly, or a new market may need to be created, which makes in-depth research difficult. Besides, Procter & Gamble sometimes comes up with bummers, which it can afford, but even a multimillion dollar company which makes a misstep into a new market can experience financial disaster. For the aggressive entrepreneur this is an ongoing fact of life.

There's Never Much Time

The time horizon for these critical decisions is dramatically different in large and small businesses as well. When I was in banking I was asked to study the feasibility of offering overdraft checking privileges as a new service to our customers. I wrote a report recommending that we do so. Subsequently I left banking to work in corporate finance. Ten years later my old bank announced the new service. A decade was required before the decision was made. True, banks move more slowly than other industries, but the decision-making process in large companies can take months or years, while for a small company it can take days, weeks, perhaps months to decide, then execute. A small company can go out of business in the time that it takes a large company to make a decision. This is one of the chief dangers for a small company trying to sell a product or service to a larger one, or for a small company trying to negotiate some kind of joint venture with a larger company.

This quick reaction time is one of the advantages of the small business. The owner can see an opportunity and follow up before large competitors can react. But the short time span also creates a volatility with which the owner will have to cope. Resources can be rechanneled almost immediately. But results can vary from expectations within a few months, leaving the entrepreneur strapped for working capital, because the small business seldom has the staying power of larger competitors. That is why the entrepreneur's mistakes can be so devastating. The larger company has well-established markets, substantial cash flow, long-term banking relationships—all of which enable it to ride through a bad decision or a market downturn. Many entrepreneurs have just enough to take care of the day-to-day expenses when business is going well. Making the wrong expansion move can put a small business on the mat. Many times I've seen trouble occur even with the right marketing move because other mistakes were made, such as underestimating the funds required for the expansion, overestimating the profitability of the new product or service, or breaking down because middle management wasn't strong enough to handle their new responsibilities.

Always—An Abundance of Pitfalls

The entrepreneur's Achilles' heel is a lack of awareness of the pitfalls hidden within what seem like the natural business decisions one has to make from month to month and year to year. Every decision or commitment—from arranging financing for new equipment, to establishing a sales rep network, to going after a new market, to hiring a new general manager—contains the ingredients which have put entrepreneurs in deep trouble or out of business. Yet some other entrepreneurs have made these decisions successfully, finding new avenues for profitable growth.

Ed Simpson's harrowing example

What happened to Ed Simpson, the owner of a transportation company I worked with years ago, is an example. In 1970 Ed started his business with a dump truck. He was able to take a salary of $25,000 for the first year. A couple of years later, he had the chance to get into contract hauling, for which he bought a tractor and trailer, financing them through the manufacturer. In the next two years Ed had phenomenal success, expanding his contracts so rapidly that he had to add twenty-three new tractors and forty trailers to keep up with the volume. He was doing well over $1 million in sales. From one dump truck to a fleet of tractors and trailers in just three years.

But Ed was in deep, deep trouble. His company had been suffering a cash deficit of around $5,000 every month. He and his wife both worked ten hours a day in the business, but they'd been able to take a combined salary of only $8,000 for the year, and with two children they were having trouble meeting their family expenses. The company's cash flow would sustain only another two months of deficits before Ed would have to close down operations. The implications for his family were obvious.

The crux of Ed's problem was in the financing of his fleet. The manufacturer's financing was written over a three-year period for all vehicles and trailers. The contracts provided for the depreciation expense on those items to be charged to the customer over the number of years accountants would allow for the useful life of the equipment, which was something like five years for tractors and seven years for trailers. This meant that Ed's payments of principal and interest had to be made in three years, while the customer was reimbursing him for the cost of that equipment over five to seven years. The consequence was the monthly cash deficit of about $5,000.

This story had a happy ending, however. A cash-flow analysis showed Ed and his banker what the root of the problem was. We were then able to obtain a Small Business Administration guarantee to enable the bank to refinance the equipment, but with a ten-year payment schedule. In one stroke we converted a cash deficit into a monthly surplus of about $2,000. Within two years Ed was so profitable he was able to take a $70,000 salary, and his wife had taken a full-time job working for another company.

Ed knew trucking. His dispatching operation was efficient. He had an excellent repair and maintenance operation. He was a competent supervisor of a crew of drivers scattered over a good-sized geographical area. As a result he was able to perform under contract very well, and his customers were willing to award him additional business. But he had no previous experience to alert him to the intricacies of equipment financing. The contracts he worked under contained complicated pricing schedules which obscured the discrepancy between his financing obligations and the cash flow he could generate from the jobs. His bookkeeping procedures were not good enough to give him the monthly financial statements which could have shown him what the causes of his problems were, but at that time Ed would not have been able to analyze his own statements anyway. Part of the turnaround of his business, in addition to the refinancing, was to set up stronger bookkeeping, along with financial statements which enabled Ed to monitor his performance and to make better bids on his contracts. Once these financial and accounting adjustments were made in his operations, Ed was able to capitalize on the good basic skills he had for running the business.

A Wide Range of Skills Is Needed

Ed's problems involved financial management, an area which causes untold grief for entrepreneurs around the world. However, business owners become embroiled in serious problems in all areas of management, not because they lack ability or intelligence, but because the operation of a small business encompasses the complete range of management skills. Few of us, including yours truly, possess all of these skills. In a large company, there are a number of factors to the chief executive's advantage. First, operations in all of the functional areas of the enterprise have been well established over the years—the market sectors, the customer base, manufacturing, banking and finance, personnel—whatever is required of management, there are longstanding procedures and relationships which contribute to getting the job done. Second, there is a staff of experienced and trained managers in each area who supply the boss with in-depth analyses and recommendations regarding a wide range of technical and operational issues. Third, the large company usually has a stable of consultants, lawyers, accountants, bankers, and advertising executives to provide guidance in areas where the internal staff doesn't

nal equity he had to build on. The third year showed substantial profits. Now, in a better retail market, he is in an excellent position to rebuild his retained earnings to what they had been in the good years and more. He was able to make realistic judgments about his sales volume, which he translated into the decisive action to save his business. The other man never faced reality—he let his feelings about what the future might be influence his decisions, with the result that he never acted decisively enough. He bet on his hopes, and the consequence was disaster.

Knowing How to Read Financial Statements

A third characteristic of the successful entrepreneur is knowing how to read financial statements. A small business is perhaps the only activity in our society where what happens is what happens, short and sweet. You either made a profit at the end of the year or you didn't. No matter what you say, what your politics are, no matter who you know—if you sustained a loss, it was a loss, and the consequences are immediate. In a large corporation, multitudes of managers make decisions day in and day out, but there's no direct tie-in with the overall corporate profit. Sometimes the Chief Executive himself seems disengaged from the process. A few years ago the Chairman of General Motors retired to national acclaim, at just about the time when all the big auto makers were managing themselves into the disasters of the energy crisis and foreign competition. When Chrysler hit the skids, the government was pressured into bailing them out. The same thing happened with Continental Illinois. There were compelling reasons for the government to do so in both cases, but the point is that no small business ever has that luxury. If you're out, you're out, and there's not even a ripple on the surface of the economy.

The entrepreneur must know where the business stands. What is the profit? Why is the profit being made or not being made? To know the answers, the owner must have timely and reliable financial statements and must be able to interpret them. I'm afraid to say how many entrepreneurs I've met who didn't know how to read their financial statements. I'm afraid to say how many operated for months at a time without any statements at all. I have even known entrepreneurs who received inaccurate statements, but who lacked the aptitude to sense their inaccuracy, only to find out later that what was reported to be a profit was really a loss, sometimes a tragically large loss. Not understanding how to read the financial statements is like flying a small plane without instruments through thick clouds over a mountain range. The successful entrepreneurs I have met grabbed their financial statements each month and read them carefully, with a nose for that bottom line.

Minding the Store

I was talking to a client a few years ago about another client whom we both knew. We agreed that Sam wasn't unusually bright or creative or particularly sophisticated about business. He knew his industry from years of experience. Yet he'd built his operation to several million in sales and had been profitable every year. "Sam minds the store," my client said. A simple act, but a profound one. A characteristic which sets apart those who succeed from many of those who fail. How many times have I heard experienced bankers say, "So and so is taking too many Caribbean vacations these days," or "Such and such an owner is paying more attention to his yacht than his business." Frequently, such are the signs that financial trouble is on the way. Paying attention to the business takes care of many problems which can torment those whose attention has wandered to other things, whether those things be vacations, law suits, industry association work, or other business ventures outside the main business. Ironically, the client who was so perceptive about Sam is now going through a period where he isn't minding his own store.

Experience, the Catch 22 of Small Business

Seasoned entrepreneurs have a better chance of making it than neophytes. The Catch 22, naturally, is how can you last long enough to be experienced, if by definition you're inexperienced when you start? The answer is that experience comes in several forms. Many owners learned management from years of work with another company, especially companies which were particularly good at certain aspects of business. Some had the knack of learning how to do things by working with businesses that constantly did things wrong. There seems to be a class of successful entrepreneurs who learned business because it was in the family—parents or grandparents or aunts or uncles who were astute entrepreneurs themselves.

Life experience has something to do with it as well. I've seen business owners in their late twenties or early thirties go under because they couldn't handle business problems at the crucial time. Perhaps a decade later they might have known themselves better or they might have had a deeper perspective on life's priorities. Perhaps they would have been able to stand up to those tough decisions requiring patience and a kind of emotional endurance that comes from knowing for sure that you're inevitably going to fail at some things, and that though it does matter, ultimately it doesn't matter. A more experienced eye can see deeper into trends, has more to draw on to interpret what is happening. And there is much truth, based on what I've seen, to the story of the race between the tortoise and the hare.

Some of the most successful entrepreneurs I have known have experienced great trouble at some point in their business careers. Once a cagey bank loan officer said, "I always feel more comfortable dealing with a business owner who has had real problems. They know what trouble is; they know trouble will come. The ones who've breezed through successfully all the way scare me. They don't think it can happen to them."

Whatever goes up can come back down. Success isn't a guarantee against failure. Frequently I've heard people say, "Well, I've been in business for five years now, so that means I'm going to make it." Wrong. You can fail no matter how long you've been in business. In one tragic case I know of, an owner of a family business which had been operating for forty years, one he'd operated for over fifteen years himself, went under. No business owner anywhere has a guarantee of anything. You have to re-create yourself constantly. One day Jerry Wolman was worth $98 million, the next day he was busted. If you've been through trouble, you know it can happen again, and you know what it's like. If you haven't known trouble, no one can tell you; you're going to find out for yourself.

The Ability to Judge Advice

Another characteristic of the successful entrepreneur is the ability to distinguish good advice from bad advice. Rare is the business owner who can operate without counsel. In fact, some have succeeded partly because of the help of an extremely astute advisor or set of advisors. Many advisors, though, lack the necessary insight into what really makes a small business work, even if they are frequently exposed to those types of companies. Simple exposure doesn't equal knowledge. There are those who will never have the knack of it, though they may be in a position to act as advisors. CPAs, lawyers, bankers, and consultants all look and talk alike, but some of them are much more astute about small business management than most of their profession.

The entrepreneur needs advice but must be able to evaluate whether that advice is sound or not. Too often the guidance from outside professionals has led to serious business problems, because the advisor, no matter how qualified in that profession, simply didn't understand the guts of how a small business lives or dies. When the advice was accepted on authority, rather than being weighted, sifted, and tested within the owner's mind, heartbreak frequently ensued. It's a matter of judgment—I've seen brilliant people, Ph.D.s in fact, who had a childlike acceptance of professional counsel. "My accountant said," or "My lawyer said," seemed to decide the matter. If the owner is in that position, then it's back into the cockpit of that airplane flying without instruments.

YOU ARE IN THE OWNER'S CHAIR

The crux of it is you as the owner, sitting in your chair, are in the one position from which true judgments can be made. It's your investment—money, time, hopes, self-esteem—which is at risk. No one else can adequately evaluate the pros and cons of a particular action, because they simply can't weigh all the factors; only you can. Add to that the fact that most advisors lack true understanding of a small business and you see the issue.

Conversely, some entrepreneurs are only too aware of this pitfall. They won't take advice from anybody. Their suspicion is arrayed around them like the walls of a fort. This approach can lead to just as much trouble as the naive taking of advice. Only that rare bird who has all the answers can succeed inside a fort; almost everyone else needs some help. The crucial factor is being able to evaluate what people say to you.

For those who endure the years of hard work and personal sacrifice, the nerve-racking exposure to risk and near failure, the pressures of decision making, the constant exposure to management tasks which entrepreneurs dislike—such as arbitrating disputes between managers—there are the unique rewards of small business ownership. We have all seen examples of the economic rewards. Many of my clients are millionaires, because the successful operation of a business creates value. A competent business owner can achieve a salary comparable to those of big-time corporate executives. But the entrepreneur also has the opportunity to create substantial net worth by investing in real estate, which shelters incomes, allows the maximum effectiveness of the dollar due to the financing characteristics of real estate transactions, and provides excellent long-term appreciation. A profitable business may allow the owner to begin with a building for the company's own use. I must underline that these are the outcomes of profitable, stable businesses where the owner has skills and insights into real estate investments. As for all things in small business, many have come to grief by mishandling these opportunities. An owner shouldn't get involved in real estate transactions, one's own building or otherwise, until the business is strong enough and the owner has enough understanding of real estate to handle the transactions effectively.

Another value is created, which many entrepreneurs underestimate, though it's a success story with which we are all familiar. This is the value of the business itself, which can be quite substantial for a company with good growth prospects, profitable operations, and a sound financial position. Frequently this value can be the greatest of all, including the salary stream over the years and the net worth one has in real estate. Many owners have sold their businesses to retire as millionaires. One of the requirements of the successful entrepreneur is to understand the balance between what can be done to create tax-sheltered investments with income taken from the business and the gain which can be created by leaving capital in to support the future value of the business.

There are rewards beyond the economic. For some, the economic goals are paramount, while for others additional factors are of consequence. Anyone who starts a business and gets it somewhere has created something. By definition you start at zero—no sales, no expenses, no assets—and from there you go to who knows where? In the process you create an enterprise, an activity with its own unique personality where people work, where customers do business, where assets and liabilities accumulate. That business reflects the personality of the owner in attitudes toward people: those working there, the customers, the community. It takes on an ethical tone; it assumes a posture toward the marketplace—aggressive, imaginative, or otherwise. It is something which can fill up a good part of a life.

Intelligently and responsibly managed, it can fill up that life with much that is positive.

Then there is that special flavor which working for yourself can give. Those who have had the experience know what it is to realize every day that what happens is an interplay between fate and what you can make of it yourself. It's your own initiative and your own judgment which counts. You have to live with your own successes and failures, but you don't have to live entrapped in someone else's limitations.

The small business is the last frontier, in my view. The entrepreneur ventures into unknown territory. Each enterprise begins with a virgin entry into the market . . . who knows how it will go? Sometimes this is an entry into a totally new market. It may be the introduction of a product which has never before existed or a service no one has ever thought of or a unique marketing and sales approach. The risks are clear. Scattered along the trails leading to the frontier, one can see the corpses of the businesses which couldn't cope. During the journey and after it's over, there is a satisfaction in surviving where so many failed and a respect for anyone who has tried.

2

The Marketing Strategy Umbrella

THE MARKETING STRATEGY UMBRELLA

The Most Powerful Way to Tell Your Story

Many entrepreneurs think that marketing is advertising. On the contrary, a successful marketing strategy assembles a number of tools that combine to tell your customers most powerfully about the products or services you sell. These tools must reinforce and supplement each other if you're to make maximum impact. Marketing strategy is an umbrella over all of the dynamics of your market place. A model of the marketing umbrella is shown in Figure 2-1.

"Cherry Pick" the Umbrella

The panels of the marketing umbrella contain all the tools that could be used to develop a marketing strategy. Each industry and each company within an industry requires a different combination of tools for effective marketing. Sales are generated in different ways in different industries, and each company has to deal with unique

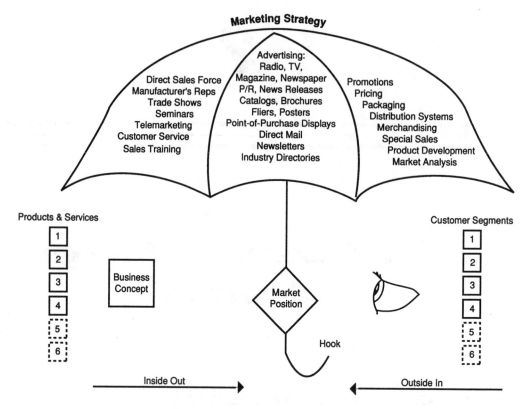

Figure 2-1 Marketing Strategy.

circumstances. To construct a winning strategy you must "cherry pick" that unique blend of tools that most persuasively tells your company's story to the exact customer segments you wish to sell to.

Each component of your strategy must be used for its proper purpose. Otherwise the money you spend will be wasted. Marketing can be extremely expensive. If you misuse your tools you pay a double penalty—not only do you waste money, but you don't get the sales that expenditure was intended to create.

Larry's Faux Pas

A prime example is national magazine advertising. I remember a business owner, Larry, who announced his new marketing campaign—$50,000 for national magazine ads. The budget included the agency cost for creating the ads and a package of full-page ads divided between two leading industry magazines. "Sales should go up this year," Larry said proudly.

Larry was headed for disappointment. The primary purpose of national advertising is to create "top of the mind" awareness for your company among the readership of the magazine. National advertising is a long-term campaign to create image among potential customers to make your other marketing tools more effective. It was unlikely that Larry's little budget would have built much awareness nationwide. It certainly wasn't designed to stimulate immediate sales volume.

Furthermore, Larry had no other marketing plan. Even if awareness had been created, Larry had no direct mail campaign aimed at the magazine readership to create leads or any telemarketing and direct sale follow-up. Even worse, the magazine readership omitted crucial customer segments Larry needed to reach but included thousands of people who had no interest in Larry's products. Larry spent money to create a speck of awareness among people who didn't count while leaving many sales opportunities unexposed to his products.

Watch the Timing

Exact timing and careful coordination of the "cherry-picked" tools of your marketing strategy will ensure that each component will reinforce the other components. This marketing power will result in increased sales. Maximum sales per marketing dollar will be achieved.

However, poor timing and lack of coordination will diminish the impact of your marketing. The absence of a key marketing tool just when it's needed can disrupt the effectiveness of an entire campaign. Good organization is as necessary to marketing success as all of the marketing tools.

The Inside-Out View

Reading Figure 2-1 from left to right looks at market analysis from the inside out. We begin by defining the products and services our company offers or plans to offer to the market. Medical Products, Inc. (MPI), a small company in the Midwest, manufactures a line of standard formulations used in biological research. They also prepare special formulas to order. They perform basic research projects under contract to pharmaceutical research departments and for universities. They are developing a line of test kits for measuring research results.

MPI's range of products and services is brought together or focused for sale to the marketplace by a business concept:

> MPI provides basic and specialized formulations and contract services in support of biological testing and research. MPI is a low-volume, high-quality, high-reliability supplier, with emphasis on responsiveness to the individual researcher's specifications and with emphasis on prompt and courteous customer service.

The Outside-In View

Buying decisions are always made by the customer. The customer sees your company from the outside looking in, the eye in Figure 2-1. This is the critical viewpoint. It's not how you see your products but how your customers perceive them that counts. To be an effective marketer you must be able to put yourself in the minds of your customers. Your message must be in their frame of reference and in their language.

Precision Tune developed a diagnostic and maintenance program to service the new high-tech car—fuel injection cleaning, carburetor overhaul, and computer diagnostics. From a technical standpoint, these services were essential to good automotive maintenance. But to communicate with the driving public, the advertising agency translated Precision Tune's technical jargon into performance problems—sluggishness, poor gas mileage, hard to start.

Constructing an intelligent marketing program starts with knowing your customers: who they are, how they think, the needs that your products or services fill. This knowledge must extend to each segment that comprises the total group, with their differing characteristics and interests.

MPI sells to researchers in virology, cell biology, molecular biology, and to the product development departments of biotech companies. They conduct research for pharmaceutical companies and universities. Each of these customer groups has different needs and different attitudes.

Market Position

A company's offerings to the market, as communicated by its total marketing program, must meet the viewpoints and needs of its target customers to create market position, as shown in the middle of Figure 2-1. This is how consumers see a company versus its competition. The sales that result are the company's market share; its slice of the total pie.

Market position can be built on. It can act like a wedge to gain greater market share. It can be lost through inattention to customer needs and blindness to the strategies of competitors, such as GM in the 1980s.

MPI's market position is distinctive. Many researchers see MPI as "the best place to buy because they will formulate to my specifications reliably." But as a small company, MPI sells to a minute portion of the total research market. Many researchers don't know of the company's existence. For them, MPI has no market position.

The Hook

Frequently, marketing programs will feature a distinctive product or service that is likely to attract attention throughout the market. The hook is not simply to generate sales of that product, but to attract attention among the customer segments to the company's entire line of products and services.

MPI has developed a new product that is a significant advance in purification. Announcement of this product is drawing attention within the entire research community. By featuring this product in all of its marketing materials, MPI has an ideal hook to draw attention to all its products and services, with the hope of expanding market position and increasing market share.

Long-Term Growth versus Decline

I have seen initially successful companies pass their peak and decline, leaving the owner destitute just when he or she should be enjoying the success from years of hard work. Long-term, sustained success is generated by a marketing strategy that is constantly recreated to keep abreast of changing markets and changing customer attitudes. The owner who falls asleep or who plays a pat hand for too long frequently suffers. The owner who has both the determination and the vision to keep current with the marketplace can make the adjustments necessary to stay on top.

MARKETING MATRIX

The marketing matrix, Table 2-1, is a quick look at the tools of the marketing umbrella according to their purpose, advantages, typical users, and measuring results. Businesses succeed or fail—with all

TABLE 2-1 MARKETING MATRIX

Marketing tool	Purpose	Advantages	Typical users	Measuring results
National magazine	Increase name awareness. Create image. Generate leads.	Efficient targeting of readers with specific interests. Monthlies are kept for weeks and passed along.	Consumer goods and services Business-to-business	Increase in calls or written inquiries. 800 number increases success.
Local/regional magazines	Increase name awareness. Build image. Inform reader of availability of product or service.	Targets specific geographical markets. Monthlies are usually kept for weeks and passed along.	Retailers/real estate/restaurants	Increase in inquiries. Higher traffic. Special, limited-time offers increase success. Code address for measuring responses.
Metro newspapers	Produce immediate response.	Short lead time for publication. Economical production costs. Wide publication coverage.	Retailers/car dealers/real estate/entertainment/health care/insurance	Immediate increase in sales or inquiries.
Local newspapers	Produce immediate response.	Short lead time. Economic production costs. Target specific geographical areas.	Smaller independent retailers and service businesses	Immediate increase in sales. Response to special offers.
National radio advertising	Increase name awareness.	Targets specific demographic groups. Effective, economical, creative.	Soft drinks/automobiles/airlines/national retail chains	Increased dealer/distributor participation. Increased inquiries. Increased sales. Response to special offers.
Local radio advertising	Increase name awareness. Increase immediate sales.	Targets specific demographic groups in a local market. Effective, economical, creative. Promotional opportunities with stations.	Retailers/car dealers/national companies doing local promotions	Immediate increase in sales. Response to special offers.

Method	Objectives	Advantages	Typical users	Measuring results
National TV advertising	Increase name awareness. Introduce new product. Create/build image.	Reaches large numbers of population. Produces instant recognition.	Beer and soft drinks/airlines/personal products/automobiles/household products/telephone services/oil companies	Increased dealer/distributor participation. Increased inquiries. Change in opinion or perception of product/company.
Local TV advertising	Increase name awareness. Increase immediate sales.	Reaches large segment of local market. Produces immediate results.	Car dealers/retailers/food chains/banks/shopping centers	Immediate increase in sales. Responses to special offers.
Public relations	Create name awareness. Change opinion.	Cost effective even with small budgets.	Banks/associations/nonprofit organizations/special-event organizers/companies with image problems	Press coverage. Public opinion polls. Membership increases.
Newsletters	Communicate detailed information about a company service or issue on a periodic basis.	Efficiently targets interested readers. Relatively low production costs. Establishes company credibility. Keeps in touch with customers.	Associations/service businesses/advocacy organizations/nonprofit organizations	Inquiries. Membership increases.
Direct mail	Elicit response. Increase inquiries, traffic, and/or sales.	Results easily measured. Very efficient, precise targeting of prospects.	Fund raisers/new-product introductions/magazine subscriptions/special sales events	Direct responses (response cards, call, letters). Sales.
Mail-order catalogs	Generate sales.	Consumers like the convenience. High sales with relatively low investment.	Hobby/gift retailers and manufacturers/clothing manufacturers/music and book publishers	Direct sales.
Telemarketing	Generate sales. Produce leads.	Relatively lower cost when compared with alternatives. Enables one-on-one communication.	Telephone services/magazine subscriptions/financial services/insurance companies	Increased qualified leads. Increased sales. Keep log books of calls for measuring results.

(continued)

TABLE 2-1 MARKETING MATRIX (continued)

Marketing tool	Purpose	Advantages	Typical users	Measuring results
In-house sales force	Call on customers for orders. Service customers; take care of problems.	Personal, dedicated representation of company. Intimate knowledge of products.	Manufacturers/real estate/service businesses/media	Increase in orders. Decrease in customer complaints.
Outside sales reps	Call on customers for orders. Service customers; take care of problems.	Lower cost than in-house sales force.	Manufacturers	Increase in orders.
Trade shows	Present new products or services to key, prospective customers.	Reaches highly interested, important prospects. Showcases products and services. Opportunity to shop and compare.	Manufacturers/wholesalers/service businesses/publishers/associations	Key contacts made. Product literature distributed. Schedule orders for coming year.
Trade catalogs	Offer a convenient, organized presentation of products to buyers and prospective buyers.	Buyers more easily make decisions. Keeps sales force focused. Used when sales force cannot visit customers.	Manufacturers/distributors	Orders are written. Requests for sales call.
Collateral materials	Provide information on specific services or products. Support ad campaign. Communicate corporate capabilities.	Freedom to create material of varying sizes, lengths, and designs.	Manufacturers/real estate developers/financial institutions/insurance companies	Increased orders. Increased inquiries.
Point-of-purchase materials	Call out and identify products, product benefits, and special offers.	Captive audience. Cost effective. Can bring immediate results at the expense of the competition.	Food and packaged goods/apparel and footwear retailers/hardware stores	Immediate increase in sales.

Product development	Create products that have or will have demand.	New products that offer real benefits and value to customers are successful. New-product development expands and diversifies product line. Keeps sales growing as times change.	Manufacturers/packaged goods/computer software	Gain in market share. Diversified product line. Diversified customer base.
Packaging	Differentiate product from competition. Make a product more attractive to buyer. Communicate benefits of product.	Tremendous power of persuasion at a relatively modest cost.	Packaged goods/self-service products in hardware, auto supply, toy, and other retailers	Good packaging moves off shelves. Poor packaging sits.
Distribution system	Determine position of product or service in the marketplace. (Wide, discounted distribution versus narrow, high-end distribution).	Product or service becomes known by the company it keeps. Carefully planned distribution adds value to product.	Manufacturers/distributors	Long-term effect not always evident. Brand loyalty builds with time.
Pricing	Establish position in marketplace. Cover all costs plus reasonable profit.	Beating competition here usually leads to success.	Every product or service has to be priced.	The market usually decides if a product or service is priced correctly. If you're disappointed with sales, rethink your pricing.
Special sales	To move inventory that is not selling or is discontinued. To attract first-time buyers.	Good reason to advertise. Attracts new customers.	Retailers/auto manufacturers/fast food chains	Immediate increase in sales. Beware of lost gross profit.

(continued)

TABLE 2-1 MARKETING MATRIX (continued)

Marketing tool	Purpose	Advantages	Typical users	Measuring results
Promotions	Stimulate sales. Increase inquiries.	Good reason to advertise. Creates excitement. A good way to involve sales force as well as customer.	Retailers/auto manufacturers/fast food chains/packaged goods	Immediate increase in sales/traffic
Market analysis	To better identify and understand customers. To study the competition.	Sound, cost-effective decisions are made when customers are identified, their psychology is understood, and when you know what the competition is doing.	Every company must analyze its markets.	Sound market analysis leads to good marketing decisions and increased sales over the long term. It leads to consistent and successful diversification of products and markets.

the varying degrees of success in between—according to how well the owner masters the marketing for his or her business.

Most entrepreneurs begin with a knowledge of their product or service. They know how to provide what their customers need. Too often these same entrepreneurs start their businesses with little knowledge of marketing. They are ignorant of the techniques that they must master to be truly successful over the long haul.

Instead of marketing mastery—the essence of modern business success—most small businesses are run with erroneous or incomplete ideas about marketing in general and marketing tools in particular. When I probe the marketing programs of such clients, I'm greeted with impatience. "I don't have time for that!" Or, "That's too complicated!" The matter is dropped there.

A business owner cannot escape the consequences of his or her decisions (or lack of decisions). Those entrepreneurs who lack the time or mental toughness to get a handle on marketing are rewarded with modest sales. Worse, their marketing ineffectiveness can lead to the loss of their businesses.

Don't Follow Ed's Example

Ed started his visual communications firm years ago. He began as a graphics studio and grew into a diversified, multi-media company with sales exceeding $7 million. His goal was to triple sales from there. He had many ideas for new products and services to reach his goal.

I asked him repeatedly about the marketing strategies he needed to keep the sales growth going. "Have the marketing strategies in my head," he snapped. Each year I urged him to sit down with me to develop concrete ways to get his wealth of ideas for new services into the right markets. He never had the time, and, besides, it wasn't necessary because he had it in his head.

Ed peaked at $7 million. His new ideas never got to market. As visual communication technology changed, Ed changed with it. But new marketing approaches and new marketing tools were needed, and Ed didn't respond to that. Sales started to fall off. They dropped . . . dropped . . . dropped. Ultimately Ed's business was struggling to generate $250,000 per month. He was in terrible financial trouble.

He entered his fifties with shattered self-esteem, loss of confidence in his business ability, and an appalling loss of income and financial worth. Don't let that happen to you.

Take the time and apply the energy to learn the intricacies of marketing. Get a handle on how to market your business. Keep abreast of the changes in your marketplace and revise your marketing strategies accordingly. That will ensure success over the long haul and not just for the first few years.

SUMMARY

Marketing strategy is more than just advertising. It is an umbrella that assembles a number of marketing tools to tell your story most persuasively. You must "cherry pick" from all the marketing tools to create a unique blend that will work best for you.

Much money can be spent for little effect. Don't commit Larry's faux pas. Watch the timing and coordinate your marketing program to achieve the maximum reinforcement of your message.

Don't forget to look at your company from the outside in. Define your targeted customers. Remember, it is *their* perception of your products and services that produces the sale, not yours. If you have a hook, use it. Use the marketing matrix to create marketing mastery.

3

Never Let Up
on Marketing
and Sales

SALES ARE THE MOTOR OF BUSINESS

Everything begins with sales. If your business can generate sales, then operations managers can produce the product or service efficiently and financial managers can manage the cash and help produce a profit. Without the sales, it doesn't matter how well the rest of it is done. Of course, the results depend on a balance of all three—sales, operations, and finance—but sales are the motor which drives the machine.

Creating a marketing strategy is at the heart of business success, yet many entrepreneurs have invented a product or are experts at providing a service, but they know little about marketing. How do you set an intelligent marketing goal? How do you define your company's marketing position? How do you develop the strategy which ties your product or service to your existing customer base, then connects the two with potential customers to create increased market share and growing sales? What role should advertising play in this strategy? Should there be direct mailings? Telemarketing?

Should your company employ a direct sales force? How should you price your products and services? Which products or services should you push ahead of all others? How should your products and/or services be packaged? Have you fallen into the trap of looking at your business from the inside out, rather than the outside in?

KNOW THE DIFFERENCE BETWEEN MARKETING AND SALES

Answering these questions is only half the battle. Once the marketing job has been done, the entrepreneur has to turn to sales, which is not quite the same. As a practical matter, marketing is the development of the context or structure with which the company will attack the marketplace (defining what the sales effort will be is part of the marketing strategy), while the sales effort is actual dealing with the customer to get the sale. This is more than a technicality. Entrepreneurs sometimes define a marketing strategy, possibly even a brilliant marketing strategy, and then prepare the operations for the influx of sales. Only the sales don't come, because there is insufficient understanding of what the direct sales effort must be for that company actually to generate the business.

On the other hand, I have seen entrepreneurs plunge into an intense selling effort without understanding the kind of marketing preparation necessary for that sales effort to work. An aggressive entrepreneur in the microcomputer industry comes to mind. Based on the rapid growth in business microcomputers, his goal was to reach several million in sales within three years of starting his company. He hired a senior sales manager and his entire staff of five from a large computer supply company. Needless to say, the monthly cost of carrying this group strained the entrepreneur's resources, but he was convinced that bringing on a sales force which had been successful for another company would quickly generate business for himself.

After three months the new sales force had produced almost nothing. All six were forced to leave the company, having quit successful jobs only shortly before, and the owner was left without an ongoing sales effort and with his cash resources severely drained. What went wrong?

- The sales force was from a large wholesaler while the entrepreneur sold directly to users. Thus, the sales team had little understanding of how this market worked. The owner paid no attention to the industry differences.
- The owner did not have the two largest-selling microcomputer lines. His sales goals were unrealistic, given the market share of those lines he was authorized to carry.
- The owner could give the sales manager no guidance as to how to attack the marketplace. The owner did not understand his market position. He wasn't able to analyze the needs of potential customers to develop a marketing strategy which would focus his selling efforts on those market segments with the highest potential for buying his products.

To this owner, sales and marketing were the same thing. Since he needed to generate sales, he hired salespeople. Since they were salespeople, they should have known what to do. Not only did he not understand what kind of marketing he needed to succeed, he did not understand what kind of sales management he, as the owner, needed to provide to conduct an effective sales effort.

The sales effort differs drastically from industry to industry. Some companies generate almost all business by means of a direct sales force which operates outside the company—for example, manufacturers of industrial products or certain types of wholesalers. Retailers, on the other hand, depend on selling to customers in the store. Other companies have no sales staff at all, relying instead on direct mailings. Others emphasize telemarketing. Many contractors get business almost exclusively through competitive bidding, while contractors in other industries may rely heavily on personal contacts that lead to sole-source contracts. The nature of a sales effort depends on how the marketplace for that industry works, and it depends on the style of the business owner and on the strengths and weaknesses of the company.

The entrepreneur has to design a sales effort which will produce the sales for that company in that industry operating with that marketing strategy from that marketing position. Nothing turns out the way it is planned; the trick is to monitor sales results to detect unfavorable developments quickly, and then take decisive action to adjust to the new sales realities. How is this done? Many companies are bankrupt today because the owner couldn't find the answer.

HOW TO DEVELOP A MARKETING STRATEGY

Begin with Your Personal Goals

The origin of a sound marketing strategy is what the owner wants to do with the business. This is one of the critical differences between small and large in our economy. Owners can attempt to do anything with their businesses they want—grow to $1 million, $5 million, $20 million, $200 million, don't grow at all. Stay at one store; develop a chain throughout the metropolitan area; develop a regional chain; go national. Acquire other companies; grow from within. Add lots of employees; stay small; operate the business yourself.

What the owner wants to achieve sets the tone for everything else. I had one client who wanted to reach $25 million in sales, then sell his company and retire. All of his waking hours were spent brooding on how to reach that goal. His expansion programs were equipment oriented, to put the company in a position to produce at high volume. I've never been sure that the industry would support that growth without diversification into some allied fields where there have been some traditionally larger companies.

Another client was in the electronics field. Sales were increasing at forty percent a year. The possibilities for growth to $10 million, and then a public offering to provide funds to get to $20 million and even beyond, were there. But the owner didn't want that. He wanted to control growth, to keep the company within management limits which would maintain the kind of lifestyle he desired.

There isn't a right or wrong in personal goals; different people are motivated by different factors. Twenty million in sales is neither a good thing nor a bad thing in itself. The issue is to understand—as the business owner whose goals are at the heart of what the company tries to do—what your goals truly are and what they actually mean to you. Frequently, entrepreneurs aren't specific about what they really want. This can lead to the pursuit of conflicting goals. For example, consider the man who wanted to reach $25 million. He also wanted to have the highest possible annual take from the business. But rapid growth requires a great deal of capital; it is necessary to maximize your retained earnings to provide funds and to supply a good base for bank borrowing. At some point the owner may have to raise outside capital to make up the shortage of funds caused by rapid growth. Naturally, this owner wanted to own 100 percent of the business. As a result, when the opportunity came to expand into diversified areas where there were potentially higher growth rates than those he had been experiencing, the owner was unable to follow up. In the pursuit of his personal lifestyle, he had stripped too much capital from the business. He wouldn't consider raising additional capital. Several million in sales growth was lost because his contradictory goals denied him the resources which were necessary to execute the expansion. Now, perhaps he'll never reach his $25-million goal.

Setting the goals, then, depends on what the owner wants to achieve, but the owner needs to articulate clearly what he or she most wants to accomplish. In this process the consistency of the goals must be evaluated to ensure that they are not going to cancel each other out, as they did with our expansion-minded entrepreneur.

Personal inconsistency can be as damaging to some as the economic damage I have just mentioned. Not infrequently, entrepreneurs can strive mightily to achieve a goal which in the achieving they find less satisfying than they had anticipated, often because it brought problems they hadn't foreseen. The dissatisfaction which results can worm its way into the operations of the business with unfortunate results.

A clear statement of the owner's goals sets up the next major issue. Are these goals feasible? They may have so much internal consistency that they ring like a bell, but as a practical matter, can they work, given the company's situation and the conditions in the marketplace? The marketing job is to reason out how the owner's goals might be realized and in the process to moderate those goals, if necessary, to bring them in line with marketing realities.

Establish the Business Concept

The second step is also a definition. Who are we? What is it that we do for people? I worked with one small company, introduced to me as a retailer of calculators and other electronics for businesses and individual consumers. I was shown the store where the owners displayed several lines of merchandise for walk-in customers. Part of our work together was to analyze their plans for advertising and promoting traffic to their store, especially in terms of the financial consequences for their profits and for their bank financing.

They also mentioned some contracts they were bidding on to supply calculators to local government agencies. As we talked, I asked them to estimate the proportion of revenues derived from business customers, from individuals, and from government sales. We checked their sales records to find that eighty-five percent of their business was with the government. As we discussed their prospects for the next six months, it became clear that ninety percent of the sales they were expecting would come from local government contracts, and, in addition, they were planning to bid on some federal contracts. In fact, the lion's share of the financing they needed would be to support accounts receivable on these contracts if their bids were successful.

They had started their company as a store. That self-image was paramount in their minds, even though retailing was only a small segment of their business then and for the immediate future. After they redefined themselves as contractors for local and federal agencies, with a small retail adjunct, there was a major shift in their marketing analysis. Advertising was no longer an issue, because retailing could never be a significant factor for them in comparison to the government work. Instead, they needed to develop a strategy for locating and then bidding on government jobs across a broad range of local and federal agencies, if they were to have enough successful bids to grow satisfactorily.

Defining the personal goals and then the business concept does not require a voluminous document. The important part of the process is clear thinking. What is it I want to achieve? Then, what kind of business do I have? Clear answers to these questions set the stage for effective marketing. The calculator company owners should have said to themselves, "We are a small supplier of electronic calculators and allied equipment to local government agencies, especially school districts in our county and to a lesser extent in neighboring counties. We respond to those government Requests for Proposal on which we can underbid our competitors because of our low overhead. We have an opportunity to expand to the college market and to some federal agencies. However, due to our small size, we cannot bid on the larger contracts because we cannot satisfy the government's financial requirements."

Another goal description might be stated as follows: "I am an audio retailer, with a metrowide chain of stores, handling upper-end lines on an exclusive basis. I offer quality products with sophisticated customer service at a reasonable price. I do not discount. To maintain my exclusive, quality image, I do not handle other types of merchandise in my stores. On the other hand, I do not carry exotic "audiophile" equipment, because I serve the broader, upper-middle-class market, rather than a specialized segment."

Make a Clear Statement of Market Position

Defining the company concept is the first leg of stating the market position. Much is said about the small company finding its niche. The niche is that segment of the market which the small company can serve profitably, but which larger companies find too small or inconvenient to enter. I think market position is a more powerful concept, because there is no guarantee that a larger company won't enter a market, and, besides, there are usually plenty of small companies competing for the same sales dollar no matter what the niche. One of the things which makes a company competitive is management's ability to define a market position and to communicate that position persuasively to customers.

The audio retailer's business concept states a market position: upper-end hi fi, but not "far out" audiophile. This distinction is important because what would appeal to upper-end buyers, in terms of merchandise, price and sales approach, store appearance, etc., is not what would appeal to the audiophile, and vice versa. At the same time, the dealer was careful to avoid discount pricing. First, the customer profile for discount-oriented customers is distinctly different. Second, the upper-end merchandise is sold by different manufacturers—who don't countenance discounting by their exclusive, quality image dealers—and it is at a much higher price range than the discounted products. Third, in addition to the incompatibility of the upper-end versus the discount operations, the dealer lacked the financial resources to go head to head with the high-volume, high-advertising, low-margin discount chains.

The market position which this retailer was able to establish was as an upper-end dealer who gave a good price for the product within his segment of the market. That market position was established by maintaining consistency throughout all aspects of the company's marketing—the advertising, the product line, the pricing, the image and location of stores, the quality of sales personnel, the customer-oriented, consultative sales approach, the warranty program. As a consequence, the dealer achieved a good, profitable expansion which came from capturing his share of the market growth plus a portion of the market share from his competition.

Developing a business concept and defining and establishing a market position are a natural part of doing business. The names and labels aren't important; it's the astuteness and clarity of thinking which matters. Companies evolve into a personality and a market position. Too frequently, though, entrepreneurs don't fully understand what their true market position is. They adopt conflicting approaches, which results in a mishmash of products, sales techniques, and advertising messages. They may aim messages at one market segment, while their customer base is being generated from another. These marketing inconsistencies often are harder to define than, say, financial problems. "Cash is short, profits are low," are frequently heard comments, but not so often do you hear, "I haven't clearly defined my market position." Nevertheless, mistakes in this phase of marketing can be the source of lower profits and short cash, because the owner is spending a higher marketing dollar for a lower sales return by advertising to the wrong customer segment, by sending out the wrong advertising message, by employing the wrong type of salesperson, by locating stores in the wrong places, or by carrying incompatible merchandise. All these factors and many more translate into a sales volume which isn't worth the range of costs needed to generate that sales volume.

Marketing position is a means of targeting the marketing efforts to that specific segment or to those specific segments of the market which the company can uniquely serve. This requires precise understanding of the qualities and attributes of the products or services, from the customers' point of view, and a good grasp of who the actual and potential customers are. The next step is to evaluate the strengths and weaknesses of what the company offers, from the customers' point of view, versus the competition. This is an ongoing process, because things change from year to year. Properly formulated, the market position will evolve out of the company's unique strengths. Then the job is to communicate this unique position effectively.

The process is applicable to specific products. Big companies do this constantly. For example, 7-UP® is the *un*-cola. For the people who want to drink Coke,® 7-UP has obvious weaknesses. But for people who prefer a no-caffeine, no-cola taste, 7-UP has a distinct advantage. The *un*-cola campaign positioned 7-UP by targeting it to that segment of the population which is its natural market.

A company can build its overall image by targeting a product or limited number of products to a specific part of the market. Take Levi's 501® jeans versus Levi's jeans in general. An owner can evaluate that one product very carefully by listing all of its advantages against its competition. The goal is to find the unique advantages which can be shown to the natural customers for that product in the marketplace.

Market Analysis

Defining the right market position for a company begins with an analysis of the customers, actual and potential, for the company's products or services. This same analysis provides the basis for setting realistic marketing and sales goals. Obviously, there are a multitude of customer groups, varying widely from industry to industry. These differences require vastly different marketing strategies and sales approaches. Entrepreneurs sell everything from high-fashion clothing to automated industrial controls.

How does one analyze the market? Most business owners have to use common sense in combination with their experience, industry statistics (when they are available and relevant), and sales information from the company's own records. The first step is to define the present customer base. Who accounts for the largest percentage of sales? The next largest percentage? The next? The retailer must know the profiles of the clientele to carry the right merchandise and to advertise the right way in the right media. The manufacturer has to know the customers by company and by industry. The entrepreneur must have a statistical understanding of the customer base.

At the same time, the entrepreneur must have a keen insight into the customer's needs. Industrial clients may be trying to control energy consumption, or they may need imprinted T-shirts for companywide safety programs, or they may need consultation concerning industrial hygiene. The list is endless. No matter what the industry, the business owner must provide a product or service to meet the customer's needs, which means that those needs must be well understood. In addition to this understanding, there must be some insight into how these needs will translate into demand for the company's product or service. We sold $2 million of masonry materials last year to our existing customer base. What will these customers buy from us this year? What new customers will we add to our customer list, and what kind of volume can we expect from them?

How does the business owner develop marketing insight? It comes from knowing the customers, whether we're talking about government technical officers, industrial purchasing managers, or single professionals aged twenty-five to thirty-five. The owner has to know who they are, approximately how many there are, and what they want that the company has or could have to sell. This knowledge comes from talking with customers; from listening to salespeople reporting back from the field or from the store floor; from having customer service personnel ask a few discreet questions; from study-ing industry market research data, if it's available.

By developing this understanding of the customer, the owner can gain the ability to look at the company from the customer's point of view—looking at the business from the outside in, rather than from the inside out. Once the owner begins to know the customers, he or she can begin to think about them in a myriad of ways. What new products might better serve their needs, as they see their needs, and as the environment changes from year to year? How would advertising approaches A, B, or C appeal to them? What must be done to keep the business before the customers, so sales can be taken away from the competition? What kind of customer service job is being done, in terms of the way the staff handles the public, the response time, the quality of service? Growth may cause business owners to get out of touch with the customer. They don't actually see how the customer is being treated. Too many entrepreneurs are focused on managing day-to-day problems—certainly something one must do well to survive—but to gain market share, the owner has to be a marketer, as well.

The Effect of Economic Conditions

Some industries are affected more violently by prevailing economic conditions than others, but every entrepreneur must be alert to the changes which come from shifts in the economy. Many business owners have come to grief because they were oblivious to possibilities that business might fall off. It's not only a question of whether business might turn down or not—most home builders, for example, know there will be downturns—but when will the downturn come? This is what makes it so difficult.

Another confusing factor in assessing the economy is the behav-ior of the economists themselves. The newspapers are full of predic-tions: GNP will be at such-and-such a percent for the third quarter; interest rates will moderate in the first quarter of next year; demand for housing is on the upswing; businesses are building inventories; the leading economic indicators are up; stock market prices will do this or that. Republican economists attack Democratic administra-tion policies; Democratic economists attack Republican administra-tion policies. A multitude of learned institutes and government of-fices make economic predictions which differ.

To the dismayed onlooker, only one fact seems to be consistent—how frequently the predictions are wrong. Recessions so often shock the experts; economic recoveries so often catch them by surprise. Sometimes it's the simple fact of the change that startles them; sometimes it's the magnitude of the change which was not foreseen. Whatever the case, the consequences to workers and employers amount to billions of dollars. To the hard-working entrepreneur, economic changes can mean anything from bankruptcy or severe belt-tightening on the negative side, to ballooning profits and an affluent lifestyle on the positive side. Many entrepreneurs experience swings from one to the other and back again. This scenario is further complicated by the fact that some industries expand right through recessions while others contract during prosperous periods, because each industry has its own cycles.

What is the entrepreneur to do? "Sure the company affects my business, but how can I predict that? Even the experts are confused. Just let me get on with business and I'll deal with the problems when they come, but in the meantime, this year is going to be my best ever. I feel it. I'm opening up a new store. I've increased my advertising. I've increased my line of credit with the bank to buy new inventory."

The essence of this problem lies in prediction. What is going to happen in the future, even in the near future, is uncertain. Some events are more likely than others. Every act we plan to undertake has a range of possible outcomes. When we get on a plane, there is one chance out of some huge number that the plane will crash. When we flip a coin . . . when we play blackjack at Las Vegas. But the same applies to whether a new salesperson will produce, whether the new general manager will work out, or whether the new product line will sell up to expectations.

The same holds for the economy. When the experts predict that GNP will be such and such for the quarter, they are really saying what they think is the most likely outcome. When the entrepreneur said it was going to be the best year ever, it was really an estimate of the most likely outcome. There are other possibilities. We all know that those other possibilities have a way of materializing. We face an uncertain future. Making predictions, and then sticking to them, is not the way to deal with the problem. Instead I recommend a different frame of mind, based on three key principles:

- First, how we feel about the future is not going to influence how things turn out. That the retailer felt it was going to be a great year won't make it so. Many entrepreneurs, however, fall into the trap of thinking that their business will go the way they feel it will. No. What happens is a function of countless variables in and out of the owner's hands. We will find out what the future holds in store only after we get there. Before the fact, it is only an estimate.

- Second, when estimating economic conditions and industry trends, we are actually assessing a set of probabilities. The economy can either decline, stay about the same, or expand. We can think about the magnitude of each change. We can then think that the chances are greater for one of these scenarios and less likely for the other two. For example, Linda, who owns an advertising agency, feels that the economy will be about the same next year. She gives it a fifty-fifty chance: about twenty percent probable that there will be a downturn, thirty percent probable that there will be an expansion.

- Third, we can structure plans about what we think will happen, and then monitor results in comparison with the plan and evaluate the economic developments when they have been established as fact. Deviations, either positive or negative, from what had been anticipated will require remedial action to bring the operation in line with the realities of the marketplace.

The Effects of Competition

Knowing the competition is an integral part of analyzing the market, both to establish a market position and to estimate what share of total sales a business might capture. The competition has a significant impact on all of marketing strategy. Who are the major competitors? What are their strengths and weaknesses? What do we have that gives us a distinct advantage against them in the competition for sales? What share of the market do they have? What share do we have?

To underestimate the competition spells disaster. One retailer was expanding very rapidly. He was selling to the middle market, positioning himself between the budget competition and the expensive boutiques. He had expanded to several stores in his metropolitan area and two stores in another city. At the peak of his expansion, a major chain entered the market on a discount basis, with a massive TV and newspaper advertising blitz. They began to open stores throughout the area, pulling in customers from all segments, especially the middle market. The retailer decided that the chain could not keep up the massive advertising blitz. He increased his own advertising budget to keep up as best he could, assuming that the chain would cut back after a year when they had achieved their desired penetration. Then there would be a readjustment, leaving our retailer in a solid position even if his sales growth had been slowed in the interim.

The chain's advertising blitz has continued to this day, some several years later. Their marketing strategy has resulted in massive sales, extensive store openings throughout the metropolitan area, and the capture of market share from every other retailer in that industry. They have driven a number of smaller retailers out of business, including the once successful retailer who didn't think they could do it.

It is also important to pay attention to the competition. The massive attack on the market by discounting has hit other retailing industries as well. A sudden, well-conceived attack on any industry by a well-financed, well-run competitor is going to hurt, but the damage will be even greater if the entrepreneur is napping. One must be up to date on the changes in the industry which could upset the balance in the day-to-day marketplace. Otherwise, an expansion might be undertaken, as I have seen happen, just when a major competitor was about to take a market share from everyone. A manufacturer might find its biggest seller made obsolete by a new product brought out by a competitor. A maintenance company might find that changes in technology have reduced the need for its services.

Pricing

Most entrepreneurs I have known have had a gut feeling for what they can charge and still sell their product or service with enough volume. Much of pricing is dictated by the marketplace to begin with. There are strategies. "Skim the cream" is what can be charged when the owner is lucky enough to offer a unique product for which there is a strong demand, allowing for an unusually high price. "Penetration" is at the other end, where the owner prices low to enter the market as deeply and as quickly as possible to get a volume position. "The middle" is the middle—trying to get the best price while still hitting the sales goal for the year. Pricing takes place in a myriad of environments, from competitive bids to industrial products to consumer retailing. For a small business, setting prices isn't textbook mechanical . . . it is usually a sweaty process of balancing how much it can be sold for versus how much can be sold.

The key is knowing what the costs are. *All* the costs. Cost of sales, selling, general, and administrative. Ultimately, all of the prices for all of the products and services must cover all of the costs, as well as leave the target profit. There are sales an entrepreneur should walk away from. In the final analysis, it is the bottom line, not the top line, that counts. I have met owners who have been excessively top-line oriented, and their companies were chronic losers as a consequence. They went after too many sales that had insufficient margins to cover all the needs.

Creating the Strategy

Marketing strategy is a way to pull all the resources of the company together to make a buck. It doesn't have to be fancy, theoretical, or business-school slick . . . in fact, it has to be intensely practical to work. Every company has a varied menu of ways to reach its customers. Frequently the problem is that these factors are employed by the entrepreneur in a disjointed way. I'm speaking of advertising (magazine, newspaper, radio, TV, industrial directory, yellow pages), word-of-mouth referrals, press releases, telemarketing, direct mailing, in-house sales, outside sales using company salespeople or industrial sales reps, product or service packaging, pricing strategies, customer service, store displays and merchandising, and special sales and promotions. Imbalance is the bugaboo of effective marketing.

A perennially winning sports team is a good analogy. Take the pro football teams which have the best records over a ten-year period. Invariably they maintain a balanced attack. They do not rely on a single aspect of the game; they have the ability to run and pass. Teams that only run or only pass eventually break down when playing a team with superior balance. But winning teams also have excellent defenses. Their special teams are sound. They execute all phases of the game consistently.

To beat the competition at the point of sale and then to close successfully requires a balanced attack. In reviewing the personal goals, the business concept, the market position, the analysis of the market, the competition, and the economic conditions, the key is to select those tools which will work in the company's marketplace. Then, fashion a marketing strategy that integrates those tools into a balanced program designed to produce the sales goals for the year.

Each phase of the program should be implemented in a way consistent with the overall strategy and personality of the business.

An example of marketing strategy

I once worked with a long-established, family-owned business which manufactured a line of proprietary electrical products. For years the company sold primarily to the Defense Department. Several years ago the owner started a distribution operation to sell accessories for the electrical devices, along with other allied products. He arranged distributorships with several major manufacturers. His concept was to offer his basic product line, plus distribution of items which were used in conjunction with the line. He could bid on government supply contracts calling for a full range of items; he could act as a distributors' distributor, with special emphasis on a military inventory. At the same time, the distribution business would open up the opportunity for some commercial sales, as well. The owner hoped to develop civilian applications for his manufacturing products.

Once the dealerships had been arranged and stocking of items was under way, the owner faced some nagging marketing problems. Long-time customers of the manufacturing products didn't realize he also handled a range of distribution items. Informing each customer as orders were placed got the word out too slowly. At the same time, the new distribution customers were unaware of the company's manufacturing line. In either case, the company was hampered by its long orientation as a service-based manufacturer, rather than as a marketing organization. Employees were used to filling orders instead of seeking out new customers. The owner had developed an integrated product line which tied together manufacturing and distribution. But no one knew about it, and the company lacked the marketing skills to promote the message.

At this point, an advertising consultant was retained, and a team was formed to develop a strategy with which to attack the marketplace. The first step was to restate the marketing concept. This company was "one quick and reliable source for electrical products" on a nationwide basis. The second step was to define the market as other electrical distributors, electrical contractors, manufacturers that used electrical devices as part of their products, government supply depots, and commercial contractors supplying military parts using these items. All these potential customers could get a full range of products with a single order, frequently faster than anywhere else because this was a stocking distributor. At the same time, the company was a manufacturer, offering its own set of integrated products. Pricing was competitive.

The third step was to address a crucial issue: How could they put out the message that all of this was available? First a catalog was proposed. A catalog would display for every customer the company's full range of manufacturing and distribution products. It would be a visually pleasing, informative document which would state the company's marketing concept and policies and list products, with example photographs and engineering specifications. But how could they get exposure in the targeted market segments? Magazine advertising was ruled out as high expense/diffused exposure. Manufacturer's sales reps were ruled out as high expense/limited exposure.

A direct mailing campaign was chosen to spearhead the marketing program. A visually distinctive mailer was designed to get across the idea of "one quick and reliable source for electrical products." This piece was mailed to thousands of companies chosen by the SIC (Standard Industrial Codes) that were in the market segments targeted for penetration. Those who responded to the mailing would be sent a catalog, and their names and addresses would be entered immediately on a mailing list to be maintained by an outside service.

The response to the mailing was about six percent. The mailing list began to expand rapidly. Catalogs were mailed out to the respondents, which put out the company's complete message to an increasingly wider circle. Distribution sales began to increase by forty percent annually. One of the marketing priorities was to respond to the returns from the mailing as quickly as possible; the company had trouble doing this initially because of sheer unfamiliarity with this kind of marketing program.

To supplement the mailings, a series of press releases were sent out, which resulted in product announcements in industrial magazines. These caused several hundred additional requests for catalogs. The mailing list continued to expand; distribution sales continued to increase. However, manufactured products did not share equally in the growth trends.

To keep the company's name in front of the customer list, line cards and rolodex cards were mailed out on an annual basis. The large direct mail campaign was tried again to addresses from SIC codes that had showed the highest percentage response to the previous mailing. Once again, the return was six percent. This time the staff, with growing marketing experience, mailed the catalogs out much more quickly. In subsequent years additional mailings targeted to specific products were tried. The response was three percent, and the owner was not pleased with the quality of the respondents.

The total reliance on direct mailing, which had launched the company into national awareness in the targeted market segments, which had stimulated distribution sales, and which had created a mailing list of thousands, was beginning to peak out. It was becoming apparent that an additional sales tool was needed to supplement the mailing strategies.

It was at this juncture that the owner looked into telemarketing. It fit naturally into the marketing strategy. The company had an extensive customer list and a larger mailing list. A systematic telemarketing program aimed at the customer list first, then the mailing list, then selected target industries enabled the owner to capitalize on the wide visibility of his company and the numerous active and inactive accounts which could be stimulated by personal contact. At the same time, telemarketing was an ideal follow-up to further direct mailing campaigns. With the hiring and training of a telemarketing staff, the company had a comprehensive marketing attack consisting of

- Well-designed direct mail pieces
- Catalogs, line cards, rolodex
- Newsletter sent to mailing list quarterly
- Ongoing program of press releases
- Advertisements in industrial registers
- A mailing list of thirty thousand respondents to mailings, press releases, advertisements
- A multiphase, ongoing telemarketing program
  — Aimed at active customers
  — Aimed at inactive customers
  — Aimed at noncustomers on mailing list
  — Aimed at targeted industries
  — Aimed at special leads
  — To follow up any direct mailing
- Carefully selected direct sales calls by senior marketing staff.

Know When to Ask for Help

This was a marketing strategy which worked effectively for one company. The effectiveness of specific tools and techniques varies dramatically depending on the industry and the company's markets. Entrepreneurs who are uncertain about their best marketing options will experience a diluted sales effort at a higher proportionate cost, an expensive double penalty. It is particularly difficult to know what kind of advertising will work best for your company, if any, if you haven't had prior experience. Do you advertise in the major local paper, which has by far the greatest readership but also the greatest cost? You're paying for metropolitanwide exposure. Should you advertise in the county paper, which is low cost but which also has limited readership? Is your product or service suitable for newspaper advertising to begin with? When is radio advertising effective? How is it used? If it's right for you, which stations should you use? Can you sell your product with direct mailing? When is magazine advertising effective, and how is it used? When is a direct sales force effective?

Due to experience and training, some people are better equipped to deal with marketing problems than others. After I have helped clients identify marketing problems, I have to call on marketing consultants to help us with the technical aspects of advertising and to bring more creativity to the development of marketing strategies. My skills lie more in general business consultation and financial advice; there are people who are just better at marketing than I am. All entrepreneurs have to evaluate their strengths and weaknesses across the range of management. If marketing is not the owner's strong point, as is frequently the case for entrepreneurs, then some help is necessary. It is important not to be obstinate about doing everything yourself.

MANAGING SALES

Start with the Sales Plan

After all the head scratching about goals, strategies, the make-up of the market, and the balanced set of tools to be employed, it comes down to, How do we get those sales on a practical, day-to-day basis? If feasible, the owner can target sales by major accounts and by expected new accounts. Some owners build their projections by individual sales rep. Others simply forecast sales on a monthly basis, taking seasonal fluctuations into consideration. These sales targets are a logical outcome of the marketing strategy adopted for the year and the resources which the owner has committed to achieving the goals.

Table 3-1 shows a sales plan developed for Zeta, Inc., a small company which was only two years old. It is a simple but effective approach which would work just as well for a considerably larger, older company. The owners projected over twelve months, which is a good planning period for small businesses. What happens beyond twelve months is too speculative to be meaningful. In fact, for some volatile industries, such as home building, six-month planning is more satisfactory.

The baseline for the projections was an analysis of sales for the major accounts during the fiscal year just completed. The owners evaluated what might happen with these accounts during the new year. They felt that most would reorder at about the same rate. A monthly average for each account was established, and then the total was adjusted for the pronounced seasonal fluctuations which were typical in their industry. The plus or minus sign over each column represents the seasonal fluctuation about the average for that month.

Zeta expected that, if no changes were made in their marketing approach, they would experience a thirty percent sales growth from new accounts. In addition, they planned an intensive direct selling campaign involving one of the owners and a new sales rep. They anticipated that it would take six months before major new accounts could be added. Since this program would begin November 1, they forecast a new $3,000-per-month account for each rep in March, and then two more in September. Smaller accounts, averaging about $2,000 between them, were also projected.

Who knows whether a plan will be successful or not? Owners who have been in business for a while can base their expectations on previous years, sometimes with great accuracy. But even for them, a new product or new advertising campaign creates uncertainty. Besides, economic conditions can change, to everyone's surprise, as we discussed earlier. Whatever the case, the sales plan sets the tone for the owner's entire operation for months to come, whether it is formally stated or just an assumption carried in someone's head. Every owner has expectations. Resources, in terms of personnel, facilities, equipment, marketing expenses, receivables, and inventory (if any) are going to be committed in pursuit of those expectations.

The benefit of having a formal sales plan is that the owner can compare monthly results to the targets. If deviations are substantial, one way or the other, adjustments to operations can be made before problems get out of hand. If you're way behind plan, then your

TABLE 3-1 ZETA, INC., SALES PLAN, OCTOBER 1991–SEPTEMBER 1992

	Oct	Nov	Dec	Jan	Feb	Mar	Apr	May	Jun	Jul	Aug	Sep	Total
	+	+	+	−	−	++	++	++	AVG	−	+	+	
Major Accounts*	15,000	15,000	15,000	11,000	8,500	16,000	16,000	16,000	13,500	8,500	15,000	15,000	164,500
Internal Growth (+30%)	4,500	4,500	4,500	3,300	2,600	4,800	4,800	4,800	4,100	2,600	4,500	4,500	49,500
Direct Sales Campaign	0	0	2,000	2,000	2,000	8,000	8,000	8,000	8,000	8,000	8,000	14,000	68,000
TOTAL	19,500	19,500	21,500	16,300	13,100	28,800	28,800	28,800	25,600	19,100	27,500	33,500	282,000

* Major Accounts, Monthly Average

SDS	1,200
PSD	4,300
WW	1,200
RP	300
MLNH	1,000
MNNN	300
AA	200
CC	300
ASDF	500
NVF	700
EP	600
RHTJ	200
LC	200
PF	200
CJM	100
AIMA	100
GRC	100
OTHERS	2,000
TOTAL	13,500

expenses are going to be too high. Monitoring results can tip you off before losses build up. If you're way ahead of plan, cash-flow problems can quickly make a bad thing out of a good thing. Prudent financing can be arranged to correct the problem before it occurs. Otherwise, the owner realizes too late that the company's position is different than had been expected. The end of the third quarter is not the time to begin a turn-around from a loss to a profit for the year. It's best not to go to the bank for a loan after you've run out of cash. The banker's first thought is, "Why haven't they planned for this?"

Knowing where your sales should be during the year, and then comparing that to where you actually are on a timely basis, is the first crucial step to management control.

Sales Management

Even if there is a sales manager on the staff, sales management begins with the owner of the business. When there isn't a sales manager, the owner wears the hat. Once the marketing strategy and sales plan have been developed, it would be nice to turn them over to someone and go on about the day-to-day business, taking up problems as they arise. If there is no one to turn plans over to, it would be nice to set them aside in a file as a reminder, and then turn to the day-to-day. In fact, this is what many entrepreneurs do, but it doesn't work that way. The marketing and sales process is intricate, dealing as it does with the relationship of the company to the outside world of customers. Follow-up is essential.

Let me give you an example concerning the manufacturer/distributor I mentioned earlier. When they entered the telemarketing phase of their marketing program, it was a crucial step. They had invested substantial sums in developing a large mailing list and a broad visibility for their company on a national basis. They needed to punch through that potential to increase sales. Telemarketing was their primary vehicle for growth at that time. The strategy had been developed on a team basis, which resulted in a reorganization of marketing, sales, and customer service to create the maximum number of telephone salespeople. Staff meetings were held to introduce the new organization and to gain support for the program, which was received positively. Training sessions were held to prepare the phone salespeople for their new responsibilities. Sales goals and specific calling list priorities were established. A kick-off date was selected.

Follow-Up Is Crucial

The owner held a follow-up meeting with the sales manager to discuss progress after the first week. Results were good, in terms of both staff attitudes and performance and the reception they had been getting from customers. During this discussion, however, a very disturbing fact was disclosed. Since the company had never been a telemarketing organization, the phone system was not designed to handle this kind of activity. Existing sales lines had to be left open for incoming sales-order calls. The lines available for telemarketing had to be shared on a rotating basis, which cut the volume of out calls to half of the staff capability. With everyone focused on the development of new marketing concepts, departmental reorganization, and the establishment of sales priorities and training programs, the telephone system had fallen through the cracks. Neither the time nor the funds were presently available for the purchase of an elaborate new system.

A very practical solution was devised. The managers of the company's other departments all had private lines. They were willing to give up these lines to the telemarketing staff, which allowed the program to proceed at full capacity after a short delay for the telephone company to make the line changes. A simple matter of switching lines around allowed the company to double its selling effort. Yet, because the change involved other managers, it was necessary for the president to be involved. This president was able to solve the problem because he was personally involved in the follow up. So often in business the successful implementation of a major commitment comes down to working out some picayune impediment that no one had thought of. Too frequently I have seen owners neglect to follow up on their commitments to find out these facts. It was assumed that having been planned and decided, the program would carry itself out. Understanding how to follow up is one of the characteristics separating those who succeed from those who fail.

The business owner has to manage the sales effort, whether it be establishing a dialogue with the sales manager, as the manufacturer/distributor did, or dialogues with the sales staff, if the owner is the sales manager. Even in a one-person company, sales management must take place—the dialogue is with yourself. In any event, sales management begins with establishing priorities which are agreed on between the owner and the staff. From then on there must be a dialogue on a regular basis between the owner and the staff about progress. Do the results show that our priorities were correct? Do we need to shift emphasis to get better results? How is the performance of each salesperson shaping up? What do we need to do to get better results? Are we dovetailing the other phases of our marketing with the sales effort to maximize our impact on the market?

Sales Personnel

One of the most difficult areas for all small business is the hiring and maintaining of an effective sales staff. Time and again I have witnessed owners struggle unsuccessfully with the problems of ineffective salespeople. There are several factors that contribute to the difficulties. By nature of the job, salespeople spend most of their time away from the company, operating autonomously and with heavy requirements for good personal organization and initiative. At the same time, the small company, either because of its meager financial resources or because of the limited sales potential of its markets, does not pay large sales commissions or base salaries, especially in comparison to large companies. As a result, the more highly talented people have a tendency to gravitate to the large companies where potential annual incomes are many times greater. Entrepreneurs have to take their sales staff from among less experienced people or from those who, for one reason or another, are not high-volume producers. Facing these problems, owners frequently have limited understanding of how to manage a sales staff, often because they themselves have had little direct selling experience. The problems are magnified because most people trying to get jobs in sales make a good impression in an interview, irrespective of how well they will do over the long haul. The owner may hire someone who seems impressive, expecting real performance. Yet the owner may be without the tools to follow up on the day-to-day effort. All of these factors result, more often than not, in a lethargic sales effort which costs the entrepreneur both in sales salaries and in lost sales volume. Often the owner realizes this failure only after some time has passed, which serves to increase both the expenses and the amount of sales which have been lost.

The Owner Must Be Involved

What is an owner to do? He or she can't afford the luxury of avoiding the sales effort because of not being good at it, not understanding it, or not feeling comfortable with it. That's akin to writing a suicide note to the marketplace. In a small company, the owner is the origin of all things. Turning sales over to someone else won't work. No one else has the hunger for the success of the company that the owner does. No one else has their investment at risk, either in financial or personal terms. If it doesn't come from the top, it won't come, at least not with the intensity and focus which a small company needs to survive and succeed. If the owner can manage the sales effort effectively, as a direct participant in the program or as the sales manager or as the president directing the sales manager, then the tone is set for intense effort from the staff. If the owner is vague, indecisive, or inattentive, the sales effort will drift. As you would expect, the entrepreneurs who are most often successful with selling efforts are those who have come from a marketing and sales background. Of course, they have other weaknesses. But for those of us who have to do it by our own bootstraps, here are some of the steps we can follow:

- KNOW THE CUSTOMER. Effective selling begins with understanding the customer's problems, then showing that we are ready, willing, and able to help solve those problems. For example, a customer who is worried about price can be shown that we can deliver good quality at a price they can afford. If an owner has a good grasp of these issues, that understanding can be passed on to the sales force.
- DEVELOP A COMPREHENSIVE, PRACTICAL MARKETING STRATEGY. This will give the sales force a sound context within which to work. Their efforts will be supplemented by the other marketing activities, and their morale will be enhanced by knowing this.
- NEGOTIATE REASONABLE SALES GOALS WITH THE SALES MANAGER AND/OR STAFF. From a psychological standpoint, it is important to gain a mutual commitment to these goals. Superficial agreement, without genuine commitment, doesn't amount to much.
- FOLLOW UP. Establish a dialogue with the manager or staff about the results. Well-organized weekly meetings can be used to evaluate the degree of success the staff is having with the present priorities. Discussions can lead to modifications in any phase of the program, to enhance the results.
- MONITOR INDIVIDUAL PERFORMANCE. Superior performance

needs to be recognized. An owner doesn't want the best salesperson to leave unexpectedly. On the other hand, subpar performance is costly. Why is a salesperson not meeting target? Perhaps some training is needed. Maybe there is a personal problem. Perhaps this is a person who will have to be let go. Some weeding out has to be done over time to build a dynamic staff.

- DEVELOP SALES CONSCIOUSNESS THROUGHOUT THE COMPANY. Some organizations get into the rut of being service oriented or production oriented. Success starts with the customer. If everyone thinks sales, then they will be sensitive to whatever they might be able to do to enhance the effort—from answering the telephone graciously to putting something extra into the product they're making or the service they're providing. They'll cooperate and help the sales staff any way they can.

- STUDY COMPANIES WHICH HAVE DEVELOPED SUCCESSFUL SALES PROGRAMS. An owner who learns what worked for other companies can do the same things or modifications of them. Search for quality seminars, articles, or books on sales and marketing. The knowledgeable owner is better off, and the same goes for the staff.

Setting the Marketing and Sales Budget

Entrepreneurs frequently ask, "How much should I spend on advertising?" That's a difficult question to answer. For some companies the total expenditure for marketing and sales can have several components—advertising, promotion expenses, travel and entertainment, sales salaries and commissions, show expenses, telephone expenses and so on. It is best to think of these expenditures as a percentage of sales. Given my gross profit, after my cost of goods, what percentage of sales can I devote to my total marketing effort, while covering my administrative expenses and producing a profit?

This percentage varies widely from industry to industry because the nature of the sales effort is so different. Retail advertising budgets run from five percent to eight percent of sales. Manufacturers work more in the range of two percent to three percent. Individual companies will differ within those ranges, depending on the owner's orientation. To this the owner must add the rest of the marketing expenses and sales costs, as described earlier. The starting point, then, is to analyze industry averages to find the range other companies have settled on as practical. A central part of the year's market plans is the estimate of expenses for each activity, to set a prudent level of expenses as a percentage of the expected sales volume. It's a balancing of what is needed to accomplish an aggressive plan versus what the company can afford.

This is where the sales plan starts to be so important. If the actual sales come in less than projected, it follows that marketing and sales expenses will exceed the acceptable percentages and some cuts may have to be made. More than one entrepreneur has lost control of these relationships, with substantial losses as the penalty. If expenses are starting to exceed budgets, it's a tip-off that the owner is trying to buy into the market. This could be a strategy for a one-time penetration, but if it happens year after year it would mean that the owner is trying to reach an unattainable sales volume, either because of the economy or competition or because the market just isn't there. That means part of the budget is going to be paid out of profits, rather than by new customers. Another reason for disappointing sales could be that the program isn't as effective as it should be. If marketing and selling expenses are too high, that would be the first place to look.

But what if there aren't any industry averages? Many business owners work in unique circumstances where no one has gathered statistics. The first step in getting a reference point is to think of any industries which might have similar marketing situations. Their averages could give a clue. If not, then the owner has to set a marketing budget by analyzing all the other expenses, subtracting those from the gross profit; then, after leaving an allowance for profit, the rest can go to marketing. (I discuss managing for profits in detail in chapter 5.)

Advertising, in particular, has a direct relationship to sales. If the nature of the industry dictates that advertising is an integral part of the marketing effort—the audio retailer versus a competitive-bid general contractor—then the owner has to decide on the percentage of sales at which to set the advertising budget. The advertising expense should follow the sales curve during the course of the year. Some entrepreneurs spend extra advertising dollars when they have some money or when they want to pump up sales. Never try to change a natural sales situation drastically with forced advertising. Stick to the percentages.

When Should You Use an Advertising Agency?

To begin with, many agencies have a minimum billing—for example, around $25,000 annually. Entrepreneurs with smaller needs can look for freelancers to create graphics and designs. Some companies have in-house talent, either on the graphics side or in someone who has experience in advertising. In these situations a combination of in-house capabilities and outside support can be developed. For many companies in advertising-oriented industries, an agency will be necessary. Don't hire an agency simply because it has a recognizable name or because the account executive is an impressive talker. The entrepreneur must penetrate the image to judge whether or not this agency has a good "feeling" for the business, which will provide creative ideas about getting the message out to customers. Otherwise, the owner may be throwing money—lots of it—away. Agencies can be very expensive. In fact, the business owner must be alert to keeping the agency expenditure, plus all advertising costs, within that percentage of sales budget.

A creative agency can have a major impact on a company's development. The manufacturer I mentioned earlier went from an unknown business to a position of national prominence with the help of its agency. Subsequently, a foreign manufacturer, looking for a distributor to introduce its products to the U.S. market, wrote the company to this effect: "We would like you to consider carrying our products, as you are obviously a leader in your industry." Some things to look for when selecting an agency are:

• Active participation by the agency's owners
• An agency with a good growth record of its own
• A creative "knack" for your situation
• A commitment as to who will work on your account
• A check of the agency's client list and comments from representative accounts
• An examination of some of the agency's campaigns, hopefully ones which are similar to your own situation
• A discussion of accounts lost during the last year and why.

In dealing with the agency, it's best to have a clearly and persuasively stated marketing and business plan for them to evaluate.

Too many business owners leave it up to the outside professional to come up with ideas. Many professionals drift in such situations, with the owner coming out the loser. The better the job the owner does of stating the overall situation—positioning the agency, in effect—the better the agency can generate creative ideas for electrifying the marketplace.

SUMMARY

Financial management is the most often cited weakness of entrepreneurs, but I have frequently seen owners struggle unsuccessfully with marketing and sales. As in every phase of management, a successful marketing program requires an understanding of how the process works in the industry. Everything begins with sales. If the owner doesn't have an intensive, well-conceived marketing and sales effort, the sales goals will not be met. A good program blends all the relevant phases of marketing into a balanced attack. Then the owner follows up—establishing a dialogue with the sales department (even if that department is only the owner; you can challenge your own thinking just as well as anyone else's), monitoring actual results in comparison to the sales plan, monitoring actual expenses in relationship to the budgets and the actual sales, and continuing to study the customers and the competition—to establish an ever-improving program.

An owner can't duck personal involvement in the development of a marketing strategy and the execution of the sales program. No one else will have the hunger for the company's success, because no one else has the investment at risk. Excellence in marketing and sales is putting your best foot forward to capitalize on everything else the company does.

4

What to Do When Growth Gets Difficult

FAST OUT OF THE STARTING GATE

Frequently a business can grow fast in the first few years. Many of the initial customers are people you knew before you started. You added to the customer base by networking with your initial contacts to meet new people. Sometimes early growth comes from one good customer you continue to cultivate for additional business, from a good reception to your first product, or from the trade area around your first store.

At some point, depending on the circumstances of your business, sales growth begins to slow. You've run through your contacts; that big customer has reached the limit; your new product has reached peak sales; you've tapped out the customer base around your store. Many entrepreneurs get stuck here for good.

Sam has been doing $1 million annually, plus or minus, for ten years. He manufactures electronic components for a stable but no-growth market. He hasn't been able to develop a new product line to create additional sales. In contrast, Jack has a service business that's in a growth industry. But he's been stuck at about $3.5 million annually, plus or minus, for years. He has no concept of how to set up a dynamic marketing program.

THE HEROIC SOLUTION

Too often, entrepreneurs try to break out of the sales box by going for the home run—a glitzy new product, a fancy new store, a burst of advertising. They bet more than they can afford in hunger for new growth. Sadly, the results are often poor. New products have a high failure rate; new stores can take years to mature (if ever); there's much more to marketing than spending money on advertising. I've seen many businesses go under after the big growth project ruined profits and drained cash flow from operations. Modest success was transformed into total failure.

THINK ABOUT GETTING RICH SLOWLY

It's not how much money you have now or next year or the year after, but how much money you have five years or ten years from now. You want to be the one standing at the finish line with a bundle to enjoy for the rest of your life. The Japanese have proven that working assiduously for market share year after year pays off, while the quick-fix sector of American industry loses out again and again.

I know many entrepreneurs who went for fast growth, despite the risks, only to lose out. They may have lived high but only for a while. Arnold started his business with $4,000. Ten years later he hit $90 million in sales. His net worth was $25 million. He had boats, planes, and women. He was the classic entrepreneur of the 1980s who took risks with other people's money to live life in the fast lane. Arnold is now penniless.

For the first several years Arnold did many things right. He paid attention to his business, developed management controls, had a ground-level vision of how to develop markets. But success got to him. He began to think he was invincible. An idea was good because he thought of it. That's when he started to play the fast-lane game to make his success even bigger. Now the history of success is left for others to write.

DEVELOP GROWTH STRATEGIES PIECE BY PIECE

Don't fail to see that your initial growth has created the platform you need for success:

- A solid customer base has been developed.
- Profitable operations have been established.
- Cash flow is under control and banking relationships are in place.
- The management, administrative, and accounting core for a good business is in operation.

Success comes from the bottom line of your business, not the top line. It doesn't matter how big the sales volume is if you can't make a profit. Conversely, profitable operations create opportunities for more success. I have a client who makes twenty percent before tax on $2 million in sales. If another entrepreneur makes ten percent on $4 million, who has the bigger business?

With profitability in mind, develop growth strategies piece by piece. Remember the platform for success you have already created. You have a management and administrative core that can handle new business, for the time being, without much additional expense. If you bring on new sales an increment at a time, say $250,000 or $500,000, you will capture the entire gross profit on those sales to go straight to the bottom line.

The results are dramatic for profits with a not-so-dramatic increase in sales. Let's say you're generating $2 million in sales, with profits of ten percent or $200,000. Let's assume you add a product feature that generates $250,000 in new sales—not a sales increase that will get you featured in magazines. But with a thirty percent gross profit, you can add $75,000 to profits with no appreciable additional costs. That's almost a forty percent increase in profits from only slightly more than ten percent in new sales. In a small growing business, enormous increases in profits can be achieved with small sales increases.

The trick is to piece together new sales in markets that diversify your sales base. Develop products, services, customers, or geographic markets that are logical steps from where you are now. Recognize that your initial product line or market area will probably mature well before you've achieved your business goals. If you're smart, you'll anticipate this and begin to develop additional sales opportunities beforehand.

Be patient when your sales growth begins to flatten. You don't have to hit a home run to break out of the sales bind. Small increases in sales can be enormously profitable. Your goal is to create a diversified but integrated set of products or services that will provide a sound base for your business and for your wealth over the long term.

In reality, developing new products, marketing for new customers, and opening new locations all require money. Sometimes the investment can be very big in relationship to your total resources. The following sections discuss how to deal with the hazards of expansion using retailers and hi-tech companies as examples.

RETAILERS: LOOK BEFORE YOU LEAP TO EXPAND

From One to Two—Look Out!

Mary is a sophisticated, tough-minded retailer. But when she came to see me, the situation was bleak. "My business is my life," she said. "I can't fail."

She'd started a store in suburban Virginia with a concept that was a hit in another city. After two years she was pushing $1 million in sales. The trouble came when she opened a store across the river in Maryland. She was hurt by the unforeseen problems that have destroyed many local retailers.

I have clients who have expanded successfully. But they will tell you, along with those who have lost their businesses, to analyze the pitfalls very carefully before you leap to expand. In retailing, especially, a disastrous expansion can't be undone.

What Are the Pitfalls of Expansion?

Location.   Many small retailers die agonizing deaths due to poor location. Mary had a good Virginia location. Her downfall came because she chose poorly in Maryland. Why? She didn't know the market. Successful expansion depends on shrewd judgments about traffic patterns, local buying habits, and where development is headed.

When you sign the lease, you're locked into the traffic patterns at that spot. Retail leases are astronomical in many metropolitan areas. The instant you lift that pen to sign, you may be dead. Do you really know how to pick that site?

Advertising. As a small retailer, you're behind the advertising eight ball. At five percent, your annual budget on $1 million in sales is only $50,000. Even $100,000 won't buy you top-of-the-mind awareness—and you'll choke at ten percent. That's why Mary was locked in by location. She didn't have enough money for advertising to make a difference. You won't either.

You can't try for high visibility in a major newspaper. Nobody will notice you. And the rates you pay are for metrowide exposure, not your locality. The switch to local media will give you more space, but the readership is drastically reduced. Spend your advertising budget wisely. But don't expect to increase traffic to your store appreciably over what your location will give you.

Managing. Your first store is successful because you're a good retailer. Merchandise is carefully selected and attractively displayed. Customers are greeted warmly, and they are well served. There is good selling on the floor. Inventory is watched. The store is neat. Attendance is good. Morale is high. You see to it personally.

With a second store, you can't be in two places at once. Mary's solution was to hire a good manager for Maryland. But she found that hiring a good manager in Washington's competitive labor market was difficult. After the store foundered, she had to spend time there because the manager was weak. Then performance in Virginia dropped because her assistant manager couldn't take charge. Mary hopped back and forth, unable to make the numbers profitable for either store. She lacked the money to hire a truly strong manager to back her up.

Hidden overhead. Rent isn't a hidden expense. But beware of the landlord's override on sales volume in big shopping centers. Achieving a profitable balance between lease cost and sales volume is tricky in murderous rent districts. A new store in a new market is always a gamble. I know of retailers who failed the moment they signed the lease.

And watch the leasehold improvements. Even experienced chain owners can overspend in outfitting a new store. Excessive leasehold improvements use up cash, exhaust credit capacity, and create burdensome debt repayments. The combination of an excessive lease with overspending on leasehold cannot be undone. If the sales aren't there, you're through.

Another hidden expenditure is inventory that "sells to the wall." Cash has to go into display merchandise over and above the surges you'll have to manage for peak season. The new store will absorb a lot of cash before it returns a nickel, but you can't make up for it this time by living a lean life. There's a manager there now, not you.

But there's more than a manager. One person can't run a store seven days a week. There must be an assistant manager. There have to be enough clerks to service customers properly and keep shoplifters from stealing your profits.

There's a fixed cost to running a store that is made of rent, principal and interest, and people, plus things like telephones. The gross profits on store sales must cover that fixed cost. Heaven forbid an economic downturn while your store is building up. Retailers definitely suffer during recessions. Sales will go down, but fixed cost stays fixed, if you want to keep the store open. And beware of competition. When a bigger, more powerful competitor opens a store in your market, sales will go down, no matter what you do.

Accounting.   Accounting and bookkeeping are the Achilles' heel of small business. In expansion, financial control is frequently lost. Trouble is brewing, but the owner doesn't know because the figures are months late. With one store, you're on top of it. You see the sales come in. You pretty much know the sales price. You watch the inventory yourself.

The second store complicates matters. You're worried about it, so you don't spend full time in store 1. But you're not full time in store 2, either. How do you know what your gross profit is? Do you have a computerized inventory system that prints out your true cost of goods? Or does your accountant plug in last year's gross profit percentage to prepare financial statements? Are you even getting monthly statements? Do you have accurate statements for each store? I have seen lives ruined by these factors.

If you don't know your true gross profit until after year-end inventory, you're flying blind through jagged mountains. Retailing is not a high-profit business. A variation of two percent gross profit to sales can wipe out your profit for the year. I know of variations that were greater than that. One gremlin is sale merchandise: How much did it reduce gross profit? Total sales volume is illusory. Gross profit is what counts.

Mary Lost Control

Mary anticipated the need for better accounting. She selected new software, along with a consultant to help install it. But among Mary, the consultant, her bookkeeper, and the outside accountant, things began to unravel. The software didn't work as well on Mary's existing hardware as expected. The consultant ran up fees making modifications. Her bookkeeper had trouble with the new system. The outside consultant was involved in other things.

Mary went six months without financial statements—the six months after her new store opened. She knew she was in trouble, but how much? When she finally got her statements, the answer was "a lot."

The Mini-Chain

Beyond two stores is the mini-chain. The pitfalls remain the same, while the management is more complex. A major new store with poor location, rent too high, and excessive leasehold can devastate an entire chain. The fixed cost of hidden overhead operates systemwide, but it is magnified by a warehouse, delivery trucks, and a set of managers at the corporate office. The owner is now a CEO who may not visit stores for months and who never gets on the sales floor. The problem of hiring and keeping good managers is multiplied by the number of stores you have.

A strong accounting system is mandatory to keep track of inventory, gross profits, and profitability, store by store. Without it, trouble will occur. A mini-chain is particularly vulnerable to attack by a large competitor. An advertising budget of half a million for a $10 million chain isn't much versus a competitor with millions to spend. And a common mistake of mini-chains is to keep too many marginal stores in operation. A sales downturn caused by a competitor or by economic conditions will create losses very quickly for a marginal chain.

How to Expand Successfully

How do you avoid the pitfalls of expansion? I don't think you can. Each new store is a risk. Somewhere along the line, even the cleverest operator will miscalculate. The answer isn't to avoid expansion altogether. You can pursue successful expansion by developing hard-nosed answers to two questions.

First, what is a realistic and complete assessment of the costs—hidden and obvious—of the new store? And stick to those budgets! Second, can you absorb the cash, accounting, and management drains of the new store from the profits and resources of your existing store(s)? Even if the new store gets off to a bad start? The trick is to absorb the drain of expansion with profits and cash flow from your mature stores. Then, expansion will lead to greater profitability, a stronger market position, and more opportunities for you and your management team to grow.

NEW PRODUCTS WON'T BE CARRIED MERELY BY TECHNICAL BRILLIANCE

The Great Pitfall

Recently I met an entrepreneur who was conducting the final testing of a new industrial product.

"What are your marketing plans?" I asked.

He wrinkled his nose. "I'm an electrical engineer . . . I leave marketing to other people."

Our new entrepreneur is ready to fall head first into the great pitfall of new product development. *It takes as much time and money—if not much more of both—to develop the market for a new product as it does to develop the product itself.*

Many cities are strewn with the corpses of R&D firms; many of them because they ran out of money before they could penetrate the market for their product.

The Technical Hazards

Developing a new product can lead to great success, but there are serious hazards on both the technical side and the marketing side. Many years ago an electronics client of mine said of his partner,

"John is one of the top design engineers in the world. He can solve any problem in contemporary electronics. But we can't always tell how long it will take him."

Estimating time and money for design is extremely difficult, even for the very best. Many projects have died in this phase. But let's say that design has been completed and that the prototype has been fabricated and then tested successfully in the laboratory. Now we come to the second great technical pitfall—testing on site.

Our new product has to work on the plant floor, on the ceiling, on production machinery, in animals, in the bodies of humans, at the retail counter, and in the warehouse. Our prototype has to do on site what we say it will, with consistency. It must be reliable.

My first exposure to a new product was twenty years ago with a client who had developed a water-jet drill that was clearly superior in penetrating hard materials to any traditional drilling system. Tests under varying conditions proved that it was faster. A $30 million market was at stake.

But after years of testing, the company couldn't prove that the water jet would be as reliable as traditional equipment. A brilliant invention with brilliant performance was unable to clear the practical hurdle of reliability. Venture capital had been raised on its promise.

The water jet exemplifies a treacherous problem for small companies trying to sell new products to big companies. Decision making by our big brothers can take months, even years. I've seen small companies go broke waiting for a bureaucracy to grind out a decision.

The Market Hazards

The successful development of a new product is at best only half the game. How is the product to be sold? Many technical entrepreneurs don't know the answer. Their new product is all dressed up with nowhere to go. Too often I've looked into the haunted eyes of an engineer or microbiologist who's realized he isn't going to make it.

The sheer brilliance of a new product won't carry the day. Products have to be sold. Thirty years ago, who had the best computers . . . IBM or Univac?

Is there a distribution system for your product, wholesalers or dealers who can resell your product with their own advertising campaigns and direct sales forces? If so, how do you sell to them?

If this is your first product, what do you offer a distributor? You don't have a corporate name to pull the product through. You don't have an advertising program aimed at the end user to stimulate sales. Don't expect the distributor to order thousands of units for initial stocking. You're going to be at the bottom of the priority list, and it's going to be a long, uphill battle to generate volume sales.

Some products are sold primarily at industrial trade shows. Others require advertising in technical magazines or industrial directories. There are telemarketing and direct mail campaigns. Some products must be sold by a direct sales force. Systems of manufacturers reps can be set up to avoid the cash drain of an in-house sales staff.

Manufacturers reps are notorious for giving short shrift to new products. This means sales management. A sales force, either inside or outside, requires systematic, weekly management from an experienced hand—someone who can weed out nonperformers quickly and who can keep the performers motivated to reach their goals.

Many products require all of the above. Success means a carefully developed marketing strategy that combines several tools, with the proper emphasis and with precise timing, into a comprehensive attack. As an electrical engineer, microbiologist, software designer, can you do that?

Can You Hire Someone to Market for You?

One answer is to hire someone to do it for you. The results I have seen have been dismal. First, an effective marketing director or sales manager can demand a salary that few small companies can afford. A middle-level salary is more likely. You get what you pay for. The tricks of bringing out a new product for a small business are frequently beyond the capabilities of a mid-level manager.

Second, there's a subtle wrinkle with major consequences: A good sales manager may not know much about developing a marketing strategy, about how to use advertising or direct mail. A good marketing director may be an abysmal sales manager. With limited funds, most small companies try to combine the two functions, with mixed results.

Third, no employee will have the incentive you do to make the product work. It's your invention, your money at risk, your future. You're the one who has the intensity and determination to overcome all obstacles. "But I'm not a salesperson," you say. "I don't know anything about marketing." You probably don't have a choice.

To Begin, You'll Probably Have to Do It Yourself

Years ago the two electronics partners felt they couldn't sell. They went through three marketing and sales directors with pitiful results. Only when they resolved to learn how to market and to sell did their company become successful.

Marketing is expensive. A $100,000 advertising budget is lunch money when you're trying to sell across the country. Unless you're experienced, sales reps can run through a year's draw, burden, and travel before you realize they're unproductive. A fancy brochure combined with aggressive direct mailing can cost $50,000, with minimum results. If you don't know how to work a trade show, the entire expenditure can be useless. Dollars flow out fast; sales come in slowly.

A few years ago, I advised two entrepreneurs with a brilliant technology to move into their basement. Since then they have won a major national award, and they have had extraordinary publicity. They're still in the basement. Sales have come slowly, and they need every nickel for marketing and for survival.

The cruelest reality is to realize that there is no market for your product. Years ago a small company set out to manufacture interferon. Incredibly, two years and $2 million later they had succeeded, only to find that interferon would never fulfill its promise.

Tips on Developing a New Product Successfully

The future of industry is based on new products, and you have to know how to develop one, perhaps several of them. Others have succeeded. You have the right to try. I have two recommendations for you.

First, when raising funds for product development, make sure you raise at least as much, if not more, for marketing. Otherwise, you'll get halfway across the ocean only to run out of fuel. It is extremely rare that sales of a new product will cover its marketing costs. The initial thrust of—six months? a year? two years?—must come from other funds.

Second, avoid basing the success or failure of your company on an exotic new product. It may not work technically. It may not succeed in the market. *The Economist* reports that companies such as Procter & Gamble, an all-time marketing great, are now experiencing failure on nine out of ten new products. The cost of failure is being carried by the success of products already in the market.

The ideal combination is to market "meat-and-potatoes" products or services that fill daily needs. Steady sales cover the overhead and help to absorb product development. If the exotic new product fails, you'll survive to develop another product for another day. Intelligently managed R&D combined with shrewd marketing will ultimately add the products you need to achieve significant success.

SUMMARY

Fast growth out of the starting gate doesn't guarantee sustained growth for the future. After the success of selling to your initial contacts or of selling your first product or service, systematic marketing becomes the name of the game.

Don't think you have to launch new products or services heroically to keep growing. Think about diversifying one piece at a time. Don't forget the retailer who leaped to expand, only to strangle on the added costs of operating in an unfamiliar market.

Remember that new products won't be carried merely by technical brilliance. Success comes from effective marketing, which requires as much clever thinking and at least as much time and money.

5

Manage for Profits

PROFITS AND THE FINANCIAL MANAGEMENT JUGGLING ACT

Financial management is the most cited cause for small business failure. Again and again I have heard entrepreneurs say, "I got my business off to a good start. I know how to manage my operations, but now I'm in over my head. Finances are getting more and more important, and I just don't know what to do."

Financial management is difficult because it's a juggling act during which the owner must keep three balls in the air at all times—profits, cash flow, the company's financial position. These three factors are highly interrelated, but there isn't a single equation which allows an entrepreneur to enter some numbers and derive a solution to financial problems. Yet so many things hinge on the financial outcome: the basic solvency of the company, the amount of salary and benefits the owner can prudently take, the degree of expansion which can be undertaken in the future, whether or not the bank loan can be arranged, how much the company is worth to investors. Effective financial management requires experience combined with knowledge of the principles of finance which are at work during the growth of a small business. Most owners haven't had the luxury of either. However, when financial problems occur, that luxury has suddenly become a necessity.

Profits Are the Key to Long-Range Health

After taxes, the profits are retained in the business to develop the stockholder's equity, which increases financial strength and enhances the owner's ability to borrow from the bank or to work out equipment leases or, possibly, to increase credit limits with vendors. A strong equity increases the company's value to outside investors or to potential purchasers. The ability to earn profits continually is a consequence of an efficient, well-managed operation, and it is seen as such by these outside parties. The profit picture can change suddenly from a profit to a loss and vice versa, but usually the situation evolves over a period of months or years. The profit position changes with less volatility than does cash flow. Reductions in expenses take several months to accumulate enough to turn a loss situation around. Declining sales or increased expenses, without corresponding increases in sales, tend to sneak up on the owner. Profit is one of the crucial balls of the juggling act which must be kept in the air at all times.

Making profits comes from paying attention to detail. Despite the obvious importance of profitability, I have found this to be one of the weakest areas of small-company management. Perhaps the best way to discuss profit management is to begin with the start-up of a business, and, then trace the process as operations become larger and more complex.

Good Bookkeeping Is the Foundation for Profits

The foundation of profit management, in fact the basis for all financial management, is good bookkeeping. The failure to set up good bookkeeping lies at the heart of more financial trouble than any other factor I have seen, and this includes some multimillion dollar businesses as well as very small ones. Good bookkeeping provides timely and accurate information consistent with generally accepted accounting principles. This allows the owner to study the financial statements to see how the business is doing, while there is still time to correct problems before they get out of hand.

But too often it doesn't happen this way. Financial statements are late, perhaps only occasionally available during the course of the year. The statements may include serious inaccuracies, misstating the company's performance, about which the owner learns only after the outside accountant prepares the final statement, some time after the year is over. What good does that do? Some statements may not be inaccurate, but they may be based on a misunderstanding of or an ignorance of basic accounting principles, which again misstate the company's performance and again about which the owner learns only after the year is over.

Why do these problems crop in an area which is so important to businesss survival? First, I think entrepreneurs try to save money by keeping bookkeeping costs down. After all, office work doesn't make money, production or sales work does. Spending money to count beans doesn't help the bottom line. As a result, the owner may keep the books as the business starts up. The dangers are obvious—how much bookkeeping does the owner know? Many of the costly misapplications of accounting principles are commited by owners. Besides, owners are so anxious for things to go well that their handling of the numbers can be influenced by their desire for good results. How much time and energy can the owner devote to the bookkeeping to begin with? The consequence is often hastily kept books which are behind in posting.

If the owner doesn't keep the books, then a low-cost employee may take on the job, frequently in addition to his or her main duties, or perhaps a part-time bookkeeper is employed. Whoever it is, the results depend on their knowledge of bookkeeping, which too often is inadequate. The result is confusion, an unclear picture of how the company is doing. To avoid this problem, some owners turn to outside bookkeeping services. Though this can work out well, again there are pitfalls. Many accounting services are operated by people who are not qualified accountants. They may have purchased a franchise. They may be computer programmers. While the owner is looking to them for accounting guidance, sometimes for general business advice, the accounting service is lacking in the expertise to provide either.

A second reason why business owners experience these problems is their own lack of knowledge about bookkeeping and accounting. In starting up a business, the owner is faced with a range of worries about getting enough sales, getting a bank loan, delivering the product or service to the customers. While all this is going on, the owner is supposed to understand accounting, too. It seems to be just too much, especially since few owners have had much exposure to accounting, either in school or in practice. It's not easy to evaluate whether your secretary/receptionist or your customer service clerk is doing a good job with the books or not. And the accounting service owner says he is an accountant; he shows some impressive samples of computer formats. After all he's a salesman; he needs to generate new accounts, too.

Get a Nose for the Bottom Line

When an owner is unsophisticated about accounting, we not only have the problem of evaluating the bookkeeping work, either inside or outside the company, but usually a lack of intensity about getting financial statements in the first place. Frequently the owner has difficulty in reading and interpreting the statements anyway. There is a strong tendency to rely on other measures of business performance, such as the cash balance, the sales volume, whether the receivables balance exceeds the payables balance, taking care of day-to-day operations problems. In this kind of frequently occurring situation, the owner allows the accounting process to fall behind. The bookkeeper is overloaded; the accounting service is running late; the CPA is trying to get to the books as soon as possible. Perhaps the delays are because of incomplete or inaccurate information supplied by the company to the outside service or the CPA.

Successful, profit-minded entrepreneurs refuse to accept these kinds of delays. They place the highest priority on getting financial statements quickly, as soon after the close of the month as possible . . . it's a standing policy. It is the first criterion in evaluating the bookkeeper's performance. It is a stipulation agreed on by the outside service or CPA. If statements are not supplied on time, the bookkeeper loses a job or the service loses an account. Nothing but timely and accurate statements will do.

These entrepreneurs have that nose for the bottom line I mentioned earlier. They know that the success of their enterprise is determined by their ability to operate efficiently. Their income, their long-range economic value, the job security of every employee rests on the company's ability to perform profitably year after year. It doesn't matter whether the owner is a scientist or a plumber, a person who works furiously for twelve hours a day or who gets to work at ten and leaves at four, a two-fisted slave driver, or a meek-mannered nice guy. A characteristic which separates those who succeed from those who fail is this insistence on getting prompt, accurate financial statements which the owner reads with an insight into what makes up the profitability of the business.

Net income before tax is the result of thousands of business transactions, even for a very small company. Some of the transactions produce revenues; some create expenses; some result in assets or liabilities or equity. It takes a careful, systematic accounting to determine where the company stands at the close of each accounting period. For most businesses the margin between a profit or a loss is very small, sometimes no more than two percent or three percent of sales. It is extremely easy to fall from a profit to a loss with such a narrow margin, but the difference can mean either a slowly improving or a slowly diminishing financial strength, if not a quickly eroding one. Those entrepreneurs who think they can keep track of all of this in their heads are kidding themselves, especially if their business gets to any size.

"Well, I'll get better bookkeeping when things become more complex," an owner might say. It is far wiser to build from a sound base. Owners who wait for more size before applying resources to their accounting regret the decision. It is a nightmare (which I'm sure some readers have already experienced) to unsnarl the problems of a poorly kept set of books, just when the company is growing and the owner has lost track of where things stand. A company can't just start off where it is; the accountants need opening balances for the new year. But if they have a bookkeeping jumble to work with, where do they start? The process is extremely expensive—the entrepreneur may spend every bookkeeping nickel which was saved to get things straightened out.

In the meantime, he or she will have to operate in the dark, because the old books are still being reconstructed. This process is slowed down because the bookkeepers need to keep up simultaneously with the mounting volume of new postings. Weeks, months drag by. When the statements are finally ready, the owner discovers that the hoped-for profits aren't there. Not only was the previous year less profitable than had been thought (perhaps it was even a loss), but all this new growth hasn't yet been worth the effort. The scenario plays on . . . the banker is unhappy to find the expansion loans haven't resulted in profitable growth; cash flow is tight because operations aren't profitable enough; trouble, trouble, trouble.

A third cause of basic problems in getting profit management information has to do with the nature of outside accounting services. CPAs or accounting services vary in quality. Certainly, CPAs have a more consistent and higher standard of accounting knowledge than the average accounting service. But knowledge is not the only issue. Some CPAs give faster service than others. Some are more involved in the development of good procedures in their clients' operations. The same goes for accounting services. The responsiveness of the outside service is the responsibility of the owner to ensure, and I think too many entrepreneurs accept whatever level of support they get, rather than insisting on standards which will give them the management tools they must have.

Cash or Accrual, How to Begin

For tax purposes, except where the IRS Code prohibits it, cash basis statements are almost always the best. Since revenues are recognized only when the cash is received, income is cut down. Who needs to pay taxes on money which hasn't been collected yet? For profit management purposes, however, cash basis statements are seriously inadequate. Many of the most important transactions in a business involve revenues which haven't been received or expenses which haven't been paid. To evaluate the efficiency of the operation—and that is what profits are, the ultimate measure of efficiency—the owner needs to see a complete picture of operations. Sales must include what was sold on a cash basis plus what was invoiced to customers. Expenses must include what was paid for in cash plus accounts payable. At any point in time, only this total accounting gives the full picture.

A common mistake with a new business occurs when the owner goes no further than the cash statement. Perhaps no more than the year-end tax return is seen. That's fine for taxes, but at the same time the owner can use an accrual basis statement, where all revenues and expenses are accounted for, to make a management evaluation of the company. Neophyte entrepreneurs sometimes make the serious mistake of giving the cash basis statement to the bank to support a loan request. No! This shows the company in its worst light—what is best for taxes, but not what should be shown to the bank. Bankers most often are looking to accounts receivable for collateral when lending to a small business, and the cash basis statement doesn't show any accounts receivable!

Cash basis statements are usually misleading. They are actually receipts versus disbursements; in essence, cash-flow statements which can deviate from accrual net income. They can show profits when losses are being incurred and losses when profits are being made. That's because of the difference in timing between billings and collections and between the receipt of invoices from vendors and the payments thereon. The owner should set up the company with the ability to use cash basis statements for taxes, where allowable, but accrual basis statements for profit management and for use with the bank.

PROFIT MANAGEMENT

Managing for profits requires the owner's intense focus on those control points which make the difference between a profit and a loss or between a good profit and a poor one. Let's start with the Zeta Company, which had developed a sales plan going into 1992, its third year of operations. Then we can trace the process through for increasingly larger companies. The Zeta Company's results for 1991 are shown in Table 5-1.

MANAGEMENT FOCUS—1: SALES

There are four points of focus for profit management on the Zeta statement. The first is the sales line. The origin of all profitability is in sales, but the company must reach the volume the owner expects, either in a formal plan, such as Zeta's, or in a figure carried around in the owner's head. Expenses will either be in line or not, depending on the company's sales success. This is why it is so important to monitor sales results constantly. The owner must know where the company stands at all times. If there is a sales plan, comparison of plan versus actual will give a prompt indication of what must be done with expenses. Profit management can and should start before the financial statement is available.

MANAGEMENT FOCUS—2: GROSS PROFIT

The second area is the gross profit margin, which for Zeta was 49.5 percent. This is a crucial management control point. Since the gross profit is what the company makes on its sales, this amount must be

TABLE 5-1 ZETA COMPANY INCOME STATEMENT
YEAR ENDED DECEMBER 31, 1991

Sales	$170,000	100.0%
Cost of Sales:		
Labor	51,510	30.3
Materials	21,590	12.7
Other Direct Costs	12,750	7.5
Total	85,580	50.5
Gross Profit	84,150	49.5
General & Administrative Expense:		
Advertising	2,317	1.4
Bad Debts	1,256	.7
Dues & Subscriptions	750	.4
Depreciation	680	.4
Insurance	2,500	1.5
Legal & Accounting	1,200	.7
Maintenance & Repairs	863	.5
Office Supplies & Expense	3,286	1.9
Rent	9,996	5.9
Salaries	35,000	20.6
Taxes, Payroll	8,477	5.0
Taxes, Other	423	.3
Telephone	2,500	1.5
Total	69,248	40.7
Net Income before Tax	$ 14,902	8.8%

sufficient to cover all other expenses and leave the desired profit at the end of the year. If the gross profit is insufficient to accomplish these two purposes, the owner has been defeated before the game has begun. Therefore, tight control of the gross profit margin must be maintained at all times. This is the other side of the coin. In addition to volume there is the profitability of the sales, measured in terms of gross profit.

If the gross profit margin is to be controlled, the owner must have an idea of what that margin should be. Otherwise, how does he or she know whether the operation is in line or not? The best way to deal with this question is to think in terms of percentages. In fact, profit management is a process of carefully analyzing percentages— the paying attention to detail I mentioned earlier.

Gross profit is what remains after the cost of goods sold. What makes up cost of goods varies enormously from industry to industry. For retailers and distributors, cost of goods is simply the price paid to vendors for product. For manufacturers the cost of goods includes labor, materials, and manufacturing overhead, which is made up of those costs in direct support of the manufacturing operations, such as plant rent and utilities, depreciation on manufacturing equipment, insurance, supervisory salaries, etc. For a management consulting company, costs of goods is direct labor, materials used in consultation, if any, and other direct costs, such as travel or outside consultants.

Costs of goods for retailers, manufacturers, and consultants are as different as oranges, apples, and pears. Yes, they're all fruit, but . . . . For this reason, what constitutes a good gross profit varies from industry to industry. The owner must understand what makes up cost of goods before true insight can be gained into how to manage for gross profit. Zeta is a graphics studio. The production of graphics is a process involving labor, a lot of expensive but small-item materials, and other direct costs, such as freelancers, printing, typesetting, etc. Some of the work is done on in-house equipment; some is purchased from vendors, depending on the particular company. Managing gross profit for the studio means keeping the board artists productive, making sure that materials are not wasted, carefully pricing outside services, and fully utilizing in-house equipment to make it efficient.

Use Industry Comparisons to Target Gross Profits

Several sources of industry statistics can provide insight into what a gross profit target should be for a company. At the same time, there are a variety of reasons why these statistics might not be a valid measure of a company's performance, such as size differences, regional differences, the fact that the industrial classification might not quite fit the business type, the existence of diversified product lines or service categories either in the industry sample or the company's operations. Whatever the case, statistics should be used for comparison with caution.

A valuable source of financial statement comparative data is an industry association, such as the National Association of Home Builders or the Contract Printers of America. That means the trade association should be the first place to look for indicators of performance. Bankers use Robert Morris Statement Studies, which are industry statistics drawn from information supplied by member banks. More than one baffled entrepreneur has looked at a photocopy of a page from this book which a loan officer has handed over with the statement, "Your profitability is lower than the industry average; you need to tighten up operations." That may or may not be the case, depending on whether the Robert Morris industrial classification is an accurate one for the business, but the guidelines for expense percentages can be helpful when the industry classification does fit.

How to Target without Industry Figures

The gross profit comes from the price which can be charged in the marketplace, as opposed to how much it will cost to acquire, make, or provide the goods or services. The factors that determine what price can be charged are often complex, but frequently the competition has a lot to do with it. Entrepreneurs fortunate enough to offer a new product or service which serves an urgent demand can set a high price, while those who are in a mature market with intense competition have to meet the market rates. There is a wide range of situations in between. At some point, the higher price begins to cut down sales volume; at some point, the lower price prohibits making a profit.

Picking the right point for pricing requires knowledge of costs. With that knowledge, the owner can set a price which will produce the gross profit necessary, with enough sales volume, to cover the general and administrative expenses and make a profit. This process involves three critical variables which the owner must understand: the price which can be charged and still maintain the desired sales volume; how much the goods will cost; how much it takes to run the company administratively, to include sales and marketing expenses and interest on loans. To be successful, the owner must acquire the judgment to make sound decisions about how customers will react to prices, how much it should take to make or provide the goods, and how much it should cost to run the operation. An entrepreneur can't answer those questions by reading a book.

Use Gross Profit to Find the Break-Even Point

One trick is extremely helpful in keeping sales and expenses in balance. Let's take Zeta as an example. After a couple of years of operations, it has turned out that Zeta required about $70,000 for general and administrative expenses. Let's say that for the next year the owners would like to add a salesperson at about $30,000 and increase other expenses about $15,000. With the new total of expenses, how much business would they have to do to break even?

The answer lies in the gross profit percentage. We know that gross profit must cover all general and administrative expenses, including marketing, sales, and interest, plus enough extra to make a good profit. We know that Zeta produces 49.5 cents in gross profit for every sales dollar, with the rest going to direct expenses. How many 49.5 cents would we have to generate to break even on the new expense level of $115,000? To find out, we divide $115,000 by the gross profit margin of .495, which equals about $232,000. This means the owners must increase sales by $62,000, thirty-six percent, just to break even. They must do better than that to make a profit. Before committing themselves to the expense increases, they must be satisfied that the sales can be made.

This method can be used to address a more specific question—how much in sales must they make to break even on the new salesperson? By dividing $30,000 by .495, we get just over $60,000. Any specific expense increase can be evaluated this way, before the owners commit themselves. It is important to analyze commitments in advance, regarding either profits or cash flow, before taking the step. Many entrepreneurs have regretted the day they decided not to look before they leaped. Perhaps more frequently, they didn't know *how* to look before they leaped. Financial planning, which we will discuss in detail later, teaches you how to look.

SPECIAL ISSUES IN MANAGING GROSS PROFIT

Produce Gross Profit by Controlling Job Costs

For Zeta, in reality, the gross profit is the sum of a thousand individual jobs. These jobs are brought in by a sales rep or reps, possibly including the owner, who price out the work to quote prices to customers. It will take a certain amount of labor, materials, and other direct costs to produce each job, whatever the quote. Profitability is a function of the reliability of the quote combined with the efficiency of the studio. Managing for the gross profit means managing the job costs and managing the reps' pricing. For Zeta to be profitable, there must be job cost analyses which summarize for the owner how each job has gone, so loss jobs can be evaluated to see what went wrong, either in the work or on the bid. If the owner has an effective program of controlling job costs, the gross profit will take care of itself. Again, this is profit management before the financial statement is prepared.

The guts of profitability for any job-based or contracting company is job cost control. This means collecting cost information—labor, materials, other kinds of costs—and then displaying this information by job, to evaluate the efficiency of the company. For a small company such as Zeta, we're talking about a simple, probably manual process, involving a sheet for each job, except for ones that are too small to worry about. Larger companies usually require a complex, computer-based program that tracks several cost elements for a large number of jobs. To the owner just starting up a business, this may seem like too much trouble, but that is not what trouble is, believe me. Trouble is losing money in your business. The best way to take a chance on losing money in a job or contract type of business is to ignore job costs.

My horror stories about this kind of error are so numerous, I hardly know which one to tell. Let's take the two owners of a rapidly growing printing company, union printers who started their own business. With aggressive selling and good equipment financing, they were able to grow to $3.5 million in sales within a few years. I met with them the night they decided to go Chapter Eleven. They had lost over $300,000 during the year just ended, their accounts payable were unmanageably in arrears, and current operations were still losing heavily.

Their financial statements, prepared by an outside accounting service, were a mess. It took several hours of restructuring before I was able to see the problem. I was shocked to learn that with a $3.5-million business these men had produced a gross profit of zero! Since their general and administrative expenses were about $300,000, that was their loss for the year.

Of course they were able to grow rapidly; they were underbidding everyone in town. Because they had neglected to analyze the profitability of their jobs, they hadn't bid in any gross profit at all. The accounting service compounded the problem by reporting results in such a confused mishmash that no one could see what was happening. Don't tell me it's too much trouble to analyze job costs; these owners, and many like them, did not survive Chapter Eleven bankruptcy because the damage that had already been done was too severe.

Work-in-Process

When a company undertakes jobs or contracts which last for months or years, the accounting can get hairy. Entrepreneurs can get terribly confused and awash in troubles if sound accounting principles are not applied in the handling of their direct revenues and expenses. In these types of operations, the importance of good bookkeeping can't be overestimated. The first problem that crops up involves jobs which start in one month and end a month or months later. When expenses are booked as they are incurred, monthly distortions can result, if the job is large enough, which can make some months look like losers while other months show outrageous profits. This is because the expenses will show up in previous months, while the revenues will be dumped in the month when the job is completed. By setting up a work-in-process account, these fluctuations can be smoothed out, because the expenses are accumulated in work-in-process until the revenues are booked.

Fixed Price Contracts

The most dangerous situations involve fixed price contracts. Here the company will undertake work, whether it be to develop a prototype instrument or to deliver an economic report or to build a six-story building, any of which may take months or years to complete. The contractor is usually entitled to invoice the customer periodically during the course of the job.

"So what's the problem? Isn't it a matter of tallying up the expenses for the billing period, and then taking those as direct expenses against the amount of the invoice, which is the revenue?"

"Yes, but what do you take for profit each billing period?"

"I still don't see the problem. Just take the total profit for the job, then, if you have twelve billing periods, take one-twelfth of the profit each time. Or wait, say you've completed twenty percent of a job by such and such a billing date, then take twenty percent of the profit at the same time."

"That's essentially the process. But what happens if you're twenty percent through the costs on the job, but you're only through with ten percent of the work. Worse yet, imagine that you've booked sixty percent of the costs, but you're only forty percent through with the work."

"Who knows that?"

"The job superintendent, the project engineer, the program manager . . . whoever has the responsibility of getting the work done. At some point, the responsible person begins to get a picture of what the job will take to complete."

"So?"

"So remember that the entire job was budgeted well before the work began, and it may take months or years to be completed. Frequently, when there is a development portion on a job, people have a tough time estimating how long that development will take. Sometimes construction projects run into unforeseen problems. Sometimes researchers in technical companies are inefficient with their work phases. Anything can go wrong."

"You're talking about an overrun."

"Yes. And if the accountant has been booking profits as a percentage of costs completed on a job which is going to overrun, then the readjustment can drastically change the profit position for the entire company. At the same time, the owner has not had a system to provide ongoing scrutiny of the job status to give advance warning of overruns. Perhaps something could have been done to fix the problems before they got out of hand."

"What's the solution?"

"The method of control is centered on the estimated cost-to-complete process. At the end of each month, after job costs for the most recent period have been reported, the responsible manager, frequently assisted by the controller, will review all costs to date, and then estimate the costs needed to complete the job in each remaining work category. A budget summary for the Domino Construction Company, with estimated cost to complete, is shown in Exhibit 5-1. As you can see, the total estimated cost is compared to the total contract cost, to estimate the profit which will be earned on the job. The company can recognize profit based on the percentage of completion to that point, using the estimated profit from the budget analysis. As the jobs progress, the estimated costs to complete become increasingly more accurate. If the process is followed diligently for all jobs, the owner and the managers will have a good handle on where the company stands."

Manufacturers

In some respects, manufacturers are similar to the companies we have just discussed: They have multiple categories of direct ex-

Domino Construction Co.	First budget	Final buy down	Change orders	Revised budget	Costs to date	Costs remaining	Est. costs to complete	Completed job costs	(Over)/ under budget
General Requirements	328,881	346,431	43,863	390,294	328,539	61,755	36,430	364,969	25,325
Site Work	379,450	303,722	11,204	314,926	191,107	123,819	100,746	291,853	23,073
Concrete	249,700	240,936	6,909	247,845	245,119	2,726	0	245,119	2,726
Masonry	46,000	57,260	12,400	69,660	61,044	8,616	8,800	69,844	(184)
Metals	17,100	11,091	500	11,591	11,590	1	0	11,590	1
Wood & Plastic	88,500	125,662	15,253	140,915	141,972	(1,057)	3,849	145,821	(4,906)
Thermal & Moisture Prot.	50,260	49,087	13	49,100	40,574	8,526	7,995	48,569	531
Doors & Windows	90,600	77,551	2,883	80,434	72,439	7,995	10,960	83,399	(2,965)
Finishes	190,700	206,605	11,689	218,294	199,432	18,862	20,150	219,582	(1,288)
Specialties	6,064	13,135	540	13,675	9,477	4,198	500	9,977	3,698
Equipment	50,000	65,338	10,496	75,834	50,018	25,816	15,216	65,234	10,600
Furnishings	184,500	144,661	8,123	152,784	132,187	20,597	16,674	148,861	3,923
Special Construction	45,000	45,000	2,376	47,376	8,434	38,942	25,500	33,934	13,442
Conveying Systems	0	0	0	0	0	0	0	0	0
Mechanical	245,600	258,675	0	258,675	250,205	8,470	4,294	254,499	4,176
Electrical	125,500	125,511	0	125,511	120,285	5,226	2,226	122,511	3,000
Subtotal Costs	2,097,855	2,070,665	126,249	2,196,914	1,862,422	334,492	253,340	2,115,762	81,152
Builder's Profit	116,145	105,335	0	105,335	85,216	20,119	20,119	105,335	0
Total	2,214,000	2,176,000	126,249	2,302,249	1,947,638	354,611	273,459	2,221,097	81,152

penses; cost of goods is made up of a number of "jobs." However, there are critical differences which can make the accounting for a manufacturer more complicated. First of all, the manufacturer deals with inventory, taken from raw goods, to work-in-process, to finished goods. Second, the manufacturer is usually making product lines which run repetitively through the plant, based on the best schedule to meet the order backlog. If the plant is well managed, the costs to produce each product should remain the same run after run, taking into consideration increases in materials prices and wage increases from year to year. But is labor operating consistently at a satisfactory level of productivity? Are materials being used efficiently? Once again, managing for gross profit requires a scrutiny of the components which make up the total, in this case the manufacturing costs by product line, which require analyses of individual production runs over time, to ensure that productivity remains high across the board and to evaluate the profitability line by line, to identify the winners and the losers. More than one manufacturer has found a product line which wasn't worth the effort.

The more we get into the idea of profit management, the more we see that an owner can't operate a business of any consequence by using financial statements alone. Profits are made by managing components of revenues and costs long before the general ledger is closed.

Retailers and Wholesalers

For retailers and wholesalers, at last, we have only one component of costs of goods, the goods themselves. Certainly this should lead to simpler accounting. Yet there remains a major problem which has caused many owners severe financial difficulty—inventory. Many product lines are carried, with varying degrees of profitability, and the mix of products sold changes. The profitability can vary substantially as well because of special sales, which for some retailers can amount to a significant percent of the year's revenues. Goods are received continuously from several, perhaps hundreds, of vendors. Prices vary during the course of a year. Sales are made to thousands of customers, frequently with pronounced seasonal fluctuations that create heavy demands on staff time throughout the company.

Keeping inventory counts is a time-consuming and complicated task. Not only must the count be taken, but the values on hand must be extended by applying the appropriate price paid to the item count.

Beginning inventory plus purchases minus ending inventory equals cost of goods sold. But to many entrepreneurs, inventory taking and costing is too difficult a process to do more than once a year. How do they get interim financial statements? Frequently by applying an assumed cost-of-goods-sold percentage, usually based on last year's results. Then at the end of the year accounts can be adjusted to the actual gross profit after the inventory has been taken.

The problem is that retailers and wholesalers often are low-profit-margin businesses, with net income before tax sometimes no more than two percent of sales volume. What if the gross profit margin for this year is two percent of sales less than it was last year? What if it is three percent less? Some months after the close of the year, the owner may find that the profit indicated on the year-to-date statements has turned into a loss. I know of one owner whose estimated gross profit percentage was six percent higher than actual on more than $4 million in sales. A $120,000 profit turned into a $120,000 loss. It was a complete surprise. Seasonal fluctuations made cash flow vary so much that it was difficult to have a gut feel for how the business was doing, especially with that kind of sales volume. Some large special sales were part of what caused the discrepancy. How much did this owner save by not having an inventory control system with accurate gross profit figures?

MANAGEMENT FOCUS—3: GENERAL AND ADMINISTRATIVE

Once the owner has established a target for gross profit—say thirty to forty percent for a manufacturer; forty to fifty percent plus for a graphics firm or consulting firm; thirty to forty percent for a retailer; twenty to thirty percent for a wholesaler—management can focus on what is required to run the corporation. Since Zeta had a gross profit of 49.5 percent of sales, this left some leeway for further expenses. Profit management for general and administrative expenses is established by setting a budget for each account, within the limits allowed by the available gross profit. Monthly, the owner must monitor expenses, both by amount and by percent of sales, to ensure that all accounts are in line. Though there is nothing mysterious about this process, many entrepreneurs have lost money because they failed to control their administrative expenses.

There are a number of pitfalls in this area of profit management.

First is the tendency of many entrepreneurs to overestimate future sales. Expenses are piled up based on expectations, but ultimately they exceed what the actual sales volume will justify. If the owner is careless about getting interim statements, or if some of the accounting problems we have already discussed happen to distort the reporting of results, then a loss will occur.

A second pitfall is simply allowing expenses to get out of hand in a particular account or set of accounts, even if sales come in on target. For example, an overly aggressive advertising program can drain off a company's chances of making a good profit, especially when the margin of net income is low to begin with. Some companies suffer from too many high-priced managers. Others suffer from an elaborate telephone system; too many office supplies; runaway legal expenses; any of which can combine with other sins to create a fat administrative budget, which will spell a loss.

These two pitfalls can be corrected by better management on the owner's part. The third pitfall is a chronic dilemma which can make entrepreneurship very difficult. I once worked with an intelligent, hard-working owner of a company, UMN Corporation, which distributed parts to retail stores throughout the Middle Atlantic states. Like many entrepreneurs, he had started his business out of his apartment, storing the parts in his bedroom. His initial capital was about $1,000. He hit the road to build up accounts, and he had good initial success. Before long he had to move UMN to a small warehouse because the apartment was quickly becoming inadequate for inventory. Sales pushed over $100,000, then $200,000. All the needs for bookkeeping, invoicing, office supplies, telephones, and warehousing began to burgeon. Cash had to be managed, inventory purchased, payments on account made, and accounts receivable collected.

Further growth required more space, a line of credit with the bank, more help in the office, a full-time warehouse person, and more time in the office for the owner (which created the need for a road salesperson). By the time sales had expanded beyond $400,000, the company had been moved to a second warehouse. As a consequence, it now cost about $135,000 to run the company administratively. There had to be so much space for inventory, somebody to handle the goods, somebody to keep the books, somebody to answer the phone, somebody on the road to sell. At twenty-five percent gross profit, the owner had to generate $540,000 to break even.

At this point, the vice began to tighten around the owner. As he pushed to go over half a million in sales, he came into direct competition with much larger distributors, who had substantial capital with which to purchase inventory. They were able to get volume price breaks from manufacturers, which they passed on to the retailers in the form of discounts. Because of their cash resources, they were able to offer extended terms for early purchases. Naturally the retailers placed their major orders with these distributors, using UMN to place smaller fill orders. The owner couldn't offer discounting because he lacked the capital to make deals with the manufacturers. He had no chance to give dating. Sales growth had become much more difficult. Now, each year as he came near the break-even point inflation seemed to have increased expenses about as fast as he had increased sales.

Though the owner ran an efficient operation, his sales volume could not support the basics needed to keep the doors open. He would have been profitable if he had stayed at the first warehouse, but that course of action wasn't attractive for a young man with ambition. In the end, his business, like many others, could not be made economically viable, given the resources with which he had to work, because the gross profit/general and administrative relationship didn't fit. Every entrepreneur needs to understand the dynamics of this relationship between gross profit and general and administrative expenses if the business is to be expanded with foresight.

MANAGEMENT FOCUS—4: NET INCOME

The fourth point of focus for profit management is the net income itself. In its first form, it is the net income before tax. This is the goal which the entrepreneur seeks at the beginning of each year, and it will be achieved if the goals in the other three areas of profit management are met. However, those other three goals should be set with net income as the determining factor. If the owners of Zeta wish to earn ten percent or more before tax, either they must reduce general and administrative expenses, increase sales while holding G&A level, generate sales at a faster rate of increase than the increase in expenses, or improve the gross profit percentage.

To achieve the net income goal, the other three goals have to be orchestrated. However, the owner doesn't have a blank page on which to write a score, because different industries operate on different economic realities. Since distributors are in the middle, they must take their gross profit between what the manufacturer takes and what their customers take. There will never be as much to work with as Zeta's owners are going to get. There is no sense in thinking of profits at ten percent to fifteen percent. What an owner can spend to operate the company must be consistent with this reality. Why be a distributor, then? Distributors, under the right conditions, can generate a lot more business than graphics studios. Zeta would be big at one million; distributors can grow to many millions.

A business owner must understand what the realities are in each key area of profitability—attainable sales goals, the kind of gross profit which can be generated, a sensible general and administrative budget—if good profits are to be maintained. Industry statistics can act as guides; experience in the business gives insight into what it will cost to make or provide. For a very small business, the owner can eyeball the targets at the beginning of each year. Since the business virtually flows through the owner's hands, he or she can tell whether or not there is a net gain as the months go by. But with just a little bit of growth, it becomes more difficult to judge. Other people are involved. They must read financial statements to figure out where the business stands. At this point, eyeballing targets at the beginning of the year isn't sufficient.

PROFIT PLANNING

Let's take Zeta's example. The owners wanted to increase general and administrative expenses by a total of $45,000. We know the break-even sales volume for last year's expenses; we know what additional sales are needed to break even on the added expenses. But what happens when we combine the budget increases with the sales plans? Will they improve their performance? Stay the same? Lose ground?

With some simple financial planning, the owners can get a sneak preview of what might happen. Planning can be kept simple by making the format do part of the work. For the profit plan, this means listing out the income statement accounts as they appear in the financial statements, and then estimating the new levels for revenue and expense right down the page. It can be helpful to list last year's income statement with percentages in the first column to give a comparative basis for estimating the new year. (See Table 5-2.)

Sales are taken from the sales plan. Obviously, the sales expectations, either as stated in a formal plan or as a gut-feeling goal, are the

TABLE 5-2 ZETA, INC., PROJECTED INCOME STATEMENT
YEAR ENDED DECEMBER 31, 1992

Sales	$282,000	100.0%
Direct Costs		
Labor	85,400	30.3
Materials	35,800	12.7
Other Direct Costs	21,100	7.5
Total	142,300	50.5
Gross Profit	139,700	49.5
General & Administrative		
Advertising	4,400	1.6
Bad Debts	2,000	.7
Dues & Subscriptions	1,100	.4
Depreciation	1,700	.6
Insurance	2,500	1.1
Legal & Accounting	1,200	.6
Maintenance & Repairs	1,400	.5
Office Supplies & Expense	5,300	1.9
Rent	10,000	3.6
Salaries	65,000	23.1
Payroll Taxes	14,700	5.2
Taxes, Other	500	.1
Telephone	4,200	1.5
Total	115,000	40.8
Net Income before Tax	$ 24,700	8.7%

driving force behind what the owner is going to commit to at the beginning of the year. Zeta's owners feel that the studio will operate during the new year with the same cost of sales percentages as the last year. General and administrative expenses are budgeted mostly at the same percentage of sales as last year, but in certain key accounts, especially in salaries and advertising, the increase sets a new budget rate for the company. The consequence, if the year went this way, is a projected net income of nearly $25,000, or 8.7 percent of sales. This is consistent with the 1991 figures.

However, salaries will increase from 20.6 percent to 23.1 percent. This increase is offset by rent, which remains constant, dollar-wise, but decreases from 5.9 percent to 3.6 percent of sales. Zeta was fully utilizing space in 1991, and the office will seem like a shoebox with the new salesperson, even though much of her time will be spent on the road. The implication is that the owners will have to increase space in 1993 if any additional staff is added. If sales do not go up proportionately to the combined increases of staff and rent, the profitability could suffer in that year. A little financial planning and foresight could prevent that from happening.

THE EFFECT OF GROWTH ON PROFIT MANAGEMENT

I have mentioned that profit management, even for a relatively small company, should begin before the financial statement is prepared by analyzing production runs, scrutinizing job costs, and reviewing the gross profit by lines of merchandise. As a company grows to multi-millions in sales, departments or divisions of operations frequently become equal to or larger than what the entire company used to do. At this point the formal, CPA-styled financial statement becomes less useful in profit management. No matter how hard the owner stares at the figures, little insight can be gained into the causes of the gross profit or what made up the changes in G&A expenses if these costs are made up of several departments and divisions, each of which has different profit and loss characteristics.

Let's say the owner is disappointed that profit was only 3.2 percent of sales, because the target was seven percent for the year-to-

EXHIBIT 5-2 DIVISIONALIZED INCOME STATEMENT

| Arrow Builders | | | | | Budget summary | | | |
| | Chestnut Hills | | | | | Bell Haven | | |
	Budget	%	Actual	%	Budget	%	Actual	%
Sales	4,025,000	100.0%	4,037,266	100.0%	5,859,000	100.0%	5,231,652	100.0%
Direct Costs:								
Land	873,425	21.7%	862,596	21.4%	1,113,210	19.0%	965,000	18.4%
Labor & Materials	2,229,850	55.4%	2,218,719	55.0%	3,105,270	53.0%	2,785,047	53.2%
SUBTOTAL	3,103,275	77.1%	3,081,315	76.3%	4,218,480	72.0%	3,750,047	71.7%
Income after								
Hard Costs:	921,725	22.9%	955,951	23.7%	1,640,520	28.0%	1,481,605	28.3%
Indirect Costs								
Gross Profit								
Financing								
Marketing								
G&A Residential								
G&A Commercial								
Other Income/(Expense)								
Income/(Loss)								
before Taxes:								
Projected Average								
Sale Price	161,000						217,000	
Actual Average								
Sale Price	161,491						209,266	
Projected Units Settled	25						27	
Actual Units Settled	25						25	

(continued)

date. Where was the profitability lost? If gross profit was thirty-two percent of sales and the target was thirty-four percent, which division or divisions caused the problem? In the listing of combined G&A expenses, where did the budget overruns take place? In sales? Division G&A? This owner has a serious problem because profitability has slipped badly, but there is no way of analyzing why, and without that knowledge the owner can't take remedial action.

For this company, the time has come to introduce management accounting to the profit management by designing reports which can be used for decision making. The old financial statement formats are designed to meet the requirements for reporting to outside parties. Owners who refuse to have outside requirements dictate how their internal financial analysis is conducted are the ones who can operate more profitably as their companies grow. This effort requires additional accounting expense, but with growth comes added requirements for management. Owners who try to scrimp on management control as their companies become larger will pay the same price in lost profits that owners of smaller companies pay for their false economies with bookkeeping.

The profit management report, Exhibit 5-2, shows what can be

EXHIBIT 5-2 DIVISIONALIZED INCOME STATEMENT (continued)

| | Regency Square | | | | | Total | | | Nine months ended 9/30/91 |
Budget	%	Actual	%	Budget	%	Actual	%	
1,660,000	100.0%	582,586	100.0%	11,544,000	100.0%	9,851,504	100.0%	Sales
								Direct Costs
288,840	17.4%	96,250	16.5%	2,275,475	19.7%	1,923,846	19.5%	Land
981,060	59.1%	348,571	59.8%	6,316,180	54.7%	5,352,337	54.3%	Labor & Materials
1,269,900	76.5%	444,821	76.4%	8,591,655	74.4%	7,276,183	73.9%	SUBTOTAL
								Income after
390,100	23.5%	137,765	23.6%	2,952,345	25.6%	2,575,321	26.1%	Hard Costs
				450,000	3.9%	426,969	4.3%	Indirect Costs
				2,502,345	21.7%	2,148,352	21.8%	Gross Profit
				(900,432)	−7.8%	(746,584)	−7.6%	Financing
				(645,201)	−5.6%	(619,752)	−6.3%	Marketing
				(484,264)	−4.2%	(417,399)	−4.2%	G&A Residential
				(46,089)	−0.4%	(40,163)	−0.4%	G&A Commercial
				(48,666)	−0.4%	(34,271)	−0.3%	Other Income/(Expense)
								Income/(Loss)
				423,782	3.7%	290,183	2.9%	before Taxes
								Projected Average
		83,000						Sale Price
								Actual Average
		83,277						Sale Price
		20				72		Projected Units Settled
		7				57		Actual Units Settled

EXHIBIT 5-3 STANDARD INCOME STATEMENT, ARROW BUILDERS, INC.,
STATEMENTS OF OPERATIONS AND RETAINED EARNINGS, NINE
MONTHS ENDED SEPTEMBER 30

	1991		1990	
	Amount	%	Amount	%
Income				
Sales of Houses	9,851,504	100.0%	5,108,274	100.0%
Cost of Sales	7,703,152	78.2%	4,002,252	78.3%
Gross Profit on Houses	2,148,352	21.8%	1,106,022	21.7%
Contract Income	268,469	2.7%	49,270	1.0%
Cost of Sales	259,736	2.6%	21,186	0.4%
Gross Profit on Contracts	8,733	0.1%	28,084	0.5%
Total Gross Profit	2,157,085	21.9%	1,134,106	22.2%
Operating Expenses				
Financial	747,375	7.6%	446,485	8.7%
Marketing	613,345	6.2%	253,306	5.0%
General and Administrative	463,966	4.7%	254,942	5.0%
	1,824,686	18.5%	954,733	18.7%
	332,399	3.4%	179,373	3.5%
Other Income/(Expense)				
Interest Income	34,545	0.4%	5,246	0.1%
Interest Expense	(49,458)	−0.5%	(54,424)	−1.1%
Net Rental (Loss)	(27,338)	−0.3%	(25,239)	−0.5%
Gain (Loss) on Sale of Assets	(1,026)	0.0%	600	0.0%
Other Income	1,064	0.0%	82,955	1.6%
	(42,213)	−0.4%	9,138	0.2%
Earnings (Loss) before				
Income Taxes	290,186	2.9%	188,511	3.7%
Provision for Income Taxes	(100,000)	−1.0%	(64,338)	−1.3%
NET EARNINGS (LOSS)	190,186	1.9%	124,173	2.4%

done by divisionalizing the results. Compare this statement with the standard accounting format, Exhibit 5-3. The management team of this company can analyze gross profit by project. They also can analyze marketing and sales expenses by project, and they can analyze the overall cost for corporate general and administrative expenses. Using the job cost report, Exhibit 5-4 (see pages 96–97), they can analyze the profitability of each house constructed and sold within each project, in order to manage for profits from the start to the finish of operations. The company operates with budgets for each house type, a profit plan for each development, and budgets for every phase of expenses, all of which are compared to actual on a continuous basis.

SUMMARY

Profit management begins with good bookkeeping. As a company grows, effort must be applied to creating reports that enable managers to analyze the causes of changes in profitability, which can't be done using the standard income statement formats designed for outside reporting. At any level of sales and growth, making profits comes from paying attention to detail, which means focusing attention on the keys to profitability—sales results, gross profit margins, general and administrative expenses (which can be broken down into many categories as the company grows in size and complexity), and the net income target itself.

"We're in business to make a profit" is the rallying cry of entrepreneurs nationwide, but managing for profits is one of the weakest areas in small-company management. Reluctance to pay for good bookkeeping and accounting, uncertainty about how to read financial statements, and inexperience in balancing the four key factors of profitability all block the owner's other efforts to achieve results.

EXHIBIT 5-4 SUMMARY OF LOTS CLOSED 1991

Date settled	Lot & location	Sales price		Land cost	%	Labor and materials	%	Profit after hard cost %	Indirect cost	%
01/12/91	BL-88		185,550	35,000	18.9%	91,812	49.5%	31.7%	5,268	2.8%
01/12/91	BL-102		177,430	35,000	19.7%	99,170	55.9%	24.4%	6,915	3.9%
02/29/91	BL-110		221,779	35,000	15.8%	121,252	54.7%	29.5%	6,158	2.8%
02/29/91	BL-113		206,785	35,000	16.9%	119,593	57.8%	25.2%	10,439	5.0%
03/02/91	BL-101		171,415	35,000	20.4%	86,308	50.4%	29.2%	5,773	3.4%
03/30/91	BL-111		190,481	35,000	18.4%	94,817	42.8%	31.8%	7,187	3.8%
03/26/91	BL-96		191,008	35,000	18.3%	95,398	49.9%	31.7%	8,629	4.5%
03/31/91	LR-100	190,954		32,970	17.3%	109,749	57.5%	25.3%	7,609	4.0%
03/27/91	LR-229	155,031		33,000	21.3%	86,190	55.6%	23.1%	5,172	3.3%
03/30/91	LR-230	155,000		33,000	21.3%	82,542	53.3%	25.5%	5,934	3.8%
03/30/91	LR-268	155,892		33,000	21.2%	93,960	60.3%	18.6%	6,201	4.0%
Total 1st Qtr.		656,877	1,344,448	376,970	18.8%	1,080,791	54.0%	27.2%	75,285	3.8%

(continued)

EXHIBIT 5-4 SUMMARY OF LOTS CLOSED 1991 (continued)

Total cost	%	Gross profit	%	Financial	%	Settlement	%	Commission	%	Points	%	Net direct profit	%
132,080	71.2%	53,470	28.8%	7,060	3.8%	1,621	0.9%	5,504	2.97%	0	0.0%	39,285	21.2%
141,085	79.5%	36,345	20.5%	6,727	3.8%	1,542	0.9%	5,250	3.0%	1,000	0.6%	21,826	12.3%
162,410	73.2%	59,369	26.8%	8,138	3.7%	533	0.2%	6,600	3.0%	1,150	0.5%	42,948	19.4%
165,032	79.8%	41,753	20.2%	6,240	3.0%	993	0.5%	0	0.0%	5,198	2.5%	29,322	14.2%
127,081	74.1%	44,334	25.9%	7,600	4.4%	898	0.5%	3,873	2.3%	3,750	2.2%	28,213	16.5%
137,004	71.9%	53,477	28.1%	7,434	3.9%	933	0.5%	0	0.0%	4,758	2.5%	40,352	21.2%
139,027	72.8%	51,981	27.2%	7,918	4.1%	1,270	0.7%	0	0.0%	4,539	2.4%	38,254	20.0%
150,328	78.7%	40,626	21.3%	11,456	6.0%	2,675	1.4%	0	0.0%	4,500	2.4%	21,995	11.5%
124,362	80.2%	30,669	19.8%	6,821	4.4%	440	0.3%	0	0.0%	2,088	1.3%	21,320	13.8%
121,476	78.4%	33,524	21.6%	6,449	4.2%	497	0.3%	4,650	3.0%	5,400	3.5%	16,528	10.7%
133,161	85.4%	22,731	14.6%	7,066	4.5%	380	0.2%	0	0.0%	4,725	3.0%	10,560	6.8%
1,533,046	76.6%	468,279	23.4%	82,909	4.1%	11,782	0.6%	25,877	1.3%	37,108	1.9%	310,603	15.5%

6

Treat Cash Flow Like Your Own Blood

CASH FLOW, THE SECOND BALL OF THE JUGGLING ACT

Cash flow is the most volatile part of the entrepreneur's financial management juggling act. A good cash balance can go bad in thirty days . . . even less. It can be reversed as quickly. I have helped owners install monthly cash-flow planning only to have them say, "We have enough cash at the beginning of the month and the end of the month, but we run out during the middle of the month." Sometimes cash flow is so volatile it requires weekly cash budgeting to gain control.

Cash is the blood of business. An uncorrected problem will weaken and kill a company, just as a cut artery will kill a human if unattended. Entrepreneurs must have a tight grip on their cash flow at all times if they are to prevent the corporate funeral that is ever lurking around the corner. More than in any aspect of small-company management, there are hidden pitfalls in cash flow which can catch an owner off guard, especially one who hasn't been through the ins and outs of it before—that Catch 22 again. How can someone start a business, yet be experienced at the same time? That's why survival is so difficult. Negotiating the treachery of a cash-flow crisis is, more than anything else, what separates those who make it from those who don't. The survivors have never been careless with cash flow.

Cash Flow and Profits Are Not the Same

I helped one owner set up an expense budget for her business. We also developed a cash-flow plan. It was crucial that both cash flow and expenses be tightly controlled because the company had suffered a substantial loss for the previous year. During subsequent visits, I would ask her how expenses were going in comparison to budget. With a smile, she would pull out the cash-flow plan to show that actual expenses were in line with what we had planned. I pointed out that we were looking at a cash-flow analysis. She needed to look, instead, at the expenses incurred during the month, as accrued in the general ledger and as shown on the income statement, to determine how she really stood from a profit and loss standpoint. But she was certain that everything would be all right: "The disbursements are pretty close to actual expenses."

Because the bookkeeper never quite had the financial statements ready, this went on for several months, during which time the owner felt comfortable with the cash-flow comparisons. When the financial statements were finally prepared, they disclosed a disaster. Advertising and promotion budgets had been badly overrun. Sales were below expectations, though cash collections had been good because the company's peak season was toward the beginning of the year.

Now another heavy loss was unavoidable, and a mountain of accounts payable had accumulated. The company was headed into a slower sales period, when cash would become short, but there was no turning to the bank with the financial statements in such bad shape. The woman's older sister, who was her silent partner, stepped in to take over the business, which, after a bit of luck and a couple of years of hard work, was salvaged.

Often cash flow can be good while losses are being incurred. This is because cash flow involves the timing of collections on accounts receivable, which for a variety of reasons can differ from when sales are recorded, and the timing of payments against accounts payable, which can differ from when the invoices are received. Conversely, a company can be showing excellent profits but be experiencing a serious cash shortage at the same time. "Going broke while they were making money," is what some grizzled veterans call this problem, which frequently occurs with rapid growth. Increasing sales volume, even accompanied by good profits, can create mounting accounts receivable, while, in the meantime, bills have to be paid. It is an imbalance of collections versus disbursements, even though revenues exceed expenses. More than one entrepreneur has lost it all in the midst of success because this pitfall of growth wasn't understood.

The Three Tiers of Cash Management

There are three ways of analyzing cash flow. What is the outlook for the next twelve months? This is essentially long-range planning for a small company. What are the immediate prospects for the next three months? This is the early warning system for trouble. What's going to happen this week and next? This is the practical framework for managing cash when it is extremely short. Ironically, the same system works for those rare circumstances when the entrepreneur has surpluses which need to be invested to earn interest. As this discussion already suggests, cash-flow management is heavily focused on what is going to happen. Profit management, though it very much involves the future, also has a management focus on the past.

For most business owners, expansion is the name of the game. Granted, each entrepreneur has a personal view of how fast expansion should take place. There are businesses which are very stable. Except for increases because of changes in price, sales year in and year out are roughly the same—for example, as gas station, a corner grocery, the local hardware store, a hair stylist. Except for the disaster of a new competitor entering the neighborhood to take business away, stability is the keynote. Though there are seasonal fluctuations to deal with, cash flows remain basically the same year after year.

But for the majority of small companies, expansion is the norm. Growth is the avenue for fulfilling the ambitions which drove many entrepreneurs to start their businesses in the first place. For some, perhaps it's a matter of keeping ahead of inflation. For others, it may be to maintain a market position in the face of competition. In a changing marketplace, it is hard to stand still. In countless ways, all

of these owners make commitments which have critical consequences for cash flow. Sometimes these consequences are apparent,
though to what degree may not be as clear. Frequently the impact on
cash is unforeseen, catching the owner by surprise. Sometimes the
severity of the problem is not fully recognized until it is well under
way. Trying to unravel a cash-flow crisis after the fact is a miserable
and highly dangerous experience.

Why Is Cash-Flow Control So Elusive?

A cash-flow analysis isn't part of the standard accounting package of
income statement, balance sheet, application of funds, and foot-
notes. Accountants and bookkeepers aren't trained to keep cash-flow
formats the way they keep a general ledger. A conscientious entrepreneur has a generally accepted income statement format to analyze
every month as an aid in profit management. Not so for cash flow.
Whatever tools are to be used have to be created from scratch. That's
something to think about, isn't it? The most volatile, vital resource a
company has, its cash flow, is not a regular part of financial statements anywhere in accounting practice.

Cash flow, itself, is a complex process. Cash management requires the integration, analytically, of the operating dynamics of the
enterprise. Cash flows are triggered by events as diverse as simple
payments to the office supply vendor as compared, say, to the inventory cycle. Inventory begins with the purchase of materials, which
are converted to work-in-process, then to finished goods. A sale
creates an account receivable, which becomes cash when the account is collected. In the meantime, the inventory cycle results in
cash when payments are made to the materials vendors or when the
payroll for direct labor is met. Analyzing cash flow in this kind of
situation requires separate scheduling for sales and collections, for
the inventory cycle, and for the more repetitive monthly expenditures, such as office supplies.

Effective cash-flow management requires planning ahead if the
owner is to keep this multitude of transactions from becoming a
mess. But many people don't feel comfortable with financial planning. In effect, it is preventive medicine, and we humans tend to deal
with problems as they arise. Like the undetected disease, cash-flow
trouble can prove fatal.

Even for the entrepreneur who wants to do the planning, it's not
easy. Formats for cash planning can be found in many books. Most of

them are workable management tools; however, it's not the format which counts. Cash-flow planning requires sound business judgments about expected sales levels, about the rate of collections on accounts receivable, about the schedule for purchasing inventory to achieve the sales targets, about the entire process of budgeting for expenses. Cash-flow planning is an orderly analysis of the uncertainties of the future, and, as such, lies at the heart of good financial management, a process often lacking in large companies, let alone small, volatile, struggling enterprises.

But preparing a cash-flow plan is only half the process. The results must be interpreted. The analysis will result in a pattern of deficits and surpluses which are the owner's best guess as to what might happen. What kind of financing is most appropriate to meet these requirements? To answer this question, the owner must consider the type of need, in combination with the company's overall financial position and within the context of the resources necessary to execute the long-range marketing strategy. Cash-flow management is not a kid's game. It is the entrepreneur's battle front, and you'd better know what you're doing.

TWELVE-MONTH CASH FLOW IS THE LONG-RANGE PLAN

What is the purpose of evaluating possible cash flow for the next twelve months? The answer is in the answer to a second question. What does the owner plan to do in the next twelve months? Let's begin with Zeta as an example. First we have a sales plan for the new fiscal year, calling for a sixty-five percent increase in volume. This is a good place to start, because all planning must begin with sales. The expected sales volume sets the level of all other activities of the company, hopefully in the right proportion to what sales actually turn out to be, as we discussed. Our second component of the 1992 outlook is the profit plan, which shows a net income of about the same percentage of sales as last year, but which includes $45,000 of expense increases. The owners were also well aware that Zeta experienced some seasonal fluctuations in sales.

With this kind of growth, combined with the seasonal factors, what will Zeta's cash requirements be? This is the purpose of the twelve-month cash-flow plan. It is extremely difficult to estimate cash requirements on the back of an envelope or in one's head. How much is needed depends on the timing of many factors. I have worked with owners of relatively small companies who understood their businesses well enough to have a good feel for the additional cash they needed. A rigorous cash-flow analysis confirmed their judgment, which for the cautious owner made the effort worthwhile in the first place. But in those situations, there were additional benefits. First, the bank loan officer was able to work more effectively with a credit request made in the form of a cash-flow plan. Second, even experienced owners can misjudge; having a cash-flow plan to compare with actual results provides an excellent safety check as the year progresses. Third, even for the owner who has a good gut feel for cash requirements, there are unforeseen needs which a systematic cash-flow analysis can disclose before the fact.

Zeta's owners, only two years into their business, felt much better about the upcoming year after the cash-flow plan, shown in Table 6-1, was completed. With the sales plan carefully worked out, including allowances for the seasonal fluctuations, the critical assumption the owners had to make was how long it would take for them to collect on accounts receivable. Based on experience in recent months, they thought an average of forty-five days would be a good basis for planning. Many of their direct wage employees worked irregular hours, based on the amount of work in the studio, so the disbursements for direct expenses varied mostly with sales volume. Most administrative expenses were on an even monthly disbursement level, as derived from the profit plan. The owners had felt they would need about $50,000 to cover their needs, and the plan indicated that this amount would probably be more than adequate. After reviewing the full set of financial plans, the bank was pleased to make these funds available to them.

Let's take a more detailed look at Zeta's plans. The payoff for the work is an overview of how the company might perform, given what the owners intend to do, looking into the near future. Insight won't come by simply staring at financial statements or listening to managers and employees talk or listening to gut feelings. Even for a company as small as Zeta, financial planning provided needed insight.

By the same token, an incisive set of financial plans can't be pulled out of a hat. What frustrates many people about the planning process is the instant complexity of trying to deal with the thousands of variables of their business all at once. This immediate frustration causes the owners to throw up their hands, saying, "You can't do planning in my type of business, it's just too complicated." That's a

TABLE 6-1 ZETA, INC., CASH-FLOW PLAN, OCTOBER 1991–SEPTEMBER 1992

	Oct	Nov	Dec	Jan	Feb	Mar	Apr	May	Jun	Jul	Aug	Sep
Receipts (45 Days)	15,000	14,750	19,500	20,500	18,900	14,700	20,950	28,800	28,800	27,200	22,350	23,300
Disbursements												
Direct Labor	5,850	5,850	6,450	4,890	3,930	8,640	8,640	8,640	7,680	5,730	8,250	10,050
Direct Materials (30 Days)	1,300	2,480	2,480	2,730	2,070	1,660	3,660	3,660	3,660	3,250	2,430	3,490
Other Direct Expenses	1,460	1,460	1,610	1,220	980	2,160	2,160	2,160	1,920	1,430	2,060	2,510
General & Administrative	9,440	9,440	9,440	9,440	9,440	9,440	9,440	9,440	9,440	9,440	9,440	9,440
Principal & Interest	900	900	900	900	900	900	900	900	900	900	900	900
Past Due Accounts	9,000	5,000	0	0	0	0	0	0	0	0	0	0
Total	27,950	25,130	20,880	19,180	17,320	22,800	24,800	24,800	23,600	20,750	23,080	26,390
Net Receipts (Disbursements)	−12,950	−10,380	−1,380	1,320	1,580	−8,100	−3,850	4,000	5,200	6,450	−730	−3,090
Beginning Cash	3,500	0	0	0	0	0	0	0	0	0	0	0
Ending Cash	−9,450	−10,380	−1,380	1,320	1,580	−8,100	−3,850	4,000	5,200	6,450	−730	−3,090
Additional Funds Needed	9,450	10,380	1,380	−1,320	−1,580	8,140	3,850	−4,000	−5,200	−6,450	730	3,090
Cumulative Additional Funds	9,450	19,830	21,210	19,890	18,310	26,450	30,300	26,300	21,100	14,650	15,380	18,470

correct answer for those who try to do everything at once, with the intention of arriving at a decision within a few minutes. In the seminars I conduct, everybody wants to give the ultimate conclusion to the problem within the first five minutes of discussion. Most of us are oriented to delivering the bottom line right up front.

"Show me the bottom line!" the hard-boiled entrepreneur exclaims, pounding his fist on the desk.

Don't Confuse Feelings with Probabilities

The important thing about any planning process is to break the task up into its major components. That is not the time to worry about ultimate conclusions; at the outset of the analysis, no one is in a position to arrive at answers. In fact, owners who are obsessed with the conclusion may influence the results so the analysis indicates exactly what the owner had been saying all along. Of course, this type of owner usually doesn't sit still for planning ahead to begin with. Since they know the answers before the fact, they might just as well go ahead and do it. This doesn't always lead to disaster. But how an owner feels about the future won't make it turn out that way. This is probably the most important part of financial management—all entrepreneurs are, ultimately, their own financial managers—and it has everything to do with psychology and little to do with numbers. Disaster-prone entrepreneurs confuse their feelings about how things will turn out with the probabilities which actually exist in their marketplace.

"I think next year is going to be a good year. Sales will be up by at least thirty-five percent . . . I feel real good about that."

TRANSLATION: There is at least a ninety-five percent chance that sales will increase by thirty-five percent next year.

MARKET REALITY: After reviewing results for last year and analyzing the needs of our existing customers, along with prospects for new customers, there is twenty-five percent chance that we can increase sales by thirty-five percent. There is a forty percent chance that we could do between a twenty-five and thirty percent increase . . . and so on.

The owners' feelings push their assessment of the chances of making it much higher than they truly are. Perhaps reaching for thirty-five percent growth is worth the risk. But frequently these owners don't realize how the probabilities truly spread for their business in the immediate future. If they had a clearer picture of the situation, they might make different decisions. I have seen that happen many times, when the owner, for one reason or another, sat still long enough to take a careful look before leaping. For those who insist that they're right, I can only point out that the Yellow Brick Road to the graveyard is the one to your left. And don't feel too bad when you get there, because you'll have noticed how worn down the bricks are as you walk along.

Start Cash Planning with the Sales Plan

Now that we've conditioned ourselves to take this decision-making process (because that's what financial planning is) a step at a time, we're in a position to get something very powerful accomplished for our own benefit. Zeta's owners, for example, accomplished the first crucial step by carefully setting out their sales plan. The owners were aggressive in setting a sixty-five percent growth goal, but they built that up a step at a time, by first evaluating current business and making the critical assumption that it would increase by thirty percent. This kind of assumption can only come from an informed, in-touch-with-the-marketplace gut feeling. It may be wrong, but it's their best guess. In many respects, planning consists of a series of gut feelings which are laid out one at a time for second guessing, then assembled into an overall scenario. This is an alternative to making one great gut judgment, then finding out after it's all over whether you were right or not.

The second critical assumption Zeta's owners made was about the new business to be generated by their direct sales calls. They tried to be conservative by pushing results back several months after the program, including their new salesperson, was scheduled to begin. Seasonal fluctuations were factored into the plan. Once the sales plan is completed, the baseline for the level of activity has been established. By breaking the process down into components, we succeed in focusing attention on a limited set of assumptions about phases of our business, in a logical sequence.

Use the Profit Plan to Set Budget Levels

Our second planning step was the profit plan, which we used to budget every expense account, according to our expected sales volume. The first critical assumption was that direct expenses would vary with sales at the same percentages as last year, because the owners planned no changes in the way the studio would be operated during the planning period. Of course, if the mix in types of work changed—more typesetting, less artist's board work, for example—then the percentages and, thus, the gross profit percentage would change, something they will have to keep an eye on. All other expenses were budgeted account by account.

With the sales plan and the profit plan prepared, we are ready for the cash-flow plan, which is the final repository of all expected company activity, in terms of receipts versus disbursements. Income statements are essentially an economic look at the efficiency of a company over periods of time. To make this "look" as comprehensive as possible, accountants use accrual techniques to recognize income when it is earned, matching to that income, as best they can, expenses when they are incurred. In cash-flow analysis, we tear the accrual picture apart to look at operations strictly on a cash basis.

The Zeta cash-flow format is the one I prefer to use. The format is important in financial planning for two reasons. First, the data needs to be arranged to highlight the crucial conclusions. Most decision makers, whether in a *Fortune* 500 company or a corner store, find it difficult to work with financial analysis. If the plans are formatted in a confusing way, the owner may not see the critical indicators on which the final decisions will have to be based. Since most owners have to have someone else help them with financial planning, often their bookkeeper or accountant, this is a frequent problem; while the results may be clear to the preparer, the preparer usually thinks and speaks a different language than the entrepreneur. A breakdown of communication just when the owner is making a decision which will affect the long-range future of the company can be catastrophic.

A second importance of the format is very practical. Trying to make estimates of what might happen is difficult for anyone. If everything has to be written from scratch on a blank page, it becomes bewildering. But an owner can make the formats work. Listing the sales accounts or categories for sales along with monthly columns sets up a format for sales planning. Using the income statement sets up the format for profit planning. Setting up receipts and disbursement categories with monthly columns establishes a format for cash-flow planning.

Receipts versus Disbursements

Since Zeta's customers, across the board, average about forty-five days before paying on invoices mailed to them on the first of the month, only one receipt category was necessary. Receipts were plotted taking the first half of the month's sales as being collected in the following month, assuming roughly even sales for a thirty-day period (after all, these are just approximations; we're not dealing with an exact science), and the sales for the second half of the month as being collected in the month after the next.

Disbursements were set up with a strong resemblance to the income statement; they are not exactly the same, however. Income statement accounts work for cash flow if the invoices in those categories are paid in the month when the expenses are incurred, and many accounts can be handled this way. There are some critical exceptions. Except for those fortunates who can take discounts, inventory purchases are usually paid with some delay, thirty days from the invoice date, sixty days, perhaps much longer than that depending on circumstances. Furthermore, the cost of materials on the income statement is incurred when the goods are shipped or the invoice is cut. This could be months after the goods were received in inventory. For Zeta, of course, materials move much more quickly than that. But for companies that deal with inventory, the cycle from purchases being booked into inventory to when they are converted into the cost of sales, as opposed to when the accounts payable are to be paid, can create cash-flow headaches, especially when the owner has to deal with seasonal fluctuations.

Another exception is interest. This is the entry for the income statement, but for the cash flow we need to know the full payment for principal and interest which has been entered in Zeta's plan. The expense for assets is treated as depreciation on the income statement. No cash changes hands for depreciation, so we eliminate that account entirely from cash flow. However, capital expenditures for equipment and leasehold improvements paid for in cash, or that require cash down payments, must be accounted for in the cash flow. Accounts payable past due from previous months must not be overlooked. In Zeta's plan, a line was devoted to these accounts; the schedule for paying out the past due accounts so the company could get on a current basis was an important part of the analysis. For companies with many dollars in past due payables, the scheduling of payments is a major portion of the planning.

The Results

Once the disbursements have been scheduled for the planning period, we are ready to calculate the results. The net receipts (disbursements) line shows the surplus or deficit for each month. The monthly status is heavily influenced by seasonal fluctuations. The effort to generate a big sales month, whether it be in purchases for inventory or high labor output, must precede the invoice. Some of these payments are in cash, some on account, but in either case the commitment is made prior to the company's own ability to invoice customers. Sometimes the build-up effort is taking place after some slow months, which means that collections may be down while expenses are up. Later the collections on high sales months start to come in. Frequently this happens when operations have cooled off and disbursements are on the decline. As a result, surpluses.

In either case, the results must be added to the beginning cash to determine what the expected ending cash will be for the month. If the ending cash balance is inadequate, then additional funds will be needed to sustain operations. The bottom line of the cash flow—now we can talk bottom line—shows the accumulated requirement month by month. We can see that the peak borrowing need for Zeta was $30,000. As we follow the cumulative additional funds line, we can see whether this borrowing requirement can be repaid during the planning period, which would be our analytical basis for applying for a seasonal line of credit, or whether there will be a remaining balance, which would suggest a term loan or a combination of line and term loan. Though it looks like Zeta can reduce the peak borrowing by about half, there is still over $18,000 in borrowing remaining at the end of the planning period. This indicates that a line of credit probably could not be handled properly. A term loan of $30,000 to $40,000 would be the safest financing to arrange, or perhaps a term loan of $25,000 combined with a $15,000 line of credit, which could be paid off sometime during the summer, as indicated by the cash flow. Because our planning is only approximate, it is better to arrange for more financing than the requirement stated in the analysis, if possible. If the results are in line with or better than the plan, then the additional amount authorized by the bank doesn't have to be used.

Cash Management Is Analysis versus Judgment

When we get to the bottom line of the cash-flow plan, which is our evaluation and decision-making point, we can bounce our analysis off our judgment. Frequently the first run of the cash flow will seem wrong to the owner. Either the deficit months are too high or too low or the peak need seems off. Let's go with the judgment—it's time to rethink the assumptions of the cash flow to find where we may have made an error in our thinking. Perhaps payables were paid too quickly; perhaps inventory purchases were scheduled incorrectly; perhaps receivables were collected at the wrong rate. When the adjusted cash flow makes sense to the owner, we have finished our work for the time being, and we have a very powerful decision-making tool.

As a practical matter, the actual monthly cash flow is not going to be what we have scheduled in our plan. Hopefully the next month will be pretty close, but there is no way the later months in the plan are going to coincide with our projection. We can't predict the future, and long-range cash-flow planning is not a prediction. It is more of a feasibility study, the purpose of which is to search for a pattern of surpluses and deficits which, we hope, will give us a range which approximates what we will have to borrow to support operations. If we can get a workable assessment of the pattern and an approximate range of borrowing requirements, we've put ourselves in the driver's seat. It doesn't matter that the monthly surpluses or deficits actually turned out to be in different months than we had projected.

Cash Management in More Complicated Situations

Zeta is a very small company. What about larger companies with more complicated operations, say contractors with many large contracts beginning and ending on different dates, or companies with multiple operating divisions, marketing departments and administrative offices, or companies with subsidiary corporations? What about companies that are undergoing major growth activities to include major purchases of new equipment, the establishment of a new operating division, the establishment of a new marketing department with new advertising programs? What about extremely volatile companies, such as a home builder whose cash-flow circumstances can change violently because of the weather, lot problems, sudden changes in market conditions?

For these companies, cash-flow planning is even more important, though more difficult. But the complexity can be dealt with by using the same concepts. Break the problem down into components, and then analyze each component separately. We start with the monthly sales plan. Then we develop our profit plan to set the level of expenses. The cash-flow planning will begin with a separate schedule for collections on accounts receivable. There will probably be an inventory plan, with purchases scheduled to maintain inventory levels at desired targets each month, based on the sales volume. The payments on accounts payable, which are created by the purchases, will then be scheduled. There may be an additional schedule of expenses that vary with sales. These schedules will all be assembled into the master schedule, the cash-flow plan, where they will be combined with regular monthly expenses and with scheduled payments for notes and for capital expenditures. The end result may have more entries on it than Zeta's, but the summary page may not look much different for a company many millions greater in sales volume. Clarity comes from simplifying, not from complicating. In cash planning, the owner must be careful to cover all the bases, and great care must be taken in making the critical assumptions which determine what the planning results are going to look like.

For extremely volatile companies, cash-flow planning is frustrating. Too many owners dispense with planning because of the apparent futility of trying to estimate performance in a constantly fluid situation. This is when cash-flow planning is imperative. In volatile situations, there is significantly more danger of serious trouble, as witnessed by the frequency of failure in the construction industry, which combines heavy borrowing with instability.

There is a way to beat the analytical problem. First, the length of the planning period should be shortened; perhaps a long-range plan for a home builder, for example, should be no more than six months. Second, plans have to be redone constantly. I have worked with a construction company where, during crucial times of the year, we redeveloped the cash plan weekly. No matter how approximate we were, our planning consistently picked up problems that we were able to deal with because we had the time to take corrective action. That cash management program alone enabled the company to get through some disastrous economic periods which caused bank-ruptcies throughout the industry.

THREE-MONTH CASH FLOW IS THE EARLY WARNING SYSTEM

The cash-flow results for any company are not going to be what is forecast in a twelve-month plan. There are too many uncertainties for us to be able to predict the future that far out. Prediction is not our purpose anyway. Instead, we are defining possible needs, to be as ready as possible to execute the year successfully. However, the worst thing we could do, at this point, is to put the long-range plan away and go about the year without additional scrutiny of our cash flow.

Since we have no formal cash-flow report in our financial state-ment package, and since cash flow is always about to happen, events can get away from us at any time. The very nature of cash flow is volatility. The worst case is to get into a cash-flow problem without prior warning, and then to have to work out of the trouble. Any kind of warning, ninety days, sixty days, even thirty days, gives the entre-preneur time to take corrective action. Banks are more accommodat-ing to owners who come in to point out that cash will be short the next month or in two to three months, along with a request for the appropriate credit to help out the situation. There are a number of legitimate reasons why cash can be short, but there is nothing legitimate about being caught by surprise, if the owner is presenting himself or herself to the bank as an effective manager.

The purpose of the three-month cash plan is to act as an early warning radar system to pick up potential cash-flow problems before they happen. I pick three months because this is about as far as one can project for a small company with any hope of being somewhat accurate. In the first month we hope to be quite close to actual, the second month will probably be more approximate, and the third month is getting into speculative territory. Working within the three-month time horizon is the guts of cash management for a small company. An example of a three-month cash plan is shown in Table 6-2.

It is important to realize that cash management is a different kind of effort than profit planning and the budgetary control of expenses. Profit management is a systematic review of results, soon after the fact, combined with a system of controlling commitments, usually through a purchase order procedure, in which the year's net

TABLE 6-2 FPH ENTERPRISES, CASH-FLOW FORECAST, OCTOBER 1, 1992

	Actual			September		Cash-Flow Plan		
	June	July	August	Plan	Actual	October	November	December
Cash Receipts								
Sidesville Office	509,686	444,996	567,002	597,500	677,497	431,900	570,000	600,200
Windsburg Office	148,037	84,824	225,783	141,600	152,902	195,300	178,400	170,800
Golden Spring Office	188,856	172,349	202,634	159,700	164,354	165,000	170,000	213,000
Ironbridge Office	202,435	76,949	213,756	198,600	139,143	149,700	141,600	164,200
Victoria Beach Office	184,657	183,213	126,973	166,200	166,117	173,800	182,900	187,200
Middletown Office	40,564	111,112	10,134	180,000	151,671	170,000	170,000	170,000
Miscellaneous	38,908	13,296	53,985	25,000	21,568	20,000	20,000	20,000
Total Cash Receipts	1,313,143	1,086,739	1,400,267	1,468,600	1,473,252	1,305,700	1,432,900	1,525,400
Cash Disbursements:								
Payroll & Payroll Taxes	805,987	806,958	815,638	810,000	825,468	845,000	780,000	835,000
Rent	185,689	182,657	179,841	188,500	175,844	175,300	187,900	188,500
Bank Notes	95,422	92,584	90,587	91,500	86,459	95,000	91,500	91,800
Personal Notes	52,112	48,527	49,851	52,000	55,888	57,800	58,400	58,400
Other	128,974	195,422	154,712	175,000	201,556	210,000	220,000	225,000
Total Disbursements	1,268,184	1,326,148	1,290,629	1,317,000	1,345,215	1,383,100	1,337,800	1,398,700
Cash Surplus (Deficit)	44,959	(239,409)	109,638	151,600	128,037	(77,400)	95,100	126,700
Beginning Cash Balance	48,745	93,704	4,295	13,933	13,933	41,970	64,570	59,670
Credit Line Draw (Payment)	0	150,000	(100,000)	(150,000)	(100,000)	100,000	(100,000)	(100,000)
Ending Cash Balance	93,704	4,295	13,933	15,533	41,970	64,570	59,670	86,370
Line of Credit Balance—End of Month	800,000	950,000	850,000	700,000	750,000	850,000	750,000	650,000
Year-to-Date								
Cash Receipts	5,894,325	6,981,064	8,381,331		9,854,583	11,160,283	12,593,183	14,118,583
Disbursements	4,986,914	6,313,062	7,603,691		8,948,906	10,332,006	11,669,806	13,068,506
Cash Surplus (Deficit)	907,411	668,002	777,640		905,677	828,277	923,377	1,050,077
Credit Line Draw (Payments)	(150,000)	0	(100,000)		(200,000)	(100,000)	(200,000)	(300,000)

income before tax is built up month after month. Hopefully the budgets will stand for some time without modification, as guidelines for performance. In comparison, cash management is chaotic. Once immediate results have been analyzed, the past is thrown away . . . who cares what happened two months ago? The plan itself will be modified constantly throughout the year.

Effective cash management is a constant interaction of what has just happened, modification of what is just about to happen in light of what has just happened, and a short-range look at what might happen in a couple of months. The format can be identical to the long-range plan, simply shortened to three months, but there must be a regular comparison of *actual* versus *plan*. I recommend a spreadsheet that would show actual versus plan for the previous month and a plan for the next three months. The actual cash-flow report is not difficult to develop, because it is a summary of the checkbook disbursements and deposits. This report can be done immediately after the close of the month, since it is not dependent on the closing of the general ledger. After each month, the oldest month should be dropped from the plan and a third month should be added. Periodically, a revised long-range plan should be prepared, perhaps every six months or when major changes are going to be made in the company's operations.

MONITOR THE BOOKENDS OF CASH FLOW

There is a grave danger in cash management: Month after month, the plans always work out. By definition, receipts less disbursements plus the beginning cash balance will equal the ending cash balance. This sounds obvious, but the danger lies in the illusion that the process is balancing out. A harassed owner, preoccupied with a hundred fires to be put out, sometimes doesn't read financial reports very carefully, in addition to the fact that the very act of analyzing financial reports may be an alien skill. If collections are down, disbursements are reduced to accommodate the available cash, again an obvious fact. But in the confusion of running a business, serious trouble could be worming in throughout that process, without the owner's clear awareness of the severity of the situation.

The cash-flow plan versus actual makes up the books of the cash management process, while the receivables aging schedule and the accounts payable aging schedule are the bookends. Receipts are a function of the sales volume, combined with the collection experience on accounts receivable. Analyzing the cash plan can only reveal that receipts are up or down, but it doesn't give a clear picture of the collection experience. Constant control over the quality of credit extended by the company is vital to the cash-flow health of the company. Slow receivables absorb cash. If the slowness has gotten to the point of bad debts, the results can be disastrous, not only to the cash flow, but to the company's net income, if the write-offs are large enough. Bad debt write-offs have a way of happening at the most damaging times.

Frequently, the cash flow is made to balance by delaying payments on accounts payable. It is imperative that the owner have a clear picture of how extensive these delays are becoming. I have had owners referred to me who have developed past due accounts payable in excess of a million dollars, with many accounts well over 120 days past due. They were like people whose fingertips only could be seen above the quicksand. Trade credit is like a rubber band which stretches to the point where the owner has gotten into enormous trouble, and then snaps.

By monitoring the aging of receivables and payables, along with careful review of the monthly cash flow versus actual and the prospects for the next three months, the owner can control the company's cash position. When problems are detected on the early warning system, there will be enough time to take corrective action. The cash flow will be seen within the overall perspective of the status of collections and the status of payments to trade vendors. Reviewing sales versus the sales plan and the actual versus the profit plan completes the picture.

CASH BUDGETING IS THE SYSTEM OF TRADE-OFFS

There are times when cash is so tight and so volatile that monthly cash plans are not useful for day-to-day management. The company could run out of funds anytime during the month, risking inability to meet payroll and with more vendors demanding payment than there is cash to meet their demands. The owner and the bookkeeper or controller are constantly discussing, "How much cash is there today? Can we pay Acme so we can get another shipment in? Can we make payroll?"

A lot of guesswork goes on. Sometimes the exchange of information between the bookkeeper and the owner gets confused, especially when they are under pressure. A weekly cash budget can help schedule the scarce cash to make the most of little, and it can help the communications between the owner and the financial manager. The format for the budget is different than the longer range plans which we have been discussing, as can be seen in Table 6-3.

The budget begins with the week's opening cash balance. After

TABLE 6-3 TRION, INC., CASH BUDGET, DECEMBER 3–28

	Dec 3–7		Dec 10–14		Dec 17–21		Dec 24–28	
	Plan	Actual	Plan	Actual	Plan	Actual	Plan	Actual
Beginning Cash:	25,000	25,000	6,935		3,305		39,305	
Collections:								
ABC Company	0	0	37,500		0		15,000	
Agency Y	0	0	22,000		0		8,950	
Clearview	0	0	0		42,000		0	
Others	1,200	650	5,000		7,500		25,000	
Total	1,200	650	64,500		49,500		48,950	
Total Cash for								
Mandatory:	26,200	25,650	71,435		52,805		88,255	
Mandatory Disbursements:								
Payroll & Tax	0	0	50,000		0		50,000	
Insurance	0	0	3,500		0		0	
Lease Payments	0	0	2,350		0		1,850	
Note Payments	0	0	0		5,750		0	
Rent	12,000	12,000	0		0		0	
Telephone	0	0	2,780		0		0	
COD	2,000	2,465	2,000		2,000		2,000	
Other	0	0	500		750		1,500	
Total	14,000	14,465	61,130		8,500		55,350	
Net Cash Available for Other:	12,200	11,185	10,305		44,305		32,905	
Other Payments:								
Materials Vendors	4,500	3,750	7,000		5,000		25,000	
Miscellaneous Vendors	0	500	0		0		5,000	
Total	4,500	4,250	7,000		5,000		30,000	
Ending Cash:	7,700	6,935	3,305		39,305		2,905	

reviewing the accounts receivable aging, collections are projected for the current week and for the next three, perhaps four, weeks. Most of the accuracy in the budget will be in the current week and the following week. Beginning cash plus collections will provide the total cash available for payments. The first category is mandatory disbursements, defined as those payments which must be made that week or the company will not be able to keep the doors open. If the payment can be deferred to the next week or longer, then it is not a mandatory disbursement. In this analysis, mandatory disbursements are payroll, payroll taxes, rent, principal and interest, and so on.

After mandatory disbursements, the net cash available is for payment against those accounts which can be handled on a discretionary basis. Certainly the pressure for many if not most of these payments is very intense, but there is still room for delay on some more than others. Usually there will be an accounts payable aging from which the payments for that week can be selected. However, before the owner can authorize these payments, the prospect for coverage of mandatory disbursements for the next week must be assessed. As you can see in the cash budget, week 1 doesn't involve much activity, except for the rent. There is sufficient cash for mandatory disbursements plus a small amount for vendors. Frequently, companies short of cash must set aside an amount for COD each week, which Trion has done.

The actual column shows that week 1 went close to plan. Week 2 involves a payroll, which the company must cover from receipts. Ample funds are expected, but if ABC Company is late there will be trouble making payroll. Since the bank line is at limit, the controller will have to keep pressure on ABC to avoid trouble. In week 3 the Clearview payment will build up cash, but the controller has elected to hold most of it over to ensure that the second payroll is covered. After that, the major payments to materials vendors will be made. Up to that point, only the most pressing payments have been made each week.

The budget system allows the owner and the controller to make trade-offs among the disbursements, based on how the following week shapes up. In week 2, for example, they were willing to run cash way down because the mandatory disbursements were low for the following week. This system enables the controller to give the owner a much clearer reading on the cash situation than the usual.

"How much cash do we have?"

"Fifteen thousand."

"What do we need to pay today?"

"Acme, Crescent, Millbrath. But we don't have enough to make it."

"How much will we get in tomorrow?"

"Well, let me see. . . . " The controller leafs through the receivables aging. At the same time, neither person is thinking ahead clearly to the situation for next week. Using the cash budget is a much better organized and safer way of managing when cash is tight. Again, it is the process of working with cash flow, combined with the receivables aging and payables aging. Each week the actual is posted against the budget and the new current week is reworked to reflect prevailing circumstances. The oldest week can be dropped from the sheet and a new week added at the end.

This system can be used for companies with cash surpluses, to maximize the opportunities for using the cash. The format can still include the mandatory disbursements category, after which the available funds could be applied first to discounts. Remaining cash would be available for general payments. Because the requirements for cash can be seen on a week-to-week basis, the owner can be aggressive in putting the maximum into surplus money market accounts until it is needed. By the same token, line-of-credit borrowing can be delayed to the maximum or reduced aggressively, based on the week-to-week picture afforded by the cash budget. A bookkeeper or controller of a small company can earn close to their salary by investing surplus funds aggressively, with the benefit of systematic cash budgeting.

SUMMARY

The importance of managing cash is obvious. But cash flows, even for a relatively small business, are complex. To be effective, cash management requires planning ahead, based on the three tiers we have discussed. They can be applied according to whether the entrepreneur is looking at the upcoming twelve months to assess the feasibility of goals and the likely amount of financing support which will be needed; whether it is an early warning system to give that needed extra time to prepare for a cash shortage in the immediate future; or whether it is a cash budget which will break down the process to the fine points which allow for the manipulation of cash from day to day.

Cash management requires a commitment from the owner and the financial staff to be systematic and forward-looking on a continuous basis. They have to be patient enough to look at each component of the cash-flow process individually, taking care to make the critical assumptions about sales, collections, the timing of purchases and payments, and special case disbursements such as capital expenditures, to provide a prudent basis for the overall plans. Those who are willing to keep this program going will find themselves in the financial driver's seat of their own business. Those who don't will too often find themselves being shoved around by events that will get increasingly more difficult to survive, especially as the company grows.

7

Keep Your Financial Balance

THE FINAL BALL OF THE JUGGLING ACT

For most entrepreneurs, financial position is the most esoteric aspect of financial management; yet ultimately it is the determining factor in a company's destiny. The status of a company's financial position evolves much more slowly than the other aspects of financial management—in effect, it is the final summing up of all the good and bad things that happen to a business over time. While cash flow changes from month to month and while profits change over several months, the financial position alters from year to year. For companies that have achieved a good financial position, it can take some time for it to erode (but erode it will with poor financial management), while a bad financial position can take a long time to correct. In the meantime the owner lives with the consequences.

What Is Financial Position?

Think about how a business operates, from a financial standpoint. As the owner you have certain objectives for the year; for example, to increase sales by twenty-five percent. This requires a whole list of resources, if the goal is to be achieved. There may be an increase in your advertising budget, perhaps additional salespeople with attendant increases in travel expenses. If you have inventory, the rate of purchases will increase to support the sales volume. Whether or not you increase general or administrative expenses depends on your present administrative capacity. You may have to increase your equipment. Expansion, at some point, requires more space. As sales go up, so do your accounts receivable.

All of these applications of resources to your expansion require sources of funding. Somebody has to pay for them. Expense increases, such as for advertising, are paid for, hopefully, from sales. To the degree that sales increase as fast as or faster than expenses, profits are maintained or increased. After taxes, profits are retained in the business, unless there are dividends, which is unusual for a small company. If expenses go up faster than sales, then profits will shrink. In the meantime the expenditures for equipment, greater inventory, and the increases in accounts receivable have to be funded. The sources for these are vendors, the bank, commercial financing companies, leasing companies, equipment manufacturers, sometimes friends or relatives, and the company's own source—retained earnings. In rare cases there may be venture capital. In other words, there is a complex mix of the investments you have made to create expansion with how those investments have been financed.

The company's balance sheet shows the array of the assets in which you have invested on one side, while on the other side are the sources of financing. To an accountant, the balance of the balance sheet means that assets equal liabilities plus equity. But we are worried about financial balance. This is the elusive concept. It means that the way your funds are invested needs to be offset by funds appropriate in kind to that type of investment. Seasonal increases in inventory, for example, can be financed by a bank line of credit. As the season slows, inventory declines and you can pay the bank out of collections on your accounts. If you purchase a piece of equipment, however, the bank line won't do, because the equipment is there whatever the season. The equipment produces a benefit over a few years, so you arrange an equipment loan that you pay off over a few years. Financial balance, then, is a matching up of how you spend your money with how you get your money.

But there is a second, equally crucial aspect to the balance. You can get money from other people, through various types of credit, or you can provide the money yourself. Entrepreneurs usually start their companies with a little bit of money, usually not enough. The overwhelming share of owner's equity, though, comes from that powerful source—retained earnings. During the history of your business, there must be a reasonable balance between the proportion of your money in the business and other people's. There isn't a precise, scientifically derived cutoff point between financial balance and financial imbalance, but there is an approximate point, and its impact is real and immediate.

An Example of Financial Imbalance

Any entrepreneur who has been in business for a while has experienced the consequences of financial imbalance, even if he or she hasn't understood how it works. There are a multitude of examples, but let's take a notorious one. Say a company is young and growing rapidly. Vendors are always eager for new accounts, so building up inventory has been easy, especially now that the company has been around long enough to establish a satisfactory credit rating. The bank provided a line of credit because the owner had enough equity in the house to support the credit. Sales are up, and the owner is pushing expansion with intensity. It is exhilarating for an owner to realize that the great American dream of starting a business and succeeding is happening.

To keep up with the expansion, the owner begins to slow down on payments to trade accounts. Initially, nothing happens because the vendors are a fragmented group in widely scattered locations. They have a variety of credit policies and a variety of credit management, from quick and accurate to slow and imprecise. Many are happy to have growing new accounts anyway. Besides, with several hundred or several thousand accounts, a change in one company's payment pattern isn't that noticeable. This situation can last for some time. As the expansion proceeds, the owner increases the bank line, but the borrowing is now at the limit of what the company, combined with the owner's net worth, can support. As the expansion continues the only recourse is to stretch every vendor as much as possible—push the vendors, renew the bank loans as many times as you can.

Now let's say the expansion hasn't been as profitable as the owner had hoped—maybe closer to break-even, rather than a good healthy profit. That means retained earnings are providing a proportionately smaller share of expansion financing as the business grows. Still the growth keeps coming, so the owner commits to further expansion, including an increase in space and some new equipment, both of which will make the operation more efficient and hence produce a greater profit for the coming year. But as the year gets under way vendors begin to complain. Increased shipments are harder to get. Now the owner must make substantial payments against past due balances, to receive goods. The owner learns that trade credit, the first and fastest source of financing, is like that rubber band I mentioned earlier; it expands easily, until it reaches its stress point, after which expansion is very difficult. Too much pressure and it will snap.

In the meantime, the bank will not give additional credit, because as the loan officer said at the last meeting, "You don't have sufficient collateral for a line increase at this time." The meeting is rather cool because the banker is not pleased with the lack of profitability. The owner thinks, Why does he start to get huffy after all this time? Couldn't he see what was happening two years ago? Why didn't he say something then? When we started the relationship, everything was smiles and handshakes.

But at first, sales for the year are good, as they had better be because the owner has increased the facilities and equipment, which require a higher sales volume to break even. And that was difficult enough last year. However, something worse happens—the rubber band breaks. The key vendors put the company on COD. In addition to paying for current shipments, the owner must also make payments against past due balances. Financial imbalance has struck. The increased sales have come in the form of accounts receivable, which can't be collected fast enough to provide the cash to buy inventory at the rate required to keep up with the sales volume. Without sufficient inventory, sales begin to level off. Financial statements begin to show losses, at the very time when success is at the door!

The Great American Nightmare

In desperation the owner goes to other banks. "If I can just get an increased loan to buy inventory, I can get sales up enough to make good profits. Right now my bank isn't cooperating. As a result I'm taking losses I shouldn't have to."

The banker looks quietly at the financial statements. It's as if she can't hear what the owner is saying. Nothing seems to matter except what the financial statements say, and they aren't the whole story. Can't anybody see that?

Nobody can. The financial statements show that trade credit is too high, that bank financing is at the limit, and that growth has not been profitable. The owner gets turned down at every bank he applies to. Ultimately, the consequence of the financial imbalance is the worst disaster. With increased fixed obligations for equipment and the increased rent, the owner can't cut back enough to meet all the requirements. With vendors starting to sue for payment, the bank threatening to call the loan, and with losses mounting, the owner has to declare bankruptcy. The great American dream has turned into the great American nightmare. Perhaps the notion of financial imbalance is esoteric, but every entrepreneur must understand it to maintain a prudent financial position for the business. This is the only way to realize the dream rather than to experience the nightmare.

HOW TO ANALYZE FINANCIAL POSITION

Debt versus Equity

In its raw form, financial position can be boiled down by dividing a company's total equity (common stock + surplus + retained earnings) by its total assets. This percentage indicates what portion of every dollar invested in the company's assets has come from the owner; the rest, of course is other people's money. Bankers define this position by using the debt-to-worth ratio, which is the total of all liabilities—current and long term—divided by the total equity. These are two ways of saying the same thing. When the banker refers to debt-to-worth of four to one, he is saying that there are four dollars of other people's money in the company for each dollar of the owner's. This is identical to saying that equity is twenty percent of assets ($4 of debt + $1 of equity means the total investment is $5; $1/$5 = 20%).

However, evaluating what that percentage means is not so simple. Otherwise our topic wouldn't be as esoteric as it is. The final determination of the adequacy or inadequacy of a company's financial position has to be evaluated within the context of the overall company performance, the type of industry we're dealing with, the owner's own net worth, and the concrete prospects the company has for profitable operations in the immediate future. Consequently, for entrepreneurs to be able to manage the financial position, they will have to be able to analyze their own financial statements and to evaluate the results of that analysis in light of some astute business planning. If that sounds like a lot of work, it is, but nobody said that financial management was easy. What people do say is that many business failures occur because the owners were not able to deal effectively with financial problems. Difficult or not, then, an entrepreneur who wishes to be successful really has no choice but to master the basics of financial management and to insist that the financial staff do the analytical work necessary for good planning and reporting.

Owner's Net Worth Analysis

In any small business, the owner must stand behind the company's borrowing by endorsing the loans. Most small businesses lack the financial strength to borrow on their own. Because small-company markets are so volatile, even a strong equity position has to be evaluated in light of many other factors, including the market outlook, competition, the company's plans, management strength, etc. The usually thin equity is most often combined with a short operating history as well. Success after two, three, or four years doesn't necessarily translate into success when operations grow to the size where the owner has to step up to the demands of running a "large" small company.

For these reasons, a company's financial strength and the owner's financial strength blend together. Banks review both in making credit determinations. John Millbanks, owner of Antiseptic Surgical Supply Company, had the financial statement, shown in Table 7-1, as of August 31, 1990.

Though John is not a wealthy man, comparatively, there is important strength on his statement. He has $160,000 of equity in his house. The estimated market is consistent with what houses have been selling for in his neighborhood. This is an asset which clearly stands behind his company. Since Antiseptic's line of credit is $350,000, John has close to half the borrowing covered with this asset. The rental properties have small equity, and the summer cottage is on the shore, well out of his bank's trade area. Most of his

TABLE 7-1 JOHN MILLBANK'S, PERSONAL FINANCIAL STATEMENT

ASSETS	
Cash	$ 5,000
Notes Receivable	15,000
Listed Securities	25,000
Real Estate:	
Residence—Market Value	225,000
Rental Homes (2)	180,000
Summer Cottage	50,000
Total	455,000
Automobile (2)—Blue Book	23,000
Personal Furnishings	35,000
TOTAL ASSETS	558,000
LIABILITIES	
Notes Payable	8,000
Real Estate Mortgages:	
Residence	65,000
Rental	150,000
Cottage	25,000
Total	240,000
Auto Loans	20,000
Credit Cards	3,000
TOTAL LIABILITIES	271,000
NET WORTH	287,000

debt is associated with his real estate, and he doesn't have money tied up in extras, such as yachts or fancy cars.

John hasn't listed his stock in Antiseptic as an asset on this statement, which was used for the bank loan. The reason is that the bank will disregard this value, since they are already taking the financial position of the company into consideration in their analysis of the company financial statements. In this respect, if John had listed his Antiseptic stock it would have been double counting.

THE FLOW OF FUNDS

"I made $119,000 net income after tax last year. Now I have total equity of $345,000 in my business, but my cash balance is only $7,000. Where did all the cash go? Shouldn't I have $345,000 in cash? Maybe my controller has screwed up my financial statements. Maybe I didn't make that much last year."

In one way or another, entrepreneurs like John Millbanks have asked me that question countless times over the years. What happens to profits in a growing business can seem baffling. There is another way to analyze financial position—the funds-flow analysis. It is the fundamental building block of financial analysis. This is the hardest analytical technique to understand, but in combination with the areas of analysis we have just explored, it provides financial insight into the unique operating pattern of a company. To have true financial control, the owner must have that financial insight into the business.

By including the sources and applications of funds in the year-end financial statement package, accountants are recognizing the importance of this concept to financial understanding. Unfortunately, the generally accepted format currently in use is extremely difficult to interpret on a down-to-earth operating basis. Many CPAs have trouble explaining the significance of a particular "source and app" statement, themselves.

For this reason, let's take a more straightforward approach for analyzing Antiseptic's funds flows from 1989 to 1990. Before we begin, we should discuss what the flow of funds means and why it can be so helpful in financial management. Getting back to what an owner does to expand the business, we spoke in terms of the investments necessary to implement the marketing strategy for the year— new sales reps and an advertising program (to be covered by increases in sales volume), an increase in fixed assets for greater production capacity, and, increases in accounts receivable and inventory caused by the growth in sales. We said that these investments had to be funded in some way—trade credit, retained earnings, the bank, and so on. We talked about the balance sheet as the repository of the consequences of all these transactions at the end of the year. (See Table 7-2).

There is a "snapshot" or static quality to financial statements. Much of the dynamic nature of the business is lost. Enter the funds-flow analysis. Here we open up the concept of the owner's investments to include every asset and liability in the company. In essence, a company is a pool of funds that is constantly in a state of change. These funds are not simply cash. Changes in cash are included among the flows of funds, but many changes in the company's balance of assets and liabilities don't involve cash. A primary example is the shipment of inventory, which creates a sale, which creates an account receivable. The funds-flow analysis would show a decrease in

TABLE 7-2   ANTISEPTIC SURGICAL SUPPLY CO.
CONDENSED FINANCIAL STATEMENTS DECEMBER 31, 1989 AND 1990

	1989	1990
I. INCOME STATEMENT		
Net Sales	2,365,287	3,093,364
Cost of Sales	1,584,742	2,041,620
Gross Profit	780,545	1,051,744
Operating Expenses	709,586	928,009
Income before Tax	70,959	123,735
II. BALANCE SHEET		
Assets		
Current Assets		
Cash	14,311	7,074
Accounts Receivable	348,223	464,005
Inventory	417,037	583,320
Other Current Assets	40,514	92,692
TOTAL	820,085	1,147,091
Property & Equipment, Net	68,515	93,224
Other Assets	18,037	24,018
Total Assets	906,637	1,264,333
Liabilities		
Current Liabilities		
Notes Payable, Bank	346,769	475,545
Accounts Payable	241,909	317,662
Other Current Liabilities	41,378	66,959
TOTAL	630,056	860,166
Long-term Debt	50,506	58,994
Stockholders' Equity	226,075	345,163
Total Liabilities & Equity	906,637	1,264,333
Receivables Collection (Days)	55	54[1]
Inventory Turnover to Cost of Sales	3.8×	3.5×[2]

[1]Industry average 39 days
[2]Industry average 4.6×

inventory, and an increase in accounts receivable. No involvement of cash, but a very important change in the company's financial condition.

The funds-flow analysis is based on a simple set of rules. An increase in an asset means a use of funds. A decrease in an asset means a source of funds. For example, the shipment of inventory was a source of funds, and this source was "used" to increase accounts receivable. The second rule is that an increase in liabilities is a source of funds, while a decrease in liabilities is a use of funds. This is straightforward: If you borrow from the bank, you've created a source of funds; when you pay the bank back, it's a use. It's best to think of a company as a pool, using the funds-flow analysis to see the pattern of sources and uses to understand what the owner has done with the business during the period in question.

How Funds Flows Can Answer Questions

Using this technique, we can answer John's question. As you can see in Table 7-3, Antiseptic's funds were used primarily to increase inventory and accounts receivable, with smaller uses for other current assets, and so on. The primary sources of funds were bank notes payable and the increase in stockholders' equity (i.e., net income after tax). John's profit was absorbed in the expansion of his inventory and receivables. That's why there is hardly any cash.

Since sales have increased by thirty percent for the year, these increases must be expected. Expansion uses up funds. But we can probe more deeply by combining ratio analysis with the funds flows. (See chapter 8.) Was the use of funds totally warranted? John's receivables collection slowed just a little, and inventory turnover declined from 3.7× to 3.5×. By dividing the 1989 turnover into the 1990 cost of sales, we find that inventory would have been about $30,000 lower if the ratio had remained constant. One day's receivable collection amounts to just about $9,000. In effect, John's cash is tied up not only by growth but by the slippage in his turnover.

TABLE 7-3 ANTISEPTIC SURGICAL SUPPLY CO., FUNDS-FLOW ANALYSIS, DECEMBER 31, 1987 TO DECEMBER 31, 1990

Source of funds		Use of funds	
Increase in Bank Notes Payable	128,776	Increase in Inventory	166,283
Increase in Stockholders' Equity	119,088	Increase in Accounts Receivable	115,782
Increase in Accounts Payable	75,753	Increase in Other Current Assets	52,178
Increase in Other Current Liabilities	25,591	Increase in Property, Equipment	24,709
Increase in Long-term Debt	8,488	Increase in Other Assets	5,981
Decrease in Cash	7,237		
TOTAL	364,933	TOTAL	364,933

We could apply a more stringent measure by using the industry averages on the 1990 results. On this basis, inventory would have been almost $140,000 less. Accounts receivable, at thirty-nine days, would have been $128,000 less. John, in comparison to his industry, has almost $270,000 more tied up in current assets than he should have, at least theoretically. In terms of interest cost on the bank borrowing or lost discounts on accounts payable, there is a penalty for this excess, plus the added risk of a heavier debt position and a tight current ratio.

SUMMARY

Financial position is where the buck stops . . . or starts . . . or keeps coming in. It is the final analysis of balance—of the ways funds have been invested, as opposed to how they have been obtained; of the proportion of the owner's money as opposed to other people's money. There is no exact formula which can be used to scientifically derive the break point between satisfactory balance or unsatisfactory balance. That decision is made by different interests, each of which will evaluate the company according to its own point of view: trade creditors, the banker, potential investors, for example. As part of each decision-making process, a positive or negative conclusion will be made about the company's financial balance, and these decisions will have a practical day-to-day impact on the company's operations. Therefore, it is critical that every business owner understand the importance of financial position, how to analyze financial statements, and how to manage for better results.

Over the years an owner can guide a business to improvement in financial position, the rewards of which will be enhanced borrowing capability, a greater control of risks, and a greater value for the business.

8

The Financial Health Check

WHEN IT'S TOO LATE

Too often I've witnessed the despair of an owner who's lost his or her business. "If only I'd known. If only I'd done the right thing two years ago." But it's too late. What would have worked then won't work now. Nothing will.

"Nobody warned me! Nobody told me what I should have done."

You're out there alone. Your CPA, lawyer, and banker are all on the sidelines, busy with their own affairs. They lack your experience in running a small business. *You* must be the first to know when trouble is brewing. By the time professional advisors see it—if they do—too much damage will have been done.

You can detect the early warning signs without being a financial analyst. You can evaluate these signs without years of experience in running a business. If you're vigilant, and if you face the facts, you'll have enough time to fix the problems. But deal with trouble early. Get into a little quicksand, and you can back out. Get way into it, and you'll be sucked under.

WARNING SIGNS OF DANGER

What are the red flags that indicate today that there will be trouble tomorrow? They boil down to a few ratios in three critical areas of business: profitability, liquidity, and financial position.

Profitability

Profits insure long-range health. Net income, month after month, year after year, is retained in the business to build equity. This establishes the capital base to support future growth. Net income is the best single measure of your efficiency as a manager. Not only should you make profits consistently, but the size of the profits in relationship to sales volume indicates the degree of your efficiency.

Problems with profits have a tendency to creep up. If you allow them to persist, your precious capital base will erode. Bills will become harder to pay, and banks will be slower to make loans. The cure is time-consuming and painful, because the only way out of losses is to cut expenses. But improvement must accrue month by painful month. Many a sorrowful owner has gone to the bank after a few months of profits only to hear, "This isn't enough to prove you've turned it around. Keep it up a while longer, and maybe we'll be able to help."

Making profits requires constant attention to detail. Excess costs can develop anywhere: cost of materials, direct labor, advertising, overhead salaries, rent. Owners of profitable businesses have a healthy respect for accurate and timely financial statements, and they know how to use them.

The profitability test is focused on trends in four critical areas. First, the percentage of cost of goods to sales measures how efficiently you deliver goods or services. Second, the gross profit that results is your most powerful resource for making a profit. The gross profit must cover all other expenses, with a sufficient margin remaining for a healthy net income.

The gross profit percentage should be stable or improving over time. If it gradually declines, so will the margin of net income. Ultimately, losses will occur. Maintaining gross profit is the first line of defense. As your business grows, managing gross profits with a financial statement alone won't work. You'll need to know the profitability of each product line, each job, each division of the business.

Only then can you keep the gross profit at the percentage you need to be consistently profitable.

Third, general and administrative expenses—any expense category after gross profit—are a matter of prudent budgeting. If gross profit is forty percent of sales, and your goal is ten percent net income, then you can spend only thirty percent on everything else. Once you've established the budget, expenses must be monitored carefully to keep them in line.

Fourth, if you maintain the gross profit percentage and you keep expenses on budget, then you'll meet the net income target. But there's a catch. If sales drop, budgeted expenses are no longer thirty percent of sales. Maybe they're thirty-five percent. Suddenly profit is cut in half! It can be worse. Frequently the market doesn't allow a pat hand with expense control. Good, timely financial information diligently monitored will enable you to make mid-stream adjustments to keep the business profitable.

Liquidity

Cash is your most volatile asset. A client once said to me, "I have sales orders heaped on my desk. In just weeks, investors will put money in my business. But tomorrow I must pay $180,000 in bills, and I don't have the cash. I'll be shut down, just when everything's taking off. It's ridiculous!" Ridiculous, maybe, but if you don't have cash, prospects don't count.

While profits insure long-range health, cash insures day-to-day survival. But cash is difficult to manage. Cash crises can occur suddenly, without warning. Sometimes cash shortages are a way of life for months or years, until suddenly the ridiculous happens and you're faced with the ultimate disaster.

Long-range warning signs of cash trouble show up in the liquidity of current assets: cash, receivables, and inventory. The basic test of short-term liquidity is the current ratio: current assets divided by current liabilities. The ratio states the dollars in assets available to pay the dollars in liabilities. The closer the ratio is to two-to-one, the greater the safety margin. The closer to one-to-one, the thinner the ice.

But what about the quality of the assets? Having lots of receivables is great, but what if you're past due? You should monitor the aging of receivables constantly. In the health check, the average collection should be steady or improving. If it gradually deteriorates, you'll be running short of cash.

Inventory is extremely difficult to manage. If your business is sizable, you need a computerized inventory control system. Accurate inventory control packs a double wallop. It prevents excessive inventory, which devours cash. Correct and timely inventory counts also yield precise gross profit numbers, both overall and for product lines. If you don't know exactly what the inventory is, you don't know what the gross profit is.

Inventory is more difficult to finance than receivables, with some exceptions. You pay for extra inventory out of your own cash, not the bank line. Worse, overstocking can led to obsolescence, which means lost income and lost cash. The health check monitors inventory turnover, which should be stable or improving. Chronically slowing inventory turnover signals cash disaster.

Financial Position

You must make many investments to grow. Expansion will increase accounts receivable. More inventory is needed to support greater sales. Fixed assets are added to increase your capabilities. These investments must be financed in some way.

Financial balance comes from properly matching the assets you have acquired for growth with the current liabilities, long-term debt, and equity you have used to finance them. It's a judgment call based on the financial position ratios shown in the health check. You must maintain ratios that are sufficient for other people to lend you money and to protect your welfare.

Financial position boils down to the percentage of liabilities to the assets of the business. Very high current liabilities means too much has been financed short term. Cash is always short. Fixed assets should be financed with long-term debt that is repaid, basically, over the life of the asset. Too much long-term debt means there'll be trouble making scheduled note payments.

The bottom line is debt-to-worth, the ratio of total debt divided by equity. Generally, banks look for debt-to-worth of three-to-one or better. The acceptable ratio of debt is greater for asset-based lending. When the debt-to-worth ratio exceeds bank guidelines, it is extremely difficult to get financing. The greater the debt, the greater the risk that you'll lose the business.

Financial position may sound theoretical, but you must be a prudent financial manager. Anyone who's been put on COD, can't get an increase in their bank line, is in default on note payments, and can't meet payroll on Friday knows that the results of financial imbalance are immediate and disastrous. Monitor your financial position regularly to guard against trouble.

GIVE YOURSELF A CHECKUP

Use the health check shown in Figure 8-1 to check your profitability, liquidity, and financial position. If just one of these areas is particularly strong, it can carry weaknesses in the other areas, but not for long. You need to shore up your performance in the weak areas as quickly as possible. Generally, if you show deterioration in all three areas, you'd better seek professional help immediately.

You can gauge your financial health by comparing your ratios to industry averages for each line item in the test. These often can be obtained through a trade group, banker, accountant, or local small-business development center. If industry ratios are not available, you can judge your performance by evaluating the trends over the last three years. You may have your own rules of thumb to use as a yard stick as you follow these trends.

The health check in Figure 8-1 includes, as an example, the results of an East Coast supply company. You can do your own analysis in the space provided. It would be wise to give yourself a financial health check every year.

Checking Your Business's Health

By comparing your business's financial ratios to industry averages, you can gauge your company's health.

The following test checks profitability, liquidity, and financial position. If just one of these three areas is strong enough, it likely can carry the other two: The sort of financial deterioration that leads to failure usually shows up in all three areas simultaneously.

A small-business owner interested in seeing how a business measures up needs to get average industry figures for each line item; these often can be obtained through a trade group, banker, accountant, or local small-business development center. A sample test, using the results of an East Coast supply, is shown below.

	Supply company				Your data			
	1989	1990	1991	Latest industry average	1989	1990	1991	Latest industry average
PROFITABILITY								
Begin at 100%	100.0%	100.0%	100.0%	100.0%	100.0%	100.0%	100.0%	100.0%
Cost of goods sold divided by sales	67.2%	66.0%	66.5%	67.0%				
Gross profit divided by sales	32.8%	34.0%	33.5%	33.0%				
General and administrative costs divided by sales	30.1%	29.9%	33.0%	29.8%				
Other expenses (including interest expense) divided by sales	—	—	—	—				
Pretax profit divided by sales	2.7%	4.1%	.5%	3.2%				

The gross profit ratio for the supply company has been above the industry average of 33% for two years. But 1990 pretax profit was almost erased by climbing general and administrative expenses. The red flag is up. The company must cut those costs.

For your company, compare the gross profit ratio with company goals and the industry percentage. Is it stable, up, or down? Look at the general and administrative costs ratio. Is it eating up too much gross profit? How does it compare with the industry percentage? How does the pretax profit percentage compare with the industry average?

LIQUIDITY

Current ratio (current assets divided by current liabilities)				1.3	1.3	1.2	2.0
Receivables collection (sales/365; accounts receivable/daily sales)*				53.0	50.0	61.0	42.0
Inventory turnover (cost of goods sold divided by inventory)				3.4	3.5	3.5	3.8

After some improvement in 1990, the sample company's liquidity deteriorated last year as receivables collection, the rate at which customers paid their bills, continued to stretch out. Inventory turnover is close to the industry average, but the current ratio has dropped.

*To determine a company's receivables collection rate, divide annual sales by 365 to get the average daily sales figure. That figure is then divided into the accounts receivable line on the balance sheet.

A current ratio above 1.6 is good, and on that score the supply company is struggling. How does your receivables collection compare with the industry average? (The shorter the better.) How does inventory turnover compare with your goal and the industry average? (The higher the better).

FINANCIAL POSITION

Current liabilities divided by total assets				74.8%	68.0%	70.1%	55.8%
Long-term debt divided by total assets				0.0%	4.7%	5.3%	11.1%
Total debt divided by total assets				74.8%	72.7%	75.4%	66.9%
Equity divided by total assets				25.2%	27.3%	24.6%	32.1%
Debt-to-worth ratio (total debt divided by equity)				2.97	2.66	3.06	2.08

The supply company's overall financial position improved in 1990 because of the year's strong profit. The equity/total assets percentage was closing in on the industry average in 1990 but fell back in 1991—pummeled by lower profits and higher liabilities. Trouble looms. The company must post a strong profit this year and improve its receivables collection.

If the long-term debt ratio is higher than the industry average, try to retire some debt; if the ratio is below the average, consider adding long-term debt to pay off current liabilities. A company is on dangerous ground if the total debt ratio exceeds 75%. An equity/total assets ratio of 35% or higher is good. To qualify for most bank loans, a debt-to-worth ratio of 3-to-1 or lower is acceptable.

Figure 8-1 Business health check.

9

Insist on Management Controls

MANAGEMENT DECISIONS INVOLVE THE PAST, PRESENT, AND FUTURE

Marketing, profits, cash flow, financial position, all the management we have been discussing involves the evaluation of what has just happened, within the context of the trends of past months and years, as orchestrated by the owner's objectives, strategies, and plans. The results are just about to happen, and they will be followed by other business events which will be followed, in turn. But nobody can predict the future. Our plans will not materialize exactly as we expected.

Most entrepreneurs take it as it comes. In many respects they do very well at it. But as companies grow, areas here and there begin to unravel on the fire fighters, no matter how tough and persistent they are. A growing company simply becomes too complicated for one person to run by the seat of the pants. If it isn't inventory getting out of hand, it's a sales rep getting out of balance between draws and commissions, or a serious bad debt, or an accounting manager screwing up the books, or a bad run of materials from a supplier causing a big shipment to be returned, or, or, or. . . . The larger the company gets, the more things there are to unravel, and the greater the penalties paid.

The fire fighter's problem with growth is not only that size brings more fires, but that taking on one crisis after another creates confusion. After a while every fire looks the same, so how does an owner figure out priorities? If the owner can only fight five but has eight to put out, which fire should be fought and which should be left to burn? Owners who take things up one at a time may take care of the five problems that could have worked themselves out, while the three that weren't dealt with may do the business in. I have seen that happen. Furthermore, guiding a business through all the problems and dangers of the hostile environment we discussed at the outset requires the ability to look ahead, to chart a course. So much of an entrepreneur's work is done in uncharted territory. Tackling problems as they pop up doesn't allow the owner to think ahead, with the result that the business can spin its wheels, revolve in circles, become logjammed with unexecuted activity. I have seen that happen.

Control comes from being able to focus on those areas that matter, while leaving the less critical problems to another day. Only so much can be done. The trick is to pick out the pressure points. The surprising thing is that an owner can get a lot more done, with less effort, by bringing the focus of management to these pressure points. The successful management of an entrepreneur's time comes from knowing the keys to bringing the enterprise home with the profits earned and the market position strengthened and vitalized.

Manage the Critical Variables

The critical variables of management control are those half-dozen or so areas in which the targets must be hit for the company to be successful, no matter what happens in all the other thousands of variables. On the other hand, if a target is missed in any one of these areas, the company will not achieve its goals, no matter how well all the rest is done. Management control, then, means having a series of reports that allow the owner to monitor performance in the critical areas in a way that permits quick remedial action to get performance back on track.

You can call this *management by objectives* if you wish, but there must be some clear-minded thinking before this kind of management can take place. What are the critical variables for the enterprise? What kind of report or reports in each critical area will enable the owner to see at a glance how the company stands? As a practical matter, what needs to be done in the accounting department and the operating departments to generate the information necessary for the reports?

For almost every small company, the critical areas of management control will include at least the following:

- Sales
- Profits
- Cash flow
- Job cost analysis
- Receivables status
- Payables status
- Inventory status
- Financial position analysis.

As you can see, this is a common-sense approach, which doesn't involve anything mysterious or highly technical and theoretical. In a small business, everything we do has to have immediate benefits, otherwise we can't afford the cost. But if we can make this control process effective, the owner can get into the driver's seat in some areas that are almost always elusive for the entrepreneur. Though financial management is complicated, with some work and determination it can be brought into focus so an intelligent person without any special training can make astute judgments based on the best information available.

Use Planning to Set Up Control

This is where planning plays a practical role in day-to-day management. Trying to find out how a dynamic small business is doing is no easy matter. Just keeping up with posting the books is an effort. But management requires more than a monthly financial statement, as we have discussed. In the process, assuming that the owner is getting good information, how do you evaluate the results? Sales are up or down compared to what? Profits at the end of the first quarter were $35,000, but compared to what? Is that good? Maybe in a seasonable business, taking a $50,000 loss in the first quarter is a good job, but how good? Operating plans for sales, profits, and cash flows establish a set of guidelines against which the actual results can be evaluated. If the deviations from plan are unfavorable, then the owner may have to make some decisive readjustments to maintain profitability and avoid cash-flow trouble. Having a plan-versus-actual format to monitor operations gives the owner some clear-cut readings; this is preferable to trying to interpret the many results without a frame of reference. Everything in management is approximate—we have to accept that fact—but plans are a road map to help find out where you are.

For management control to work, it must make sense to the owner. If there are managers who will be involved in certain aspects of management control, obviously that part of the system will have to make sense to them, as well. Otherwise there will be a bunch of reports that take time to prepare but that are never used for decision making. In these cases, it would be better not to have a system at all, because it would eliminate the cost of gathering the information and dispel any illusion that an effective management control program exists.

Again, Formats Are Important

Let's start squeezing, here, to move to the more practical and specific from the general. Format seems a strange topic with which to start being more specific, but it is all important. I recall a frustrating discussion I had with a client several years ago.

"It's time I got a computer. I'm going to get an IBM."

"Phil, before you do, let's take a careful look at it. You've worked hard to establish a damn good management control system. Every month you can evaluate the results with a lot of insight, because the reports are tailor-made to your management style. You should select a computer system that will enable you to keep this system going."

"I don't see why an IBM system can't do it."

"Sometimes the software requires changes in the formats of the reports."

"So we'll change the reports. I'm tired of all the frustration and expense of the manual system."

"You'd be amazed to see what that can do to decision making. If the information comes to you in a way that doesn't highlight the crucial indicators of performance, you may miss the point. You may not make a crucial decision because something slipped by you. It is time to automate your accounting, but don't throw the baby away with the bath water!"

Phil shrugged and dropped the subject. After all, it was his decision to make, but on the subject of management control he was less astute than in the other phases of his business, even though he had come to rely heavily on the control system he had working for him. As you can guess, the new system did not feed him the full range of information he had been getting. This, combined with some other problems in the conversion from manual to computer, resulted in a gap of several months when Phil was without a clear understanding of where his business stood, just at a time when a major growth spurt took place. Phil was beside himself during this time, because control was critical to his management approach, even if he was unsophisticated about what had to be done to preserve his system. Fortunately the company made it through the expansion without serious problems, though if there had been trouble, Phil wouldn't have known much about it until it was too late. With a great deal of hard work on the part of his financial staff and with a different computer system, an effective control program was reestablished.

Running a growing enterprise is a tough job. A constant stream of problems runs the gamut of management, from inventory control to personnel problems, from legal troubles to product development. The owner is a master in some areas and virtually ignorant in others. His or her attention span for any single problem is limited to a short burst of intensive thinking, after which the next problem pops up on the screen. Financial and management control is one of the areas most entrepreneurs find difficult. Analytical data—columns of numbers, ratios, budgets—seem to be difficult to work with.

If the owner has to analyze and reinterpret the financial data presented, then the chances that the significance of the figures is going to be lost, because most entrepreneurs are not trained to do this kind of analysis and because time pressures won't allow enough attention to the problem. Thus it is imperative that the control reports allow the owner to see the significance of the situation at first reading. To do this, the data must be presented in a focused manner.

THE CONTROLLER'S BOOK

In the fast-paced day of a growing enterprise, something is always going on. There are daily sales results, weekly sales reports. There are reports of daily cash. Managers talk of developments in their areas of responsibility. Two weeks, possibly three after the month ends, the accounting department produces a financial statement. Perhaps there are labor distributions, possibly contract status reports or some computer runs on inventory and accounts receivable which come across the owner's desk with or before the financial statements.

Typically the owner gets this kind of fragmented view of the enterprise. Fragmentation will destroy management control. Just the act of assembling all the reports into a systematic overview of the company's performance is an important function of control. That is why I strongly recommend a controller's book, divided into sections for each critical variable. This allows the owner to study all important areas of the business as a set, to gain an understanding of the overall position of the business, how the critical areas are interrelating, where the weaknesses are, where the strengths are. In this way management attention can be focused on priorities for reaching goals. The shocking fact about management control is that it doesn't take much management time for evaluation and decision making regarding the most critical variables of the company. No more than an hour a month, perhaps, to read and decide, once the reports have been prepared and presented. Of course, unless the owner wants to work in a vacuum, he or she must also effectively communicate the decisions and changes in policy to key managers and employees.

Furthermore, it is an arduous and relatively expensive task to collect the data and process it for the reports. The design of the reports takes skill and insight into how management control works. For the owner to get into a position where this kind of fingertip control of operations is possible, at least from the analytical side of it, a significant commitment has to be made. Most entrepreneurs won't make this commitment. But how much is it worth to have control of the business? What kind of price tag would you put on being able to detect problems, either as soon as they occur or possibly before they happen? For a small business, perhaps, a controller's book is overkill, but when does a company cross over the dividing line between small and getting bigger? Some businesses blow through two or three stages of growth in a year or two. What was little is now really a "large" small business. I have seen the controller's book work. I have seen a comprehensive profit planning system open up a company to substantial growth, both in sales and in the development of management capability for the owner and key managers. I have seen owners stay out of trouble because they were able to monitor the critical variables of their business month by month. I have seen owners get into trouble because they didn't pursue an overview of their business on a continuous basis.

Control Takes Place When the Owner Insists

Back comes the Catch 22 of entrepreneurship again. If an owner isn't familiar with the process of management control because he or she is a salesperson or a technical person or what have you, then how can management controls be set up in the first place? This is a very difficult question to answer.

Developing management control begins with the owner's recognition that it has to be done. If the owner is determined, then the commitment to developing control will carry through to those in the company who will have to set up and operate the system. The expense of doing it will be acknowledged as worthwhile. But a very significant practical problem remains. Who knows how to do it? Usually the person who will have the job is the accounting manager, the controller, or the outside accountant. Some accounting-trained people are very good at developing management controls, others are not—just because someone has a degree in accounting doesn't mean that they can do the management control job. In addition, accountants tend to work in accounting formats, thinking problems out in accounting terms. Their analyses may be insightful, but the typical entrepreneur approaches the same topics with a different thought process, which frequently causes a breakdown in the communication between the owner and the accountant, with the result that an important phase of control is lost.

Controls Must Fit the Owner's Thought Process

The management control system must be tailored to the owner's thought process, if the decisions are to be made with true insight into the status of the critical variables. This means that the owner must insist that the controller's book consist of reports which he or she can understand. A format may have to be reworked several times before the owner feels comfortable with it. At the same time, the owner must make every effort to become more conversant with the basics of financial management. There must be enough self-discipline to allow a systematic review of the critical variables in the controller's book.

Someone has to be given the responsibility for keeping up the book. Usually it is the controller. Keeping the management reports on an accurate and timely basis and assembling them into a single presentation, rather than a piecemeal flow, requires coordination. The book won't keep itself.

Use of Art of Summarizing Information

Another key to good control is the art of summarizing information. The owner of a growing company can get bogged down by too much detail. Computer reports are potentially very bad in this regard. What the programmer thought was good information when the system was being created may not be relevant to a fast-moving entrepreneur. Many business reports in software that small businesses buy with their IBM, DEC, WANG, or other computer are going to require manual reworking to be effective management tools. Frequently the reports have to be replaced altogether. Too often the owner gives up the computer reports, leaving them to keep the general ledger and to send out invoices, which is helpful, but far short of what an effectively utilized computer can do.

The three layers of management control reports are shown in Figure 9-1. The layer of reports for top management should be focused on highlights. The owner should be able to track a problem into a second layer of reports that give more data, to find out what is going on. This is the middle managers' layer of reports. The third layer of information is the data base itself, usually the raw stuff in the accounting department, which the bookkeepers are posting and balancing. If the control system is good, the owner and the managers can research problem areas down to this level to find answers. In "small" small companies the owner is top and middle management and is involved in raw data, too, such as the checkbook. As companies grow from the point where the owner has a finger in everything to the point where there are layers of management, the development of an efficient and concise management control system becomes increasingly important. Many aspects of the controls are replacements, in a sense, for the owner's previous physical presence on the floor. If the managers know that the owner is tracking information in a certain area of performance, they know it is important, even if the owner isn't there to tell them.

In a good system, the owner can follow a specific
problem all the way to the raw data to get to the
bottom of things.

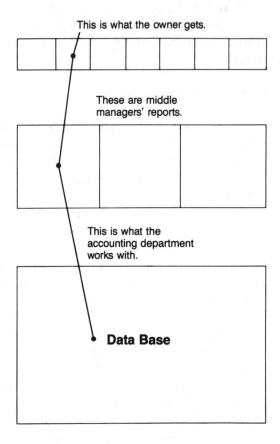

This is what the owner gets.

These are middle
managers' reports.

This is what the
accounting department
works with.

Data Base

Figure 9-1 Layers of
management reports.

HOW TO BUILD THE CONTROL BOOK

Sales Analysis

Let's work through the controller's book a section at a time. Monitoring sales results is a crucial process. Usually the sales section of the
management control has two components, a weekly sales analysis
and a monthly, perhaps quarterly or year-to-date, summary. Sales
results can be reported against targets for the period and/or against
the results for the same period last year. Most entrepreneurs are on

top of results in this section. In fact, when I help owners develop a controller's book, we usually find that sixty to seventy percent of the reports are already being used. The task is to create the missing reports and to gather all the reports together in the book.

The important feature of sales reports is to focus the attention of the owner and the sales manager on the specifics of performance, rather than on generalities about how things are going. Sales results should be evaluated weekly. In some companies, especially retailers, there are daily summaries. The results are summarized and evaluated for the month. There is much to consider—performance of individual sales reps or store owners, performance by product line, analysis of activity by major account. Through the evaluation of results, the owner can develop an assessment of how each critical factor of the sales and marketing effort is doing. Is the advertising campaign dovetailed with the telemarketing effort? Are there weak links in the rep network? Is each store manager doing a strong job? Are each of the major product lines selling well? Monitoring sales results yields answers to these questions, along with the personal evaluations of the owner. Throughout, the up-to-date knowledge of sales performance allows the owner to reassess the validity of the profit plans and the cash-flow plans, which are so dependent on actual sales meeting the targets.

Profitability Analysis

A summary example of profit planning is shown in chapter 3. Using a divisional income statement, with actual-versus-plan stated for the month and year to date, allows the owner of Arrow to discuss progress with the division managers. Each division statement shows breakdowns of the accounts in more detail to enable managers to better control expenses, while the owner concentrates on the overview, unless a more specific issue needs to be discussed. In a good system, each manager can go to the general ledger to analyze variances in any of his or her accounts on an expenditure-by-expenditure basis. Corporate expenses, or corporate G&A, are left for the owner and controller to monitor. For expense control, G&A, again, should be broken down in more detail than the summary.

I am against allocating corporate expenses, or corporate G&A, to the individual divisions. In my view, divisions should be looked at on the basis of those revenues and expenses that can be directly, or indirectly in some cases, tied to their operations. Corporate expenses have to be allocated by some arbitrary factor, because there is no direct tie-in to the divisions. Perhaps that factor will be based on the division's percentage of the corporate sales, perhaps payroll, or perhaps square feet. Whatever the case, the expense allocation is artificial. There is no concrete basis for the assignment of the president's salary or the annual audit or the annual legal bill. Arbitrary allocations are dangerous because the results may be misleading. Divisions can be made to look better or worse than they would standing on their own. With a client I had a few years ago, the division allocation of corporate expenses was a political football. The company was losing money. After allocation, the three corporate divisions looked about even in performance, but the managers, who were also stockholders, argued among themselves about the validity of the allocation method. The general manager was not objective, having previously been head of one of the divisions. Before any allocation, one division was a clear profit maker, one was at a break-even, and one was clearly losing money.

If each division is analyzed according to its contribution to corporate expenses, then the division performance is clearly stated. A critical management control point is highlighted—the amount of total division contribution available for corporate overhead—which allows the owner to weigh one against the other. Besides refusing to face facts about the true division status, this management control focus was what my client was not getting.

Sometimes the owner is the culprit in causing low profitability by spending too much at the corporate level, while the divisions are profitable in their own right. Of course, divisional statements are effective when the owner manages all the components, because the same questions about comparative profitability need to be answered no matter how many managers are involved. Profit planning is effective when there is only a single corporate statement to evaluate. Profits need to be managed through careful attention to detail, no matter what the structure of the company is.

The Budget Process Must Be Coordinated

The controller or some other knowledgeable person should act as manager of the budgets. The delivery of accurate and timely profit management documents to the management team is a complex task that requires an able coordinator. This job begins with the preparation of the annual plan, which requires explanations, as necessary, about the results for the previous year, including discussion of any adjustments the outside accountants made to the company statements. During the budgeting process, the controller must document the critical assumptions made by each manager and by the owner, to ensure that the accounting is handled properly after the year is under way. During the year the controller must analyze the monthly statements to screen for variances, both to keep the owner apprised of unfavorable developments and to catch variances caused by accounting transactions, such as an annual insurance premium which comes due during one month. The controller's job is to spread unusually large annual expenses over several months or to be able to explain why a variance was caused by an accounting event, rather than because of an overrun. There may be some budget system journal entries to convert data from the accounting general ledger into the most effective format for management control.

Budgets are fine, but they don't make things happen by themselves. When owners are their own managers, the entire profit plan is theirs to make or break. It must be the owner's plan, to which he or she is committed, or else it will be an academic exercise for the controller or accounting manager. As the company grows to where managers can assume responsibility for budget centers, the same requirement for commitment holds for them. Division managers' commitment to their budgets can be ensured by seeing that they are given responsibility only for revenues and expenses over which they have a significant degree of influence.

A word about having managers involved in the profit planning. Many entrepreneurs don't like to have others see their financial statements. This is understandable. But as one of my clients said after he had brought his managers into the budgeting process, "Now I don't feel like I've been reading my financial statements in a closet anymore. I've got four people to help me get that profit."

As a company grows, achieving superior growth and profitability goes beyond one person's ability. Managers can play a much more effective role in contributing to that growth and to those profits if they are allowed to see how their area of responsibility is doing with the same kind of insight that their owner needs to run the company as a whole. This information can be given to them without having to disclose the overall performance of the company, if the owner chooses not to, because the managers don't have to see the corporate expenses.

Another downfall of budget programs is failure to control expenses at the point of commitment. An owner can have a dandy budget, but if several engineers, for example, can order materials or take trips to retain consultants, all in good faith but outside budget authorizations, budgetary control is out the window. Some kind of sensible purchase order system is necessary to keep these kinds of expenditures within budget. Without the purchase order system, budgets will be constantly overrun. More than one owner has scratched his or her head wondering why.

Cash-Flow Analysis

It is important to keep an eye on the actual cash flow versus the plan. Small companies have limits to their cash-flow capabilities. Only so much can be done relying on cash generated from daily operations. Periodically acute shortages develop due to seasonal fluctuations in sales or due to sudden spurts of growth. These shortages are funded by bank loans combined with stretching accounts payable as much as possible. Heavy special requirements, such as capital expenditures or certain kinds of merchandise inventory held for resale, can be supported by special-purpose financing, such as equipment loans, leases, and floor-planning arrangements with commercial finance companies.

A company's ability to generate cash from daily operations added to what it can prudently borrow from all its borrowing sources equals the maximum cash capability. Managing cash flow is the process of keeping the actual cash needs within this maximum capability. At first, if the need exceeds this capability, the minimum penalty is the embarrassment—and the precedent, which damages the company's credibility with financing sources—of reneging on its obligations. If a company literally doesn't have the cash, it doesn't pay. What is not paid? Payroll, a bank payment, a check promised to a vendor? Maybe most companies have this happen once in a long while. Maybe it happens a couple of times. Maybe it happens frequently. As a company moves from rarely to frequently, it moves from understandable human error to financial instability. When an owner is experiencing financial instability, what is the next step?

Perhaps we should say that managing cash flow is the process of keeping the company's actual cash-flow needs prudently within the company's maximum cash capability, because we want to leave a margin of safety. We want to protect ourselves against the human error of underestimating the requirements we will have during a certain period. We want to protect ourselves from unexpected events, such as a sudden recession or the invasion of our market by a powerful competitor. Cash flow is tricky, though, because a sudden desirable event—extraordinary sales growth—can create cash shortages beyond our capabilities just as the sudden recession can.

The three-month cash-flow plan is the most powerful way for an entrepreneur to keep cash-flow requirements under control for the immediate future. Understanding why cash flow actually deviated from the plan for the month just ended, in combination with the estimates for cash flow over the next three months, gives the owner a constant picture of the fluid, changing nature of the company's cash flow. An example from Antiseptic Surgical Supply is shown in Table 9-1.

If the plan shows deficits coming up, the first question is whether or not the company can handle them. If so, the job is to keep the needs within the projected requirements. If the deficits look greater than the present resources, the owner will have to make some changes in operations to cut back the requirements—maybe slow down orders for inventory, maybe slow down on the rate of payment to certain vendors, maybe put extra pressure on collections, maybe ask the bank for a line increase, depending on what is most appropriate. Then, periodically, the twelve-month plan can be developed to take a longer-range look at requirements, to determine whether the long-range requirements are going to be within the company's capabilities. The cash-flow analysis is an indispensable part of the controller's book. The effectiveness of this kind of cash management depends on the skill with which the cash plan is prepared and the astuteness with which the owner evaluates the results and makes the decisions. This kind of effectiveness comes from practice in using the system. Owners who have used this approach for several months get very good at it.

Job Cost Analysis

Gross profit is a major focus for profit management. But the financial statement gross profit is an aggregate of many factors. The divisional income statement allows the owner to see the gross profit for each unit of the corporation. Even divisional gross profits,

TABLE 9-1 ANTISEPTIC SURGICAL SUPPLY CASH-FLOW PLAN
NOVEMBER 1991 TO JANUARY 1992

	October Plan	October Actual	Nov	Dec	Jan
Receipts					
Collections	300,000	281,520	223,400	277,000	263,000
Other Income	3,100	3,100	3,100	3,100	3,100
TOTAL	303,100	284,620	226,500	280,100	266,100
Disbursements					
Advertising	850	0	850	850	850
Auto Allowance	800	400	800	800	800
Bank Charge	60	4	60	60	60
Business Taxes	500	0	500	500	500
Car & Truck	1,600	1,266	1,600	1,600	1,600
Commissions	21,000	19,490	15,800	19,390	18,410
Contract Services	1,500	2,033	1,500	1,500	1,500
Convention Expense	0	0	0	0	0
Delivery Expense	1,890	1,768	1,890	1,890	1,890
Dues & Subscriptions	130	460	130	130	130
Entertainment	700	327	700	700	700
Freight	4,300	3,323	4,300	4,300	4,300
Insurance	2,950	−3,271	2,950	2,950	2,950
Interest	7,500	7,544	7,500	7,500	7,500
Lease Payments	3,750	3,750	3,750	3,750	3,750
Miscellaneous	800	0	800	800	800
Office Supplies	500	622	500	500	500
Operating Supplies	1,000	1,033	1,000	1,000	1,000
Payroll Taxes	2,600	2,929	3,000	3,000	3,000
Postage	300	492	300	300	300
Professional Fees	500	340	500	500	500
Rent	6,500	6,500	7,300	7,300	7,300
Repair & Maintenance	250	632	250	250	250
Salaries	26,300	25,756	29,000	29,000	29,000
Telephone	1,150	1,813	1,150	1,150	1,150
Utilities	900	78	900	900	900
Trade Payables	175,000	153,400	187,000	190,600	240,000
Installation & Repair	4,500	4,298	4,500	4,500	4,500
TOTAL	267,830	234,987	278,530	285,720	334,140
Net Receipts					
(Disbursements)	35,270	49,633	−52,030	−5,620	−68,040
Beginning Cash	3,742	3,742	53,375	1,345	−4,275
Ending Cash	39,012	53,375	1,345	−4,275	−72,315

though, are aggregates of products, jobs, contracts. The first line of defense in profit management comes in controlling job costs. If the company doesn't operate jobs, there are the gross profits on individual product lines. The controller's book should have a summary of job, product, or contract profitability if the owner is to have the opportunity to intervene at the operating level, where the gross profit is made or lost.

Each owner needs to have a gross profit target or a target for contract profitability or job profitability. A detailed report of job costs for each product, contract, or job may be too much for the owner to digest, if the company is large enough, but a good summary report will permit a screening of performance from which the owner can pick out substandard profitability for investigation. In the meantime, the job managers or division managers, as the case may be, can study very detailed job cost runs for the operations under their direct control. In this way, management toward the overall corporate goals can take place as the year goes along, rather than the frustrating and dangerous position too many owners find themselves in after their year-end statement as they ask, "Gross profit is down by three percent of sales . . . why?" Not only do they lack the tools to analyze the problem, without the cost analysis, but the damage has already been done. The management of Arrow can reconstruct how gross profit was made or lost on a house-by-house basis. The production manager has additional reports to analyze by phases of construction, to control costs down to the most detailed basis.

Owners and managers of job-type operations, such as construction or development contracts, have to be alert to a curve ball in job cost analysis—committed costs. Take the development of an electronic instrument, for example, At the time of analysis, say halfway through Phase D, the accounting department has booked contract-to-date costs for labor, materials, and other direct costs. The owner and the project engineer can reason through the work left to be done, and then add the estimates to the costs already booked to get an estimated cost to complete, right? Wrong! Frequently the project may have materials and services on order but not yet received. If the owner and the engineer aren't careful, they may overlook these cost elements, which sometimes significantly affect the ultimate profitability of the job. When a company faces this kind of situation frequently, a column designated for committed costs is a vital part of the job cost analysis, to ensure that nothing is overlooked.

The analogy for a retailer or wholesaler is the gross profit analysis-by-product line. This kind of analysis requires a perpetual inventory system, which virtually means a computerized inventory system, because manually keeping individual stocking units, though not impossible, is a big job. Managing inventory at this level of detail seems like a formidable task to most entrepreneurs. Estimating gross profit based on last year's performance is usually the choice for small retailers or wholesalers. What they save is the cost of an inventory system, either clerical or computer costs. What they lose is the ability to analyze profitability by product line, knowledge of actual gross profit as the year progresses, and the tight inventory control which comes from knowing the stocking levels item by item every month during the year.

Accounts Receivable

Except for retailers, accounts receivable are a crucial aspect of management. Even if the owner has stringent requirements for extending credit, growth will expand receivables. If the growth is rapid enough, the owner will have to borrow to support them. If growth were the only problem, receivables management would be simple, but that isn't the case. As with every aspect of small-company management, there are many potential problems.

There may be the one large bad account, or perhaps a group of bad accounts, which can cause a write-off large enough to threaten a small company's existence. Not only will the write-off be devastating for cash flow, but the income statement may show a loss. Explain that to the bank just when you need a loan to cover the shortfall. Banks are eager to lend to support profitable expansion, but they don't like to make loans to offset the owner's management mistakes.

But an owner doesn't have to lose money to get into trouble with receivables. Too many chronic slow-pay accounts can back up a cash flow to the point of disaster. No matter how badly the cash is needed, these accounts can pay only so quickly, because they have financial management problems of their own. It's usually the squeaky wheel they pay, and you'll get yours if they need your goods or services any time soon, but it will take time and effort. Slow receivables mean slow cash, higher interest paid to the bank, and greater risk due to higher borrowing per sales dollars produced.

The difficulty with accounts receivable problems is that they sneak up on you. One day the status is okay. The busy owner goes on to other things. Next month the change seems slight. Business is up, activity is frantic. Next month receivables are up, but so is business. Next month, next month . . . then the controller comes to say cash is getting short. Perhaps there is trouble making payroll. Another scrutiny of receivables shows that things have gotten out of hand. Collections are averaging fifty-five days instead of forty-two. Some accounts have large past due balances. With the bank line at the limit and with creditors slowing down on shipments because payables are stretched way out, there is trouble to work out of, step by painful step.

Controlling Receivables

To control receivables an owner needs, first of all, a sensible credit policy which limits exposure yet allows enough flexibility to promote sales growth. The policy should begin with a credit check of new accounts to screen out bad credit risks at the beginning. There should be a maximum credit limit for each account, based on their credit rating and the company's experience in dealing with them. This provides a chance to control the problem before it gets started.

The second component of receivables control is the collection program. There must be monthly accounts receivable aging if there is to be any control over accounts receivable. Someone must be responsible for analyzing the monthly aging to designate the slow-pay accounts, which must be prodded by telephone calls, letters, etc., to reduce past due balances. Sometimes the owner has to get into the collection act when the account is big enough. Usually receivables problems can be isolated to a handful of slow accounts, which, if collected, could add substantial cash to the company's account. Keeping receivables clean is an ongoing program. If the effort eases off, receivables collection will begin to slow. Ultimately there will be a cash problem.

To keep track, the owner needs a summary report to monitor the aging trends. This can be boring, because the aging may look okay for months. But keeping an eye on the aging will prove worthwhile if the problem can be avoided before it begins. Monitoring receivables aging may require nothing more complicated than the format shown in Table 9-2.

The owner can compare this monthly profile to a target based on the ideal receivables picture, focusing greater attention on collections with the first sign of slippage. For the company represented in Table 9-2, a credit problem has developed, with nearly eighteen per-

TABLE 9-2 ACCOUNTS RECEIVABLE AGING
MARCH 31, 1991

Item	Amount	Percent
Current	$117,522	36.7
31 to 60	78,745	24.6
61 to 90	67,706	21.0
91 to 120	17,632	5.5
120+	38,988	12.2
TOTAL	$320,593	100.0
Problem Accounts		
ABC	$ 15,000	
DEF	7,500	
GHI	6,800	
ETC.	25,000	
OTHERS	12,850	

cent of receivables over ninety days, which represents $55,000 in uncollected cash. Adding the amount over sixty days moves the total of slow accounts to over $120,000, or thirty-eight percent of the total accounts outstanding. That's equivalent to a good chunk of a line of credit.

Accounts Payable

Suppliers offer a temptation when money is tight: Stretch the rubber band almost, but not quite, to the breaking point. Then keep it there, paying off the squeaky wheels, until cash loosens up to the point where the owner can pay down some of the past due. Most business owners have gone through this exercise more than once, to grow, if not to survive.

But the trade credit sword cuts both ways. Financing expansion or helping out during a temporary cash shortage are both valid reasons for stretching the trade, but how does the owner know, for sure, that the cash shortage is due to these causes? Perhaps cash is short because of basic losses from operations, which means that stretching the trade is only digging the hole deeper. Without a decisive correction in operations, stretching trade credit is simply collecting blood in a bucket from a dying body. Besides, who knows exactly when the rubber band will break? Being put on COD by major suppliers is the first step to the ultimate disaster.

Why Is Cash Tight?

When cash gets very tight, you'd better know the reason why. Is it the season? Is it growth? Is it a temporary problem, say, because of a large past due receivable? Or does the company have serious operating problems which need to be corrected immediately before the damage is irreparable? Past due accounts payable can be an indication of any of these possibilities. The owner who doesn't know exactly what the profit picture is, who is confused about the company's financial position, who hasn't been monitoring cash flow, who has lost track of receivables collection, who doesn't know whether sales are on target or not because targets were never set, won't be able to answer the question, "Why is cash tight?"

An owner who can't answer that question—and I mean a truthful answer, not a self-delusion—can't make the right decision about what to do. There is a paradox here because many entrepreneurs, at this very moment, are desperately stretching trade, not paying their IRS payroll withholding taxes, putting off any payment they can, to keep the doors open. But why is cash so tight? More often than not there has been woefully inadequate financial control, perhaps no financial statements for months, no knowledge of job costs, no understanding of the receivables aging, just a bulldog effort to keep the doors open and push the day-to-day operations along. But where is a company headed, if day after day the operations add up to a loss?

Know why cash is tight. Take remedial action to fix the problem. Have the financial self-discipline to keep the accounts payable aging within boundaries that are comfortably short of the trade credit breaking point. The monitoring system can be identical to the accounts receivable format shown in Table 9-2. With insight into the financial condition of the company and the maturity to maintain a prudent financial position, the smart business owner can stay out of trouble.

Inventory

The most difficult asset for the business owner to manage is inventory. Inventory management requires precise data about every stocking item in terms of quantity and dollar amounts on hand, items on order, open orders outstanding, and recent activity. The sheer effort to record this information boggles the mind. The thought of doing it manually is appalling; horror stories abound about computerizing inventory, with the enormous effort and the countless errors—it can take six months before the printouts can be used with confidence!

But inventory is something that grows and grows. A company which does $500,000 in sales, with an annual turnover of 3.5×, maintains year-end inventory of about $140,000. A couple of years later, if they've doubled sales, inventory is at $280,000. Not so bad. A few years later, at $2 million, they have $560,000 in inventory. Now that's getting to be a pretty big investment. But at $3 million they're carrying an inventory of nearly $680,000. Big bucks. At what point during this company's growth is it worthwhile for the owner to get inventory under tight control?

Going from half a million to $3 million in sales happens all the time. For companies that handle substantial inventories, the investment will become massive with growth. What the owner was able to monitor in his or her head at $500,000 won't be accessible at $3 million. Without inventory reports, dollars are certain to be tied up in dead merchandise that has slipped through the cracks for a number of reasons. There may be overstocking in some slow items, understocking in some fast-moving items. The lowering of interest from reductions in inventory levels, the benefits from improved service to customers, the reduction in risk because of reduced heavy borrowing to support excess inventory . . . the benefits of inventory control make the cost worthwhile.

The controller's book can have summaries of inventory status: the largest dead items, and the total dollars in dead items; an ABC summary of the fastest, middle, and slowest-moving items; the overall turnover compared to the owner's goals. Once the owner has good inventory reports, improvement can come from the determination to pay attention to the inventory. The key is to get the reports.

Financial Position

At least once a year the owner should reflect on the key ratios concerning profitability, liquidity, financial position, and the owner's own net worth. To have an intelligent review, the owner will need to set targets for the gross profit, operating expenses, net income, current ratio, etc. The owner should have an intelligent plan for investments and net worth outside the company. The review should be focused on both the performance for the year at hand versus the targets and the trends over the last three years. The ratio guidelines are like the plots of a course. If the owner can navigate within these guidelines over the years, the company will arrive safely at its destination with a good value intact.

INTERNAL CONTROL

It is important not to confuse management control and internal control. I'm not playing a "buzz word" game with this statement. The difference between the two can be deadly serious for the entrepreneur. Management control is what we've just defined, and tight management control is crucial to financial health. But there is always the danger of theft or embezzlement. The management control system we've discussed won't guard against these problems, though the symptoms of theft or embezzlement might show up in the financial analysis.

Employee misconduct of any magnitude doesn't happen too often. I've run across only a few cases in the last fifteen years. But the frequency isn't the issue . . . it's the consequence when it does happen. The loss of a substantial sum may be something a small company will never recover from. Several years ago, I met with an owner who was desperately short of cash. He had respectable marketing prospects, but his cash shortage was causing problems with suppliers. He was pinched severely across the board and having a tough time making profits as a consequence. Some two years before, he told me in a sad voice, his accounting manager had embezzled $100,000 from the company. The owner had never been able to make up the difference. Imagine your business slowly running short of cash. Imagine learning you had lost $100,000 which could never be replaced. It might not be a stranger who is the threat, either. I know of one case where a father, acting as corporate accountant, embezzled over $100,000 from his son's company. Suspicious as to why cash was so tight, the controller and I went through the cancelled checks together.

Internal controls consist of a series of sensible checks and balances to guard against employee misconduct. Small companies are particularly vulnerable to this kind of problem because so many employees wear several hats. This is especially true of the bookkeeper, who frequently opens the mail, makes out deposits, reconciles the bank statements, posts to the accounts receivable, posts to the accounts payable, writes checks . . . see the possibilities? And with so many small companies not keeping good inventory records because of the extensive effort required, who's to know how much is walking out the door, especially if we have some part-time help during the peak season? Frequently the same person who writes purchase orders is the person who checks the merchandise into the warehouse.

Quick Steps to Internal Control

There are a couple of quick steps to internal control. One, as many entrepreneurs know, is for the owner to open the mail. As the company grows, this may not be feasible, but then a person can be selected for the task other than anyone who handles the funds. A second check is the reconciliation of the bank statement. Perhaps someone other than the bookkeeper, possibly the owner's wife or husband, the outside accountant, or the owner's administrative assistant, can do the reconciliation. At a minimum the owner can be the first one to open the bank statement, which may create a psychological barrier to misconduct. If the owner opens the mail, the bookkeeper reconciles the bank statement, and the bookkeeping clerk handles the bank deposits, we have separated the handling of the funds in a way which can make embezzlement more difficult, especially if the owner signs the checks or cosigns the checks. In a "large" small company, the additional accounting personnel facilitate the separation of receipt activities, disbursement activities, and bank statement reconciliation, which lies at the heart of good internal control.

Protecting inventory from theft has two components. One, of course, is physical security, which for a small company can be difficult because of the shortage of space and the need for many people to have access to the stocks—people wearing more than one hat again. I remember a first visit to a new client, during which I strolled into the warehouse and browsed at will among the shelves, some of which were stocked with small, relatively high-dollar items. No one knew I was there. I think there was one employee in a distant section who was paying no attention to me. The bay door of the warehouse was open to the parking lot, adjacent to a well-traveled street. Anyone could have walked in!

The other aspect of inventory security is a good management system, with accurate data to evaluate. When you don't know what you have on hand, how do you know why you're short? If you do know how much you have on hand, is a shortage due to computer error or . . .? Control needs to be extended to the receipt of shipments, where the packing slip, purchase order, and shipment contents should be reconciled. Hopefully there is enough personnel to have a check against one person writing purchase orders and also receiving the merchandise.

Good internal control depends on intelligent safeguards combined with alertness on the part of the owner and the key managers. In addition, the company's outside CPA can be used to advantage. As part of the preparation of the annual statement, the owner should ask the CPA to review the company's internal controls, with a letter suggesting where these controls can be improved. The small additional cost involved is a reasonable insurance premium to pay for better protection against theft or embezzlement.

MANAGEMENT CONTROL AND COMPUTERS

The Starting Point

Pursuit of management control always leads to computers. The bookkeeping, accounting, and the business data base that generate most management information rely on an effective computer system operated by personnel who know how to use it. This is true of simple businesses as well as complex ones.

The task is much more complex than simply buying a computer. Countless times I have seen business owners "wrapped around the axle" of a fouled-up computer system, sometimes to the point of jeopardizing the survival of their business.

Harold's company was growing fast. Harold wanted timely management reports that gave him critical information about performance. As his business grew, the computer system became inadequate for the volume.

"Pick your new system carefully," I said. "You could lose the management information you've relied on so much in the past."

"No big deal," Harold said. "We'll adjust."

Without further thought, Harold purchased the immediate upgrade of hardware and software from the company that sold him his first system. He relied on the name of the hardware manufacturer. The result was disaster. Not only did he lose management control through inadequate reporting, but his growth overloaded the upgrade so quickly that his accounting system broke down.

The failure was due to insufficient understanding of the new system and due to inadequacy of the new system itself. Harold went without any financial information for six months while his accounting personnel had to reconstruct data going back several months. The breakdown occurred during a major growth spurt, during which Harold had to fly blind.

Select Software Carefully

Software is the key to a successful computer operation. Select software first, *carefully*. Then acquire the hardware that is best for your needs. Don't pass off the evaluation and decisions about your new computer system to other people. Stay involved. Make sure you understand what you're getting. Study all of the management reports you'll receive from the system. Do they include the information *you* need in the form *you* can understand?

Don't let a salesperson or a systems person tell you what you should have or how the information should look. They don't have to run the business (they don't know how to run a business). You do. Don't let the salesperson pass you off by saying, "Oh sure, it'll do that." Insist on proof that the system will do what you want. If it falls short after you buy, it's too late.

Compare the pros and cons of several systems. Make sure the software has been written for your industry. It's a good idea to visit a company similar to yours that is using the system you're evaluating. Beware of brand-new systems. Buy one, and you may be the guinea pig for all the debugging the vendor has yet to do.

Check out the vendor. Some software companies are tiny and financially unstable. They have trouble responding to the needs of customers after installation. I know one entrepreneur whose software vendor went bankrupt and skipped town while he was halfway through installing the system. The owner had to operate with half a system until he could afford to buy a replacement.

System Conversions

"An ounce of prevention is worth a pound of cure" is nowhere truer than in computer conversions. As your business grows, you will inevitably face conversion to a new system. Don't take a swan dive from old to new. Plan.

The accounting manager of JKT Corporation started loading data into a powerful new system the day after it was installed. A dynamo, the manager worked steadily for weeks. When the production planning and inventory system went on line, the managers found serious errors in the reports. The system was unusable.

Further analysis disclosed that the accounting manager had not properly planned the coding system for data entry. After coding was properly set up, all of the data input had to be redone. The system went on line months late.

SUMMARY

I've talked to many entrepreneurs about management control and the importance of financial management, including good business planning. Many have shrugged their shoulders and said that it wasn't necessary. I don't know what happened to their businesses, obviously. They left me with a sense that it seemed like too much effort and expense. Certainly, paying a consultant to design management controls and maintaining an accounting staff to operate the system is an expense, one which doesn't produce a dollar in sales volume.

I have also talked to many owners who were in serious financial trouble, some of whom survived and some of whom did not. A basic cause of the trouble, which was almost always present in these companies, was the lack of management control, the absence of good information about where the company stood.

"If only I'd met you two years ago!"

Perhaps if they had met me two years ago, they would have shrugged and said it wasn't necessary. I'm not sure that the expense is really why so many entrepreneurs resist management controls. After all, an efficient accounting department is necessary anyway. Reasonable fees paid to a consultant are tiny compared with total sales. I suspect that many business owners avoid management controls or financial management methods because they don't want to be controlled themselves. The management control is of them; the financial management is of them. The information they get may coerce them into changing their decisions—frequently it does! These owners may not get to do what they feel like doing. For others perhaps it's the fear of the unknown, the avoidance of something that seems strange and different.

I think too, that systematic financial management seems to clash with the entrepreneurs success image—the Silicon Valley boys who went from their garage to $100 million in three years and are now flying around the world in their Lear jets wearing blue jeans and sweaters.

Maybe so. Maybe many of them had good management controls from the onset. All I know is the look of tragedy in the eyes of many business owners as they realized their life work, their livelihood, and their economic net worth had turned to so much dust in the wind. Having been on the scene, I can tell you that these owners would be in business today if they had committed themselves to the simple management controls and the financial management methods we have been discussing.

10

Make the
Banking System
Work
for You

THE HEART AND SOUL OF SMALL-BUSINESS FINANCING

When cash runs short, suppliers will give a little time. Along with
suppliers, there is the bank. Yes, there are other sources of funds,
such as equipment leases, commercial financing, floor planning, but
the suppliers and the bank are the heart and soul of small-business
financing.

We have discussed some aspects of trade credit. Now we stare
the major source of small-business financing in the eye. But what do
we see? There are as many perceptions of what a bank does and what
bankers are like as there are entrepreneurs looking for loans. For
many owners a bank is a bank; they don't realize that banks differ.
Some owners have a very high opinion of their banker. They can talk
about the many times when their bank has helped, just at the right
time. There are those who literally hate their bankers, who can speak
of the negative attitudes and lack of cooperation they have experienced to the detriment of their business. I have seen bankers save

businesses which seemed to have no hope by making loans in the face of extreme adversity. I have seen bankers push companies under by denying credit when there seemed to be some hope the company might survive.

Some entrepreneurs have a flair for dealing with the bank. For others it is a terrible ordeal. No matter what the case, bank financing is crucial to small-business success. You must be the one who gets the key loan which triggers a growth spurt. You must be the one with whom the banker fights side by side to save the company when things go wrong. Developing a strong, creative banking relationship is a tricky, ongoing process which requires a knowledge of how the banking system works and skill in making that system work for you.

KNOW THE DIFFERENCES AMONG BANKS

Attitudes Toward Small Business

In dealing with banks, it is fundamental to realize the enormous differences among them. Some banks are aggressive lenders to business. Others are timid about making business loans, frequently because they are specialists in consumer lending or perhaps because they are more comfortable in real estate financing. Many banks are negative in their policies regarding small businesses. They see the high failure rate of small companies as an unwanted risk, and they do not like the limited collateral that many small businesses offer to secure loans. Some large banks want to minimize small-business loans because of the costs of analyzing the loan request and of the subsequent monitoring required. For the sake of public image, such banks aren't going to advertise these facts, but it will be a consistent reality in their handling of loan requests from small companies.

It is a recognized fact that it takes as much or more of a loan officer's time to process a $100,000 loan as it does to process a $1 million loan. Larger companies are more established, with greater market stability, stronger financial positions, and more collateral for security. To make a loan to a small business, in comparison, more analysis and evaluation are required. This also means that a more experienced, therefore more expensive, loan officer will be needed to handle the small business. This kind of officer can make a lot more money for the bank by dealing with several large companies. Many big banks consider themselves wholesale lenders, which means that they want to specialize in providing large loans to large businesses. If they can book numerous multimillion dollar loans, the processing is more efficient and the volume can be substantial. It takes ten $100,000 loans to make up that one larger loan, and for a big wholesale bank a $1 million loan is chicken feed.

A Small Bank for a Small Business

Other banks see small businesses as a desirable growth market. Frequently these are medium-sized or smaller banks that cannot compete with the big banks for the large loans. Even with the middle-sized banks, the small business can be squeezed out. These banks like to talk of the "middle market," composed of companies with at least $5 million in sales up to $100 million, roughly. Though the guidelines get blurred and bloody in the fight for accounts, generally the great big banks aren't as aggressive in the middle market, while middle-sized banks can compete better there in terms of the size of loans and the kinds of services they can offer.

For small banks the best market is small companies, because their maximum lending limit, by government regulation for all banks, is fifteen percent of bank equity. Thus, the maximum loan a small bank can make might be $100,000, $250,000, or $300,000, and so on, depending on the size of the bank's equity. These small banks simply cannot service the needs of larger companies—even "large" small companies have to deal with somewhat larger banks. As a matter of policy, most banks, including big ones, do not like to lend their maximum to any one company. This is to avoid the problem of having one big account go bad, which could make an appreciable dent in the bank's reported earnings for the year. As a consequence, a small bank will be more reluctant to grant credit which is getting close to its maximum loan, unless the bank is very familiar with the company. For this reason, a rapidly growing small company will probably outgrow its small bank.

Attitudes Toward Industries

However, the issue is more complicated than this. Certain banks are more comfortable in some industries than others. Let's take high-tech companies, for example. Some banks thrive on lending to high-tech growth companies. Other banks avoid them like the plague, because they see a greater threat of failure in bold new ventures in comparison with the more ordinary businesses that serve established everyday needs, which the banks have had long experience in financing. Frequently these banks are reluctant to deal with high-tech companies because they can't grasp the technology being developed. Furthermore, there is an inherent skepticism about a technical person's practical business capability. On the other hand, some banks have developed special capabilities in dealing with a particular industry, such as residential construction or automobile dealerships. For an owner in that industry, that's one of the banks to go to first. "One banker's meat is another banker's poison," is an ongoing reality in getting bank loans.

Generally speaking, then, small businesses fare better with small banks. Also, some middle-sized banks have a special interest in small businesses for the sake of long-term growth. After all, some of those little fellows are going to be pretty big five or ten years from now. And, occasionally, a big bank may have a special interest in the small-business market. To be successful in getting a loan, therefore, the entrepreneur needs to find out which banks are aggressive about making loans to small businesses and which banks should be avoided because of their lack of interest in the small-business market. The owner should also be careful to avoid banks, if any, known to be unfamiliar or uncomfortable in dealing with the industry in which he or she is operating, while seeking out any bank with a reputation for dealing with that industry.

How Do You Find Out Which Is Which?

It's usually pretty obvious which are the biggest banks in town; they have branches everywhere and advertise constantly. Also, an owner can ask for an annual report on a bank in which there is some interest. If the bank's assets total in the billions, it's a big one. If the bank's assets total between about $10 million and $100 million, it's small to smallish. Over $100 million to several hundred million, and it's in the middle market. An owner can also ask the loan officer or branch manager how large the bank is; they should be willing to say.

Now that we have an idea of sizes, we need to find out about the bank's specific attitudes and policies toward small-business lending and about industry specialties, if any. This isn't as easy. There are two basics ways of doing it. The first is to inquire of other business owners about banks they might recommend. Their experiences in dealing with particular banks might be a reliable tipoff as to what to expect with the same banks. Sometimes CPAs know how some of their clients have fared with certain banks. Accountants and other professionals who deal with entrepreneurs may know which banks are active lenders to small businesses. Keep in mind that the CPAs and lawyers may not deal with the banks directly, as a business owner has to. Their advice may be well-meaning, but not as good as that of another entrepreneur who had to get the loan.

The second method is for the entrepreneur to find out by going to three or four banks to apply for financing. Particular attention should be paid to the banker's attitudes about the size of the business and about the type of business. Does there seem to be a sincere interest in the owner as a person? Is there an attempt to understand what makes the business tick? Is there a feeling that the bank wants to establish a relationship that will promote the company's growth and profitability to the owner's and the bank's mutual benefit in the years to come? As the request is turned down or accepted, the owner has to make the definitive comparison among them. But if the request is approved at more than one bank, the choice of bank may have serious long-range consequences for the business.

Don't Pick a Bank Because It's on the Corner

In selecting banks to apply to for loans, an entrepreneur should not choose a bank simply because it is on the corner. Doing business with a bank because the bank's location is convenient is one of the biggest mistakes entrepreneurs make. The crucial issue is getting the best banker for the company, in terms of the lending relationship. Small businesses can prosper when their banker is an understanding and intelligent financing partner in the company's long-range growth. Finding this relationship usually takes some searching. Sometimes the search can last for years until the right match is found. Sometimes entrepreneurs never find the right banker for them. Being able to get the right loan at the right time is worth dealing with a banker miles away. Deposits can always be made at the corner bank and transferred to the distant bank, if necessary. This is frequently the case with retailers, who have to make daily deposits. For other types of companies it is not so urgent. The payroll account can be kept at the local branch for the convenience of employees, while operating transactions can be taken care of at the bank which provides the business loans. Whatever the case, the priority should be the ability to borrow sensibly.

DIFFERENCES AMONG BANKERS

Bob Pastore's first loan

Bob Pastore started his business with $10,000 and a lot of determination. He was able to take a low salary at first, because his wife had a good job. Sales started slowly, which enabled him to run the business for several months with his initial investment plus some trade credit and his sales receipts. Before long, sales started to increase, which required more inventory. Bob started to have trouble building his stocks because of a cash shortage. It was time to apply for a line of credit.

As good fortune would have it, a vice president from one of the banks up the street came to call. He was enthusiastic about Bob's business. He was most interested in looking into the possibility of a line of credit to help Bob purchase inventory. Bob thought that $25,000 might be necessary, which didn't seem to faze the banker at all. He asked for some kind of statement on the business, even though it was just getting started, and he asked for Bob's and his wife's personal financial statement, even providing a form for them to use in making one up. Bob mentioned that most of their assets were in their house, which had a market value of $143,000 based on what houses were selling for in the neighborhood. Their mortgage was down to about $75,000. This seemed to make the banker happy.

Bob sent in his financial statements to the bank's main office, where the vice president worked. About a week later, the banker called to say, very cheerfully, that the line of credit was approved, subject to the personal signatures of Bob and his wife. In the same breath the banker went on to say how pleased he was to welcome Bob as a new account and how much he was looking forward to working with him in the future. After Bob and his wife adjusted to the idea of personal signatures, Bob felt very pleased with his new banking relationship, which gave him confidence that he had the financial backing to deal with the sales growth he was experiencing. This wasn't the largest bank in town, but it did have several branches. Bob's impression was that the bank was middle-sized but very aggressive, judging from the way they had gone after his business. That seemed to bode well for the future.

Bob's second loan

The rest of the year turned out to be about what Bob expected. Sales continued to increase, which required additional inventory. By year-end Bob was using the full $25,000 line with the bank, but he was still short of cash. At the outset of the new year Bob did some thinking. Every indication was that sales would continue to grow. He decided to hire someone to handle the books and take care of office work, so he could spend more time on sales and in running the business. He would also need a full-time warehouse clerk to handle the goods.

Armed with his year-end statements, which showed a modest profit, Bob went to the banker, who greeted him very cordially. The banker agreed that Bob had had a good year. Bob explained that he was still running tight on cash. He explained, nervously, that he would probably not be able to make payments against the line of credit for a while. In fact, he was going to need an increase in the line, perhaps to as much as $50,000. The banker seemed unconcerned about the lack of payments on the line. He looked in Bob's file, asking whether he'd had any changes in his personal financial situation; Bob replied that there were none, except maybe the mortgage was paid down a little.

The banker seemed very relaxed. He continued to express pleasure with the year's results. He thought there would be no problem with increasing the line to the full $50,000, but if Bob would give him an updated personal statement, he would let him know in about a week.

True to his word, the banker called about a week after Bob had turned in his personal statement to say that the increase in the line had been approved. However, because the business was still new, they would have to place a second trust on Bob's house, which would not bear interest. The purpose of the second trust was to act as collateral for the loan. The banker assured Bob that it was a common practice in making loans to small businesses. All the banks in town did the same kind of thing. Again, the banker warmly congratulated Bob on his success, expressing pleasure that they were continuing to do business together. Almost as an afterthought, the banker mentioned, just before he hung up, that he would look to Bob to make some payments against the line later on in the year.

Bob immediately called his accountant, who said he believed most small-business owners had to accept a second trust on their houses early in their business history, based on what he'd seen with other clients. At first Bob's wife was reluctant to let the bank take a second trust, but after they'd discussed it for a few days, they agreed that they had to put what they had behind the business, because it was their future. Sales were going so well that it seemed a good investment.

Loan three is no dice

Again the year went just about as Bob expected, except that in the last few months sales were increasing so fast that he and his staff were having trouble keeping up with the business. Cash, as always, was short, but now even more than ever. Bob hadn't been able to make any payments on the line of credit, but the banker had not called about it, so Bob assumed the situation was about the same as last year.

Bob made some very aggressive decisions during his soulsearching before the new year began. He would add two clerical assistants to the office staff, an assistant in the warehouse, and he would need a road sales rep to help him keep up with the exploding number of new accounts. With some apprehension, because he was still new in dealing with banks, Bob realized he would need a very substantial line of credit if he was to reach the targets he was setting for the new year. He would ask for $100,000. Considering the warm treatment he had received over the last two years, he felt his request would be approved, though it did seem like a great deal of money.

The banker was pleased to see the year-end financial statements, again showing the strong sales growth and another modest profit. So far the meeting was like the previous ones. Bob breathed deeply, and then asked for the line increase to $100,000. The banker's expression didn't change much, but Bob noticed that he shifted in his chair at the mention of the new line amount. He asked about Bob's personal finances, which Bob, again, said had not changed much from the last statement. The banker put on his reading glasses to leaf through Bob's file. He glanced at the year-end statements. He noted that Bob had not made any payments against the line. Bob acknowledged that fact, but he said that the growth had consumed all his cash, and since the bank had not contacted him about it, he had assumed the situation was okay, the way it had been the previous year.

The banker didn't respond to that directly. Bob thought he detected a cooler attitude, but nervous as he was, he hoped it was his imagination. After all, nothing was being said that hadn't been said in previous years, the company was doing well, and Bob had paid all his interest right on the date due. The banker asked for an update on the personal statement and again said he would get back to Bob in about a week.

This year, however, there was no word from the banker after a week had passed. After ten days, Bob called. The banker said that a decision would be forthcoming in a few days but that the larger credit required an additional officer to review the situation, and, as Bob's company was new to him, it had taken a little longer than usual.

After several days had passed, Bob grew apprehensive. Then he was stunned to receive a letter from the banker declining the line increase due to the insufficient collateral available to secure a loan of that size. Furthermore, the banker pointed out that Bob had not curtailed the principal of the loan for two years, and he was asking for an orderly clean-up of the line during the coming year.

Up the well-known creek without a paddle

Bob was near panic. He had made commitments. His year was predicated on reaching the sales targets, which he had no chance of reaching without the line increase. How could he make payments on the line? Every nickel he had was tied up in the sales growth. How could the bank do this to him, after such a warm, supportive relationship for the last two years?

He called the banker—why the sudden change after two problem-free years? The banker tried to be friendly, but Bob could tell he was nervous. First, he wanted Bob to realize the decision was not his to make. Another man had the authority for loans over $100,000, and he was very exacting in his analyses. The fact was that Bob did not have sufficient collateral to justify a loan of that size.

Bob blurted out that he was being cut off in mid-stream. He had a growing business, commitments had been made for more personnel, what was he to do?

The banker hesitated and then said he hoped Bob wasn't overextending himself because he still had to pay off the $50,000 this year. Without waiting for Bob's answer to that one, the banker went on to reflect that maybe Bob would just have to cut back on operations for a couple of years until he could generate more net worth in the business. Or maybe there was someone who would invest in the business to help it grow.

Bob hung up, furious. He stomped around his office, slamming the door shut, so the office staff couldn't hear him swear like he hadn't for years. But anger didn't help. He calmed down later, to find himself still without the funds needed to make the new year work. He either had to cut back severely, letting legitimate sales growth go and dismantling a part of the organization he was building, or he had somehow to come up with the additional cash. Outside investors were out; he didn't know anybody with extra cash to invest. His only chance was another bank, and because of the way this relationship had developed, he didn't really know how to go about it. Besides, if his own bank felt this way, why would a new bank see it any differently? He knew he had to try, though. Surely there was somebody who would see the merits of his situation. He felt that he was getting the short end of the stick.

What Went Wrong?

Just as banks tend to look alike, so do the men and women working there. Bank officers dress conservatively, with pinstripes and subdued colors. They talk the same language about deposit accounts, so much over the prime interest rates, security for the loans, personal guarantees. They all seem to be assistant vice presidents or vice presidents. They all seem to handle a loan request the same way, asking for financial statements, including personal statements, asking about how long you've been in business and what kind of business you're in, asking for some time to study the request before they decide.

In fact, there are enormous differences among bankers, even with the same title from the same bank. Though Bob was dealing with a vice president from the main office, in fact he was not dealing with an experienced loan officer. Bob was dealing with a business development officer, a banker's term for salesperson. His job was to get out and beat the bushes for new accounts. At no time did he ever commit to a loan on his own, even the small first loan. He took a week to review the situation, which really meant that he referred the credit to another officer who helped him make the decision. As is the case with many bankers, Bob's account officer did not know how to read and interpret financial statements very well. After he had made contact with Bob to interest him in dealing with the bank, someone else decided on the loans.

Bob's crucial miscalculation was to think he was building a working relationship with the bank that could be counted on to expand as his business grew. In fact, the initial decisions were not made on the financial status of the business at all, other than the fact that he was making a profit. The initial loans were based on the equity in his house. The bank was not paying much attention to the business, other than to dismiss the corporate assets as insufficient collateral for the loans. Since it was a relatively small amount, they looked the other way when Bob failed to make principal payments against the loan in the first year.

In the second year, Bob's loan was close to the limit, based on his equity in the house. Bob did not realize that he had reached his borrowing maximum with this bank. The loan officer warned him to make payments against the new line amount, because it was a larger loan, and the bank would insist on having payments against it during the year. However, the banker was not sufficiently clear, and this, combined with Bob's inexperience, led to an oversight that lasted for the entire year.

When Bob went in for the third increase, he was playing a totally different ballgame. For the first time an experienced loan officer—a man he had never met and about whom he knew nothing—was carefully analyzing the financial status of the business. This man did not know Bob, and his entire decision was based on the numbers, not what the business development officer had to say about the company. Loan officers are strongly inclined to dismiss anything business development officers might say about an account, due to their lack of expertise in making business loans—as hard to believe as that sounds.

A Fundamental Reality in Dealing with Banks

Many bankers have limited authority in making loans, no matter what their title, age, or appearance might suggest. Many of these officers are the primary point of contact for the small-business owner. Furthermore, these officers have a limited ability to read and interpret financial statements. This might be difficult for someone outside the banking system to understand, but many bank officers who deal with businesses every day fall into this category. Whatever they might advise, suggest, or indicate in advance about the entrepreneur's finances or the likelihood of getting a loan from the bank must be heavily discounted. Frequently these types of officers are branch managers or branch officers. Their primary duties are the administration of the branch and the development of new business in their designated area. Loan decisions are frequently made in conjunction with a senior loan officer at the main office, or an area loan officer who handles a number of branch loans.

This means that the development of a good personal relationship with the branch manager, which is not harmful by any means, is, nevertheless, a waste of time as far as credit decisions go, because the decision is in the hands of a stranger once removed from the situation. Though the branch manager or business development officer, in Bob's case, can have an influence, the experienced loan officer is likely to discount much of what they say, as I mentioned. The loan officer will be most influenced by his or her personal judgments about the financial statements and the financial trends of the business.

This is a very bad situation for an entrepreneur. It is vital for the loan officer to have a feeling about the owner, a sense of involvement in the business, some insight into what makes that business tick. When the loan officer is isolated from the business, as was the case with Bob, the decision is impersonal and almost totally focused on the numbers in the financial statements. Every entrepreneur knows that the financial statements don't tell the full story about the business. This means that in situations like Bob's, the decision will be made with great emphasis on the statements and limited awareness, if any, of the special factors that are building to make this business a success. In a well-presented loan request, the marketing analysis, marketing strategy, and sales plan should account for at least fifty percent of the loan officer's decision. In the basic instruction manuals for making bank loans, the character and the competence of management are stressed as key factors to evaluate in making a good decision. How can that be done, if the loan officer has never met the owner?

In getting a loan, the entrepreneur must be alert to the differences among bankers, as well as banks. The owner must recognize when he or she is dealing with the business development officer, essentially a salesperson without lending authority or lending expertise. The owner must recognize when he or she is dealing with a branch officer, whose primary job is administration plus some business development. Even when dealing with a loan officer who has authority, it is important to understand what that level of authority is. A loan officer who can lend up to $50,000 would have to confer with another officer to make Bob's third-year loan request, which would still put Bob up against someone he didn't know, although he would have been represented by a loan officer in this case rather than a salesperson. That is one step better, because the relationship he would have built with the loan officer would be working for him in a joint decision with another officer.

A Strategy for Getting a Loan

The owner's first step is to select three or four banks to apply to for the loan, emphasizing those banks which are most likely to be interested in the business. The second step is to probe for a loan officer who has the authority to make the decision about the loan. The goal is to deal directly with the officer who will make the decision, to develop the personal give-and-take necessary for any long-term business relationship. This is why small banks can be so satisfactory for small business, because the bank president is usually the chief loan officer. Though the president may have to go to a loan committee made up of Board of Directors members, he or she usually has strong influence on the final decision. If the owner detects that this is not the case, then he or she is dealing with a weak president, which should be avoided if possible.

Banks differ significantly in how credit decisions are made. Larger banks tend to delegate more authority to lending officers throughout their system, while middle-sized banks tend to centralize authority in a few higher-up people in the main office. Small banks tend to focus all lending activities in the president, who usually has to take loans to a committee of the Board of Directors. Setting up a desirable bank relationship depends on developing a personal relationship with those who make the loan decisions so vital to the company's future. The first priority is to deal directly with the decision maker; if that is not possible, it is important to deal with a bona fide loan officer who can represent the case effectively to the other officer or officers who will be involved in the final decision. It is important to avoid dealing with a salesperson or branch officer as the point of contact; usually, neither has the experience or training to play a strong role in the credit decision.

Getting a loan is vital, but as Bob found out, this is only part of the story. A single loan is only one of a series of loans. When the critical time came for Bob, disaster struck, because the bank had no intention of participating with Bob beyond what his personal assets could sustain. If Bob had realized this, he could have been building a relationship with another bank which might have been more willing to work out a loan with him, based on that relationship and the growing sense of confidence in Bob as a businessman. As it was, Bob's bank had evaluated neither him nor his business in any depth, until the loan request became large enough to require the effort from them.

Enter the small business owner's banker

At a neighborhood potluck dinner, Bob happened to talk to a neighbor up the street who also ran her own business. The neighbor was quick to understand the problem. She offered to introduce Bob to her own bank, which was a small one, located on the side of town where the neighbor had operated her business for several years. She could deal directly with the bank president, who was very knowledgeable and active in financing small businesses. The neighbor hoped Bob would be able to work something out there—at least he would get some good advice.

By Wednesday, armed with his neighbor's introduction, Bob was able to get an appointment with Bif Edwards, President of Southlawn Bank. Bob pulled off Route 232 into an area of modern industrial parks, dotted with cranes where some more office buildings were going up. The bank occupied the ground floor of an office building on one of the main roads. Bob entered the lobby dressed in his best suit and carrying a folder with his financial statements. The receptionist directed him to a secretary at the rear of the lobby, where there were two large, glass-enclosed offices. The secretary cordially invited him to sit in a comfortable chair for a short wait, asking if he'd like some coffee. Bob glanced into the offices, trying to figure out which was the president. He picked the one on the left, who looked a little older, perhaps a few years older than Bob.

Suddenly the officer on the left hung up the phone and came striding out of his office toward Bob, arm extended. He shook hands with a hearty grip.

"Bob, I'm Bif Edwards. Come on in my office and tell me what's going on!"

Bob followed Bif into his office, already feeling hopeful. This was a man, he thought, who would talk his own language. Bif motioned for Bob to set his coffee on the edge the desk.

"Did you have any trouble finding your way?"

"No. Your secretary's directions were excellent."

"Good! Tell me a little about your business."

This banker takes a different approach

Bob outlined his company's background, when and how he had gotten started, the product lines he handled, how sales had been growing. As he talked, he noticed that Bif was listening carefully. He could already sense the difference between this banker and the other. Bif was much more interested in what made Bob's business tick. And Bob could tell from Bif's eyes that he understood where Bob was coming from.

"What do you attribute your growth in sales to?"

Bob smiled. He'd been wanting to explain that to someone for a long time. So far, his scheme in starting the business had worked beyond his expectations. As Bob discussed his ideas, the banker seemed to like them.

"What brings you here to us?"

Bob took a deep breath and plunged into the story of his relationship with the larger bank. He had thought over how to present this side of it, and decided to simply tell it as it had happened, including how his request for the $100,000 line of credit had been declined. When he finished, Bif smiled.

"I can understand your consternation. I'm sorry to say this kind of story happens often. Let's see if I can help. Do you have some financial statements for me to look at?"

Bob handed the folder over. He was experienced enough to have gathered together three years of his business statements and a recent personal financial statement. Patient but nervous, he waited as Bif studied the papers. He could tell that this man was reading them carefully, as compared to the other banker, who never seemed to give them more than a quick glance. Bif gave every indication that he knew exactly what he was doing. After he had gone through each corporate statement and the personal statement, he looked across the desk at Bob.

"I like what I see. You've done a good job getting your business under way. How do things look for this year?"

Bob described his plans for expansion, indicating that he had committed himself to hiring the new employees, including the salesman. He went on to say that sales were already increasing, which was creating a terrible cash strain, since he was still operating with the old $50,000 line.

Bif leaned back in his chair to look Bob in the eye.

"I'd like to work something out with you. But we need to take a different approach. The line of credit is the wrong kind of financing for you, because you're a high-growth company. There's no way you can repay your line during the year, and your loan officer should have realized that."

He paused to look out the window, thinking.

"If we set up a term loan, with repayment over a seven-to-ten-year period, this will give you cash to grow with and a repayment schedule which won't strip the cash right back out again."

Bob sat at the edge of his chair with elation. As soon as Bif outlined his plan, it made sense. Why hadn't the other bank officer thought of it? He was impressed with Bif's ability to get to the meat of it so quickly.

Bif started to shuffle the statements into a pile which he put back into the folder.

"I tell you how we'll do it. I'm not in a position to lend you $100,000 for seven years, without something to strengthen your collateral. You're just a little too new, equity in your business is a little too thin, and there's not quite enough equity in your house to cover me. This is what scared your bank off. But you've done a good job, you have a good year coming up, and your company is shaping up nicely. We're going to get you the loan."

"I'd like you to submit your application to me for the $100,000. I'm going to approve the loan, subject to getting a Small Business Administration guarantee. Let's make it a ten-year loan. I work with the SBA quite often, and I'm confident I can get a favorable decision from them."

"What do I need to do?"

"You'll have to put an application together using the SBA forms, which I can give you. It will require making some financial projections, which you can have your accountant help you with, or else we can recommend someone to help you. I'm particularly interested in your business plan, because I want to double check whether or not the $100,000 will be enough. Also, I'd like to see your improve your profitability this year. Some financial planning will be helpful to you, I believe."

A new banker, a new loan, a new future

Bob was willing to do whatever was necessary to get the loan. The thought of doing some planning, with Bif to look it over and advise him, seemed most attractive. Bif warned him that the SBA loan process took some time but that given his present need for cash he would do everything he could to speed it up.

Bob used the consultant the bank recommended to help him with the loan package. The cash-flow plan they put together indicated that more like $125,000 would be needed to support the growth, which Bif readily agreed to. True to his word, Bif worked hard to get the SBA to approve the guarantee as quickly as possible. He was frustrated that it took thirty-five days, causing Bob some anxious moments, but the funds were finally disbursed, and Bob went on to have a fine year. The term loan provided a cash infusion which fueled the company's growth for the following year as well. Subsequently, his improved profitability and strengthening financial position enabled Bob to refinance the term loan in the third year without an SBA guarantee. At present, Bob Pastore is running a diversified business with sales of many millions annually. He can well remember the turning point in his business when he went from a banker who couldn't work with his business to one who could.

HOW TO PREPARE A PRESENTATION FOR FINANCING

The Basis Is a Business Plan

A good presentation for financing is really a well-thought-out business plan, intelligently presented. Why is it necessary to prepare a business plan for getting a loan? Setting aside the benefits of doing the planning in the first place, we know that bankers are cautious about making loans to small businesses because of the limited history to evaluate, the shortage of collateral to secure the loan, and the uncertainty about the future. Bankers are well aware of the high failure rate of new enterprises. Except for situations like Bob's, where the personal collateral was sufficient to secure the initial loans, the loan officer will be cautious about reviewing any application made by a small business. Obtaining a loan can often be extremely difficult, as Bob eventually found out. A good presentation can rarely convince a loan officer to make a questionable loan, but a bad presentation can deter him or her from making a workable loan. In the loan officer's eyes, a small business loan is frequently a borderline decision. In borderline situations, a good presentation can tip the balance because it demonstrates to an experienced loan officer that the entrepreneur grasps the management requirements for running an effective business, not only at the present time but for the foreseeable future.

The Three Benefits of Planning

Just putting together a presentation for presentation's sake isn't the answer either. Bankers see countless presentations, and those which haven't been thought through carefully by the owner are obvious. It's better just to supply financial statements and a cover letter than to submit a superficial presentation. But a good business plan is a powerful tool for getting a loan. Actually, the business owner can accomplish three purposes in developing the plan. The marketing analysis and clear-minded thinking necessary to develop an effective marketing strategy and sound sales plan; the careful development of the profit plan; and the assembly of all the components necessary for a comprehensive cash-flow plan are also fundamentals of the marketing and financial management we discussed at the beginning of this book. In effect, this process is a feasibility study of the owner's goals and objectives for the year. Does the marketing strategy make sense? Is the sales plan attainable? Does the profit plan indicate that the game will be worth the candle? What will our cash requirements be, as best we can estimate them, and is the borrowing need within our financing capability?

A clear statement of these findings will knock the banker's socks off. This isn't a presentation for financing, but a hard-hitting, decision-making plan by which the owner intends to run the business. The loan officer will see this in the whites of the owner's eyes, and it will have an effect. This second purpose of the business plan, if executed effectively, will enlist the banker's enthusiastic support as a member of the financial team during the course of the business year. A business plan format is particularly effective in working with the bank, because it states the key factors in the decision in the loan officer's terms—marketing outlook, profits, cash flow—all within the context of the company's present financial condition and past performance. It is classic commercial lending combined with classic corporate management.

Once the feasibility study has been made—and frequently the business owner will have to adjust the goals and objectives because of what the profit plan has indicated or according to what the cash-flow plan shows—and once the bank has agreed to the financing request, the plan becomes the backbone of management control. Now the owner can have sales plan versus actual, profit plan versus actual, cash-flow plan versus actual, plus the other critical variables he or she wants to monitor in the controller's book. Deviations can lead to remedial action to get the company back on track, along with modifications in the plans. This is also an ideal format with which to go back to the bank later for modifications in financing. Experienced loan officers know that actual never goes according to plan. They want to do business with entrepreneurs who are on top of the changes. If the owner goes back for more money because the requirements were underestimated, but with a modified plan to be presented in advance of the additional needs, there is a likelihood that something can be worked out. If the owner goes back in the midst of the cash crisis needing money yesterday, he or she is saying, "I was caught by surprise, I didn't anticipate what was happening, I didn't have the financial control to arrange my requirements in advance . . . please bail me out!"

The Psychology of a Winning Presentation

The goal of the presentation is to convince the loan officer to say yes to the loan request. It is very helpful in getting this "yes" to understand the loan officer's thought processes in making a credit decision:

- It is critical that the loan officer understands the business—what the company does, and how that works in the marketplace.
- The loan officer must believe that the owner is capable of managing the business effectively. How long has the owner been running this business? What had the owner done previously? How have previous financial obligations been handled? The loan officer must believe that the owner will stand behind any financial commitment that is made.

- The loan officer must be satisfied that there is a sound marketing strategy.
- There must be a realistic sales plan and a demonstration on paper that the owner knows how to make that plan work.
- The financial statements need to show a satisfactory financial position and trends heading in the right direction.
- The loan officer will carefully review the key assumptions on which the owner has based the profit plan and cash-flow plan. The intelligence with which the owner has constructed the marketing and sales portions of the planning will have created the basis for the financial plans, along with some key financial assumptions, such as receivables collection and inventory schedules.

The financing request will be evaluated within the context of all the steps just listed. The loan officer will decide whether or not the request is reasonable, given the sequence of these considerations—marketing, sales, financial position, financial plans—and the loan officer will evaluate whether or not the type of loan being requested is best for the company, given current circumstances, growth objectives, and the immediate marketing outlook. A competent, experienced commercial loan officer can make this kind of evaluation better than anyone else. It is the guts of his or her profession. That is why developing a strong, long-term relationship with a good loan officer is so important; a skilled banker can make a significant contribution to a growing company by acting as a financial advisor, providing counsel as to the types and amounts of financing needed, and helping to monitor and evaluate financial trends.

The purpose of the presentation is to lead to the final yes by creating a series of yes responses from the loan officer at critical junctures of the business plan. ONE: "Yes, I understand how your business works." TWO: "Yes, you have a good marketing strategy." THREE: "Yes, I believe you can meet your sales plan." FOUR: "Yes, I think your financial position is okay." FIVE: "Yes, I think your profit plan is feasible." SIX: "Yes, I think your cash-flow plan is a reasonable estimate of your cash requirements." SEVEN: "Yes, I will make the loan." By securing a yes response from the loan officer in each intermediate step, your chances of getting a yes at the close are very great, unless you are requesting some outrageous amount of money.

The conference provides an opportunity to engage the loan officer in the financial management program of the business. During the discussion of the loan request, the owner should invite the loan officer's comments on the plans. This can lead to some intelligent consultation, assuming the owner is dealing with an experienced and knowledgeable officer. It can have the healthy effect of drawing the loan officer into the team which is being assembled for success. If the loan officer feels personally involved in the development of the business, the owner has an important ally at the bank.

A PRESENTATION OUTLINE

Company Background

This section describes the business for the banker. It could begin something like this: "Antiseptic Surgical Supply, Inc., was incorporated in 1981 for the purpose of selling surgical equipment and supplies to doctors, hospitals, and clinics throughout the Cleveland metropolitan area. The company is solely owned by its founder, John Millbanks. Sales are generated primarily by a direct sales force of six people on a commission basis. Sales for 1990 were $3.1 million, with profits before tax of $123,000. Brochures showing the most important product lines are attached as Appendix A. A list of major accounts is shown in Appendix B."

The background section can go on to give some details about the company's location and its facilities—square feet of warehouse and of office space, number of employees, etc. The purpose of this section is to give the loan officer a clear idea of exactly how the business operates, plus a few facts about the size and scope of operations. The section may be longer if the company's business is harder to understand; for example, a state-of-the-art electronics manufacturer or a microbiological research laboratory. For these types of companies, it is extremely important to translate the technology into straightforward, layperson's terms, so the loan officer can grasp the technology and how it "works" as a business activity. A cardinal sin of many high-tech companies is to present their material to bankers in the jargon of their discipline, which can create confusion. A confused loan officer is not what you want. On the other hand, the owner can score points with the bank as a technical person who can talk about the business in "English."

Background of Key Personnel

This section is especially important when dealing with new banks. It is a brief synopsis of the owner's resume, emphasizing experiences relevant to managing the enterprise effectively. If there are other managers who hold critical positions, it is helpful to include them in this section, to give the loan officer insight into the depth of management.

Marketing Concept

Having oriented the loan officer to the type of business, the owner can now define those special factors which make the company effective in the marketplace. The section could begin something like this: "Antiseptic has established itself as the leading independent distributor of surgical products in the Cleveland area. The company emphasizes a professional, well-informed approach to selling equipment, followed up with prompt, personalized service. Supply inventories are the most complete in the area. Prices are competitive, but we are not a discount dealer. Our emphasis on value-added service has developed a loyal clientele, because the doctors prefer dealing with an independent, professional-minded distributor, as opposed to the national chains, which tend to be less personal and which tend to push their "house" products. A full-line equipment repair and maintenance service is also provided."

The purpose of this section is to answer the loan officer's questions about how the company has achieved sales growth in recent years and how the owner expects to continue growth in the future. The section should cover all the elements crucial to the development of the company's marketing position, now and for the immediate future. It should present the marketing strategy by which the owner intends to move beyond the present position to achieve the growth objectives, with emphasis on how each of the marketing and sales tools (direct sales force, advertising, telemarketing, direct mail, etc.) will be used.

Market Analysis

This section is a presentation of the best data the owner has on the make-up of the markets. Who are the present customers and what is the sales volume with them? Who are the potential customers and what sales volume might be done with them? How big is the total market currently? What kinds of growth trends are expected in the market for the next year and over the next few years? Who are the competitors and what are their strengths and weaknesses in comparison to the company's strengths and weaknesses? The factors outlined in this section are the evidence on which the owner has built the marketing strategy. Therefore, the consistency between what is presented in the marketing analysis and the concepts of the marketing program will convince the loan officer that the owner knows what he or she is doing. Of course, it's also a good way for the owner to test his or her own decision making before going to the bank.

Sales Plan

The logical outcome of the previous sections is the projection of monthly sales for the planning year. In this section the owner should specify how the actual selling program will work. Strategies are crucial, but how does the owner intend to succeed at the point of purchase? The reasonableness of the sales goals can be judged by comparing expectations to past performance in light of current market conditions. An entrepreneur can project more growth than has been experienced in recent years if it can be shown that changes in marketing strategy are likely to produce a greater rate of increase. Whether this happens or not will be decided in the future, but some marketing plans calling for faster growth are more convincing than others. I keep repeating that the chief beneficiary of this hard-nosed planning is the business owner, who gets to convince the loan officer in the process. Preparing a sound business plan is the biggest bargain in management.

Financial Background

Before getting into the financial plans, it is necessary to orient the loan officer to where the company stands financially. Bankers are heavily influenced by the past, so this necessity should be dispensed with at the outset of the financial portion of the presentation. In fact, the loan officer will test the validity of the financial planning and the reasonableness of the loan request by analyzing the current financial ratios and the trends of the last three years. A brief summary of the recent performance and reference to the financial statements attached to the business plan are sufficient. In addition to the company statements for the last three years, the owner must submit a recent personal financial statement. If receivables are a major asset to be financed, a recent accounts receivable aging analysis should be attached. The owner can call attention to the highlights of the financial statements, but it is the banker's job to do the financial analysis.

Profit Plan

This is the first installment of the financial plan. It is the demonstration that the business plan is going to be sufficiently profitable to justify the commitments. The profit plan can be attached as an exhibit. The purpose of the text in this section is to call attention to the crucial assumptions underlying the profit plan:

- Percent increase of sales over last year
- The ratio of gross profit to sales and why
- Level of marketing and selling expenses
- Level of general and administrative expenses, and how it compares to previous years
- Resulting net income before tax, and how that, as a percentage of sales, compares to previous years
- Comparisons of expense percentages to industrial averages, if appropriate.

Cash-Flow Plan

This is the payoff of the loan application. The cash flow is a result of all of the other sections of the business plan. The cash-flow plan can be attached as an exhibit, with the text again outlining the key assumptions underlying the plan. For larger companies there may be subsidiary schedules to the cash flow, showing how receivables are collected; inventory purchasing schedules; and, in the case of contracting companies, perhaps the work and invoicing schedules for major contracts.

With the sales plan as a starting point, it is important to specify the key assumptions for the loan officer. These are the timing of collections on accounts receivable; the scheduling of any major purchases, such as inventory, equipment, and lease-hold improvements; the timing of payments on trade accounts; other major expenditures; and routine operating expenses, such as rent, payroll, and telephone, which are usually paid on a current basis. It is important to include payments on past due accounts payable over and above the normal payments scheduled in the plan. Additional consideration should be given to collections of past due accounts receivable, in the same manner, if there is a collection program under way that can produce those results.

The text should outline the major findings of the cash-flow analysis. Are there seasonal fluctuations requiring a line of credit? Is there an ongoing need for funds due to the growth rate, which indicates the desirability of a term loan? Perhaps a combination of the two is most appropriate. Principal and interest payments on the loan or loans requested must be included in the cash flow. If the loan amounts plus receipts from operations can cover all disbursements, then the owner has proven on paper that the company has the ability to repay the principal and interest on the loan requested. The cash-flow plan is the best tool available to the owner for assessing cash requirements. At the same time, it is the most powerful vehicle for requesting a bank loan. Therefore, great care should be taken in working out the critical assumptions underlying the analysis.

The Financing Request

This is the final section of the presentation. It is the formal request for financing, which can be stated something like this: "Antiseptic Surgical Supply requests a $125,000 increase in its line of credit for the purpose of financing the growth in accounts receivable and inventory caused by the increased sales volume. Repayment will continue to be on a revolving basis, as outstanding receivables are collected and new receivables are generated. Collateral will be in the form of accounts receivable less than ninety days old and inventory. The owner and his wife will continue to endorse the loans."

WHAT BANKERS MEAN BY CREDIT-WORTHINESS

The first hurdle in obtaining a bank loan is to be accepted as credit-worthy. This initial judgment by the loan officer is made according to the following criteria:

- The business integrity of the applicant
- Evidence that the owner is competent to run the business at the planned levels
- A satisfactory financial condition, based on the banker's ratio analysis of company statements
- A realistic set of goals and objectives for the months ahead. The more complex the business situation, the more necessity for the presentation of a detailed plan.

If these basic requirements are met, the loan officer's decisions become a matter of determining the type of loan the company requires, of assessing the amount needed to achieve the owner's goals, and of establishing the maximum amount the bank can lend to the company at that time. These decisions are a blend of financial analysis weighted heavily by judgment. This process underlines the importance of two factors we have discussed previously: Deal with a seasoned loan officer, who will be better able to counsel you on your borrowing requirements and who will have more clout in the bank's credit decisions; prepare a business plan which will systematically lay out the critical factors to help the loan officer make a positive decision on your request.

TYPES OF BANK LOANS

Getting a loan from the bank is much more than getting the dollars needed. The right amount of dollars in the wrong type of loan can be disastrous. The near bankruptcy of Ed Simpson, described in chapter one, is an example of sufficient dollars in the wrong form, though it originally was manufacturer's financing rather than bank financing. Instead of three-year equipment financing, Ed needed long-term debt. In fact, given the great rate of expansion in his fleet, he needed ten-year money, which required an SBA-guaranteed loan.

John Millbanks, in his previous banking relationship, had experienced a squeeze from the wrong type of loan, just at the wrong time. He had been working with a line of credit which had been provided by his bank for some time, but, in recent years, he had had trouble with the loan committee because he was unable to make appreciable payments on the loans. The terms of the line called for him to pay down the line completely for at least thirty days during the course of the year. This was because a line of credit is to support seasonal increases in receivables and inventory, which will decline in slow periods when the bank must be repaid.

However, John's business had entered an extended growth period which required long-term increases in his levels of receivables and inventory. These increases prevented him from making substantial repayments on the loan. Furthermore, the loan officer was irritated because he was always asking for more money. In essence, John was continually in the "doghouse" with his bank. This situation changed dramatically after he was introduced to another bank that offered him a revolving line of credit. This line was designed to be in place throughout the year, as long as he had accounts receivable less than ninety days old plus fresh inventory, both in sufficient levels to secure the loans. Not only did this relieve the tension caused by the previous payment requirements, but getting increases each year was much easier. Basically John had to show profitable growth, combined with increases in the current assets, which would justify the greater credit limit. He was able to go from a $200,000 seasonal line to a $350,000 revolving line by changing banks. Within two years he had increased his revolving line to $600,000. The new financing facilitated his growth, while the old financing retarded it.

Use Cash-Flow Planning to Identify Loan Needs

The cash flow doesn't give precise answers, but if it is constructed properly it will show the pattern of needs and will indicate the approximate amounts required. Fluctuations in surpluses and deficits during the year indicate the need for a seasonal line of credit, in approximately the amounts shown at the bottom of the plan. The amount of borrowing remaining in the final month of the cash-flow plan indicates the need for a term loan and the approximate amount required. Sometimes, as with Zeta, a combination of seasonal and term debt is required. It's not just the need at the end of the plan, but the peak borrowing during the course of the plan that must be taken into account. Though we're talking small amounts in the Zeta plan, it is a classic example of how the cash flow works. Larger companies simply have more zeroes at the ends of the numbers; also, of course, a lot more work has to go into developing the plan.

Without cash-flow planning, the credit request becomes a matter of the owner trying to get the maximum loan from the bank and the loan officer trying to give the minimum loan to the company.

Obviously, this situation lacks the teamwork needed for a good credit relationship. The careful consideration of what might be the best type of loan and the double checking to ensure that sufficient credit has been arranged both get tossed out the window. Under normal circumstances, many seasoned business owners and loan officers can make adequate estimates of the amount of loans required. Their judgments begin to go awry when the growth rate begins to go up dramatically—say over twenty-five percent annually—though this rate varies significantly from industry to industry. The mistakes made in financing rapid growth can be very damaging. For this reason, cash-flow planning is mandatory in high-growth situations.

The Demand Loan

The simplest form of bank financing is the demand loan. This is a note for thirty, sixty, ninety, 120 days, or whatever, to be paid at maturity and that's that. If the company's relationship with the bank is good, the note can be renewed once or twice before it is paid. Once the loan is paid, a new loan will have to be applied for all over again. Usually this type of loan is for a special purpose, such as paying year-end taxes or year-end bonuses, for which the company is temporarily short of funds. The prospects are excellent for repayment of the loan within a brief period of time, as operations generate the necessary cash.

An owner can get into trouble by chronically renewing the note or by being in and out of the bank asking for temporary loans, either of which indicate a different kind of borrowing need or, worse, that the owner is not a good financial manager. This is not the impression to create at the bank! Periodically renewing notes doesn't harm anybody's image, but the owner builds a reputation for reliability when principal and interest is paid promptly. That kind of reputation is "money in the bank."

The Line of Credit

An owner who is in and out of the bank asking for temporary loans probably needs a line of credit. This is a loan arrangement, not legally binding on the bank, incidentally, by which a company can take loans up to a certain amount, say $100,000, during the course of the year. The purpose of the line is to provide cash when the company is increasing its accounts receivable and/or inventory due to the season. An example would be a retailer building up inventory for the Christmas season. Once the season has passed, the company is operating in a lower sales period, during which time the requirements for inventory are much reduced. At the same time, the cash is coming in from the higher sales of the previous period. This cash is the source of repayment for the line of credit. Lines are to be repaid completely at least once a year, and they must stay out of use for at least thirty days before further loans are made.

This clean-up period establishes that the borrowing arrangement is strictly seasonal and that the company does have the capacity to repay the loans in full. Failure to do so indicates that this is not a line-of-credit situation or, worse, that the company has some kind of financial problem. Companies with good banking relationships can occasionally get by without paying out the line in full, but this problem spells trouble for the banking relationship. Sometimes the solution is to restructure the loan by making it a revolving line with no annual payout requirements, as with Antiseptic Surgical Supply, or to convert the line into a term loan with payment over a period of years. To a knowledgeable loan officer, these types of problems are business as usual if they are handled in an open, give-and-take manner. Nobody is infallible. Early in the relationship, trying to structure a loan for a small business is frequently guesswork. If the business is managed competently, the solution to loan problems can be worked out. However, the identical problem can lead to a nasty experience if the owner is dealing with an unsophisticated loan officer, if the owner is handling the transaction in an adversary manner, or when the relationship with the bank is impersonal.

Annual Review for Lines of Credit

Each year the bank will review the line relationship. This review consists of an analysis of the financial statements for the year just completed plus a consideration of any plans the owner has developed for the forthcoming year. An update of the owner's financial statement is reviewed. If there are no unfavorable developments, the line will be renewed for another year. An increase in the line amount is the same as any other credit request. It must be analyzed and approved or disapproved according to the bank's credit procedures, just as if the owner were asking for a brand-new loan. Of course, a good working relationship with the bank can promote a favorable conclusion. However, the preparation of a business plan, outlining the favorable developments of the last year and presenting the owner's intentions for the new year, can be a powerful way of obtaining an important increase in a line of credit. Bankers do not take a significant change in any kind of lending relationship very lightly.

Just because a line of credit has been approved for a year's period doesn't mean the owner can automatically borrow under the line. If the financial situation deteriorates during the year, the bank may cancel the line privilege at any time. Usually advances under the line are in the form of demand notes for ninety-day periods, after which they must be renewed. Renewal is fine, subject to the annual clean-up requirement, but a deterioration in the company's condition can also cause the bank to refuse renewal on the notes already outstanding. Hence the old saying, "A line of credit is an umbrella you can use only when the sun shines." Putting the notes on a demand basis enables the bank to get out of the loans when it has to, as well as enabling it to alter the interest rate every three months, depending on changes in the prime rate. The owner benefits from this when the prime goes down and pays for it when it goes up.

The Term Loan

A term loan is a specific amount loaned by the bank for a defined period of time, say three years, with payments of principal and interest in equal monthly installments. Sometimes payments are quarterly. In recent years most term loans have had a variable interest rate, adjusted according to changes in the prime rate. Sometimes the interest is fixed. Sometimes the bank gives the company its choice of fixed or variable, depending on the situation. Occasionally the loan may have monthly payments scheduled for a longer period, say ten years, but with the loan payable in full in five years. This creates what is called a balloon payment at the end of the fifth year. This feature is rare for a small business.

Because term loans are a formal commitment of the bank for an extended period, they require an extensive loan agreement, which spells out the terms and conditions. Usually the bank will establish negative covenants, agreements by the business owner not to do certain things, especially regarding the payment of dividends, limits on capital expenditures, limits on officers' salaries, etc. The owner will agree not to undertake any of the forbidden transactions without the bank's approval. Failure to obtain the approval will put the loan in default, subject to payment on demand. In addition, the agreement will specify financial ratios that the company's financial statements must satisfy, such as debt-to-worth ratios, current ratios, minimum levels of receivables and inventory, etc. Failure to meet these specifications also puts the loan in default. Of course, failure to make principal and interest payments also puts the loan in default.

As with any other loan, the bank's position regarding problems with a term loan will depend on the quality of the relationship with the company, assessment of the owner's integrity, and how well the business is doing in general. Capital expenditures and increases in salaries are usually approved if they are reasonable and the company is doing well. The negative covenants are not there to straitjacket the owner but to protect the bank from unfavorable developments. By the same token, failure to meet ratio requirements will not cause the bank to call the loan unless the company is in dire circumstances or the owner is acting unethically. Problems can always be worked out among reasonable people. They never get worked out when someone gets unreasonable.

The Purpose of Term Loans

Term loans are designed to assist companies which need cash for long-term growth. The company may have to make extensive leasehold improvements in existing plan or office facilities. Perhaps the facilities need to be expanded. The company may have to make capital expenditures for new equipment, say a three-color press or a computer system. The improvement of fixed assets or the acquisition of new fixed assets requires substantial funds, and companies that can make these expenditures from their own cash flow are rare. In fact, it is important not to invade cash for extensive capital expenditures, because this will create a cash shortage that can hamper and possibly cripple the expansion in daily operations, which the expenditures were meant to create.

The essence of term lending is to match the repayment of the funds used to support an expansion to the rate at which that expansion will generate cash. Ed Simpson's trucks generated cash flow over a seven-year period, due to the terms of his contracts. His financing had to be for no less than seven years. If a printer adds a three-color press, it will generate revenues as soon as the sales force lands jobs. If we assume the sales force is effective, the press may start to push capacity after about a year. How long will it take to pay the loan? Let's take a look at the hypothetical analysis in Table 10-1

TABLE 10-1 ANALYSIS OF ANNUAL DEBT
COVERAGE HYPOTHETICAL PRESS

Item	Amount
Average Sales per Year	1,000,000
Direct Costs	650,000
Gross Profit	350,000
Selling & Marketing Expenses	120,000
General & Administrative	100,000
Net Income before Principal & Interest	130,000
Add Back Depreciation	100,000
Total Cash Flow for Loan Payment	230,000
Principal & Interest on Loan	165,000

for a $500,000 press, which has been financed over a five-year period at thirteen percent interest and which the CPA is depreciating over a five-year period.

First we take the revenues from printing jobs, then subtract the direct printing costs—labor, materials, depreciation on the new press, and plant overhead. This is still not the net amount to apply against the loan, because the gross profit on sales must be used to cover the machine's share of marketing, sales, and general and administrative expenses if the company is to remain viable from year to year. After deducting these expenses, we have a net income before principal and interest. Since depreciation is actually a write-off of the cost of the machine over an estimated accounting life, we still have the cash we didn't pay for the depreciation. We can add that cash to the net income before principal and interest to get the operating cash flow generated by the machine. You can see that only a portion of the machine's sales will be left each year to service the loan. Therefore, we must schedule the loan payments within the machine's capacity to repay after all company expenses have been covered. This case shows a five-year payment schedule, which would provide a margin of about $65,000, or a ratio of 1.4 cash flow to 1 of debt retirement. This ratio is a little tight. A seven-year loan would be safer.

In real-life cash flow, the situation is more complicated because the analysis doesn't take into consideration that some of the machine's sales will still be tied up in accounts receivable, although some of the expenses will still be accounts payable. At the same time, we haven't evaluated the inventory management situation in terms of how much extra cash is or isn't being tied up in materials. The operating cash-flow analysis is a good shortcut to estimating a machine's or a company's term loan capabilities, but the day-to-day reality of cash flow brings us back, again and again, to good cash-flow planning.

The Working Capital Pitfall

The use of term loans to finance equipment purchases or leasehold improvements is obvious. Rapidly growing small companies and their bankers sometimes stumble into the pitfall of using lines of credit to finance growth in accounts receivable and inventory in the mistaken belief that since these are current assets they should be financed with short-term loans. The reasoning is that receivables and inventory are constantly liquidated and regenerated through daily operations.

Figure 10-1 shows the hazard in that type of reasoning. To operate effectively, a company must carry a certain level of receivables and inventory proportionate to the sales volume. Rarely do companies drop to zero sales even during their slowest period, though I have a retail client whose sales do drop to essentially zero for about three months. Yet his inventories don't go to zero. There are always a couple of hundred thousand which have to be carried over to the next year.

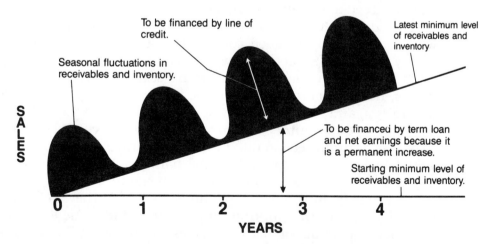

Figure 10-1   The working capital pitfall.

Most businesses which drop to some low point of sales during the slow season still require receivables and inventory of some amount. We could label these amounts as the minimum level of current assets that must be maintained in the business. In effect, these amounts are just as "fixed" in the business as the furniture and equipment, because they must be in place for the business to operate. Somebody is always buying for credit, and there has to be some inventory for people to buy, even if the activity happens to be low during that period.

The pitfall is activated by growth. As you can see in the figure, the expansion in sales pushes up the minimum level of current assets from year to year, on top of which there is the seasonal fluctuation. A line of credit won't be repaid by the minimum of current assets because this amount doesn't shrink. It is a floor below which the requirements can't go. These minimum receivables and inventories must be financed by long-term sources of funds— retained earnings, term loans, or the revolving line of credit.

The Revolving Line of Credit

The revolving line is an in-between or bastard loan which certainly isn't a line of credit in the classic sense but which isn't a term loan either. However, it can be very effective financing for a growing small business with plenty of receivables, though it is often more expensive than the other kinds of loans. A revolving line of credit allows a company to borrow up to a limit, say $350,000, as long as the loans do not exceed a certain percentage (usually seventy-five to eighty-five percent depending on the circumstances) of accounts receivable which are considered good collateral—usually those no more than ninety days old. Sometimes, when companies have a good overall relationship with the bank, including satisfactory financial statements, the loan officer will increase the revolving line by including advances against inventory. These usually do not exceed twenty-five percent of total inventory on hand, because banks consider inventory to be less desirable collateral. It is hard to control; it can be stolen; it would have to be resold before the bank could realize cash; it is difficult to verify the actual amounts on hand.

The clever thing about revolving lines is that they address some critical factors of the working capital pitfall. Since the line is based on a percentage of eligible receivables, it will expand and contract with the seasons, taking care of the fluctuating requirements of the company. At the same time the revolving line need not be cleaned up during the year as long as eligible collateral is available. In this case, the line acts like a term loan. Thus, its advantages over a standard line of credit are significant. Yet it still acts like a line in some ways, because it can be renewed annually, possibly with an increase, subject to the yearly financial review. Actually, a line increase can be requested at any time during the year that circumstances warrant increased financing. This feature makes the "revolver" much more flexible than a term loan, which is committed at a set amount and at a set payment schedule for several years. Changes in term loans require an application for refinancing, more involved and cumbersome than the request for an increase in the revolving line.

How Revolving Lines Work

Revolving lines can be very strictly or loosely administered, depending on the strength of the relationship the company has with the bank, the relative financial strength of the company, and the bank's lending policies. Most programs require the company to establish a "lock box" at the bank. This is an arrangement whereby all the company's customers mail their payments on account to a post office number collected by the bank. Checks are credited to a clearing account after they have been presented for payment through the federal reserve system. At this point the funds are applied to pay down the loan, since they represent liquidations in collateral. As the company cuts new invoices, they become eligible as collateral for additional borrowings under the line. Additional borrowings are deposited in the company's operating account. Thus, we have a "revolving" credit which is constantly being paid down and renewed.

In the strictest of situations, the company's requests for new draws must be accompanied by a cash budget showing the cash requirements for that week. Usually the transactions under the line are done on a weekly basis according to a loan report that summarizes payments on outstanding accounts, new invoices, and reductions for past due receivables, all done to derive a new eligible balance against which the company wishes to borrow. In some situations banks are more informal about policing available collateral. They require reports less frequently and they are lenient when receivables balances drop below the requirements for the loan amount outstanding. These more relaxed situations are usually found when the bank and the customer have had a long and successful relationship.

The bank has the right to audit the company's accounts receivable records whenever it chooses. Of course, the bank can stop the process at any time by refusing to recognize new invoices and continuing to apply payments against the loan amounts outstanding. Banks can also apply cash in the company's account to loan amounts which are in default. Bitter confrontations have occurred when banks have taken such action after determining the company's financial position has become unsatisfactory.

In recent years, banks have set up asset-based lending divisions that specialize in these types of loans. Because of the tight controls and the continuing turnover in the collateral, ABLs can be more aggressive in lending to marginal businesses than the standard commercial loan offices. In addition, the loan procedures require a specialized administration for handling and auditing the accounts. These additional requirements plus the greater risks involved in asset-based lending result in higher interest charges. The greater cost to the company has to be weighed against the availability and flexibility of the borrowing relationship.

HOW TO ASSESS YOUR BORROWING CAPACITY

There are three fundamental criteria for establishing the maximum a company can borrow:

- The debt-to-worth ratio
- The sufficiency of available collateral (including the owner's assets)
- Cash-flow analysis.

The determination of a company's debt capacity is a matter of financial analysis weighted heavily by judgment. A good loan officer will use all three of the basic criteria. Weaker and less experienced officers will depend primarily on the first two factors. Because judgment plays such a heavy role in the decision, there are no precise cutoff points. A company's debt capacity will not be $233,427.25 under all conditions and in the eyes of every loan officer who is asked to make the judgment. Some companies have better relationships with their banks; some banks are more aggressive than others; some companies have better prospects for profitable growth than others.

Debt-to-Worth Ratio

This is the moment when financial balance comes out of the ivory tower to make a difference on the ground floor of a business. The balance sheet is at issue when debt capacity is being determined. In raw terms, the owner bargains with lenders on the ratio of his or her money in the business to other people's money. For bank borrowing, this is stated in terms of the debt-to-worth ratio, which we defined in chapter 5 as total liabilities, including current and long term, divided by total equity. If an owner had, say, total current liabilities of $225,000, and long-term debt of $75,000, then the total liabilities would be $300,000. If equity were $125,000, dividing this amount into total liabilities would give a debt-to-worth ratio of 2.4-to-1. Many banks will state a maximum allowable debt-to-worth ratio—three-to-one, four-to-one, based on their aggressiveness and the type of industry involved. Asset-based lending divisions will accept a much higher debt-to-worth than the commercial loan division.

The way to find out whether a loan increase is within the bank's guidelines for debt-to-worth is to make a simple projection. Antiseptic Surgical Supply asked for an increase of $125,000 in its revolving line. Let's look at the company's assets and liabilities, shown in Table 10-2, to see what the effect will be.

Our quick looks shows that the increase in the revolving line to $600,000 would change the debt-to-worth from 2.66-to-1 to 3.02-to-1, which would fall right on the limit for a conservative bank. In addition, the profitable operation of Surgical for 1991 would increase retained earnings by possibly another $100,000, which would improve the ratio.

Sufficiency of Collateral

If the applicant's debt-to-worth checks out satisfactorily, the loan officer's attention will turn to the collateral available to secure the loan. Accounts receivable are best, inventory is second best, equity in fixed assets is third best. However, equity in improved real estate of good quality would move ahead of inventory as collateral. Most companies don't have much of that, but when they do it will make a difference when arranging loans.

At year-end 1990, Surgical had accounts receivable of $464,000. At eighty-five percent they could have supported borrowing of

TABLE 10-2 CHANGE IN DEBT-TO-WORTH RATIO
ANTISEPTIC SURGICAL SUPPLY CO.

	Before	After
CURRENT ASSETS		
Cash	7,000	7,000
Accounts Receivable	464,000	464,000
Inventory	583,000	583,000
Other Current Assets	92,000	92,000
TOTAL	1,146,000	1,146,000
Property & Equipment, Net	93,000	93,000
Other Assets	24,000	24,000
TOTAL ASSETS	1,263,000	1,263,000
CURRENT LIABILITIES		
Notes Payable, Bank	475,000	600,000
Accounts Payable	317,000	317,000
Other Current Liabilities	67,000	67,000
TOTAL	859,000	984,000
Long-term Debt	59,000	59,000
Stockholders' Equity	345,000	345,000
Total Liabilities & Equity	1,263,000	1,388,000
DEBT-TO-WORTH RATIO	2.66-to-1	3.02-to-1

$394,000, assuming they were all eligible. The bank allowed Surgical to borrow up to twenty-five percent of inventory, which added another $145,000, for a total borrowing of $540,000. Though Surgical qualified for the full $600,000 on a debt-to-worth basis, collateral would support only $540,000. This would be the cap until later in the year when seasonal fluctuations plus growth increased accounts receivable and inventory to allow up to $60,000 in additional borrowing. When establishing maximum loans, the requirement for sufficient collateral takes precedence over the debt-to-worth ratio.

For small, rapidly growing companies, banks will lend beyond debt-to-worth or beyond collateral limitations when the owner has a substantial net worth in relation to the loan, if the business outlook for the company is good. As companies grow, it takes a very substantial net worth for an owner to offset shortages in collateral. John Millbank's net worth of $287,000, as shown in chapter 5, is becoming modest as the line reaches $600,000. However, if the company's debt-to-worth were 3.25-to-1 when the limit was 3.0, the equity in his real estate might persuade the bank to grant the loan.

Cash Flow

A vital concern for the loan officer is the source of repayment, and the cash-flow plan is the best vehicle for assessing a company's ability to repay loans. Again and again, we return to the importance of cash-flow planning. A carefully prepared cash-flow plan is really a feasibility study of the owner's plans for the year. If the sales plan has been prepared realistically, if the profit planning has been sifted through carefully, if the cash flow's key assumptions—receivables collection, inventory schedules, payment rates on accounts payable, timing and amounts of capital expenditures, timing of increases in personnel—have been made with good judgment, then the cash-flow plan will indicate a pattern of cash deficits and surpluses which should be the ballpark within which the game will be played for the planning period. The cash flow can put the owner in control of the game, and it can bring the banker on as an enthusiastic team member.

AN IMPORTANT THING TO KNOW AS YOUR LOANS GET BIGGER

Banks frequently make a number of loans to a single business. All the loans are added up to determine the total financing extended to that business. Therefore, if the owner asks for an increase in a line of credit of, say, $50,000, the bank will not evaluate that request as a $50,000 request. By policy, the loan officers must evaluate the request on the basis of the total loans outstanding. If the total loans were $250,000 before the request, then the loan officers would evaluate the owner's request as a $300,000 loan. It is important to remember this fact, because a seemingly small loan request, under these circumstances, is actually a large request.

In fact, it is slightly more complicated. If the company's loans consisted of a $100,000 term loan and a $200,000 line of credit, but the line of credit had only $150,000 outstanding, the loan officers would still evaluate the request to include the full line authorization, irrespective of whether or not it was being used. Thus, the request would actually be for $350,000. Sometimes a small request will move the total loans up to a higher loan committee, which may not be as receptive to the company's request as the loan officers who have been handling the account all along. A smart owner keeps informed about the credit approval procedures at the bank, to anticipate any problems a new financing request might cause. The issue is never to take a loan request for granted.

OWNER'S GUARANTEES AND SECOND TRUSTS

The most unpalatable feature of getting a bank loan for many entrepreneurs is the requirement that both the owner and the spouse personally guarantee. Legally, of course, the owner is better off not signing anything personally, because in the event of a bankruptcy the liabilities would end with the corporation. However, such is not to be with bank loans. It is standard practice for the banks to require both signatures; this, of course, prevents a devious owner from putting assets in the spouse's name to shield assets from liability in the case of default.

The bank's position, which makes sense, is that the entrepreneur should believe in the business enough to put everything on the line for it. In the high-risk environment of a small enterprise, why should the bank take a risk the owner isn't willing to take? More fundamentally, if an owner is personally liable for the company's borrowings, he or she can't walk away from the business as easily as if there were no personal encumbrance.

But personal guarantees are easier to swallow than a second trust on a house. Banks frequently resort to this measure when lending to a business with a marginal financial position. By *marginal* the bank may mean a high debt-to-worth ratio, a thin collateralization for the loan, or financial ratios at the low end of industry averages. Second trusts also can come into play when the loan amount is very large for the size of the business. Perhaps the ratios are good, but heavy growth is predicted for the upcoming year. Term loans frequently require second trusts because the formal commitment of funds to a small business for several years is a risky loan when one considers the volatility of small businesses and their susceptibility to sudden failure. Like the personal guarantee, accepting a second trust on a house as collateral for a loan is something an owner has to do to get the financing. It is helpful to apply to other banks to see if a more lenient bank can be found, but banks tend to be consistent in their policies requiring personal guarantees and second trusts.

SBA LOANS

The loan guarantee program makes up the lion's share of SBA financing. Its reason for being is the reluctance of many banks to make long-term loans to small businesses because of the risk. The SBA guarantee is an inducement for the bank to make the loan, because the bank's share of the loan loss in the case of default is only ten percent. In addition, the bank can sell the guaranteed portion of the loan in a secondary market, which frees up the bank's funds to make other loans and gains the bank a fee on the total transaction.

The mechanics of the transaction for the entrepreneur are usually as follows:

- The business applies to the bank for a loan.
- The bank decides it can't handle the loan, because it is too large or because the limitations of the company's ability to repay would require a term loan of several years.
- The bank suggests an SBA-guaranteed loan and gives the owner the SBA forms to prepare.
- The owner prepares the application for an SBA-guaranteed term loan and submits it to the bank.
- The bank approves the term loan, subject to the SBA guarantee.
- The bank applies to the local SBA office for the guarantee.
- The SBA approves the guarantee, notifying the bank by letter.
- The bank notifies the owner. The bank can disburse some funds against the guarantee as soon as it has the SBA letter.
- The SBA lawyers prepare the loan documents and send them to the bank.
- The bank disburses the funds and administers the loan until it has been paid in full.
- The bank will apply to the SBA for any changes in the loan agreement during subsequent years.
- The only time the SBA would become directly involved is in the case of default, when the company's assets must be liquidated to pay off the loan.

A direct SBA loan is extremely rare. These are loans made by the SBA with its own funds. To be eligible, the business must show proof of having been turned down for financing from two banks. This is not a requirement for the loan guarantee program, as some entrepreneurs mistakenly think. The direct loan funds are so limited and the process takes so much time that it is not feasible in most cases.

The Pros of SBA Financing

Frequently, a deserving, rapidly growing small business can't get adequate financing for its expansion from commercial banks. The company may be too new for the amount requested. Often the loan repayment must be over seven to ten years to avoid loading the company with an annual debt burden in excess of its cash-flow capacity. Rarely will a bank make loans of that duration to a small business. The future is too unpredictable. In these cases the SBA guarantee is a vital resource. Ed Simpson wouldn't be a prosperous businessman today if it weren't for the SBA guarantee program. I know of several substantial, medium-sized businesses that were launched into their first major growth phases by a well-timed SBA-guaranteed term loan.

If operations expand profitably, SBA loans are like any bank loans. Actually, the covenants written by the SBA are similar to the covenants of a standard bank term loan. The ongoing administration of the loan is handled by the bank. Periodic modifications in the loan agreement, such as the release of collateral for line-of-credit financing, can be obtained if the company has performed well. Refinancing of the term loan can be obtained from time to time, again, if the company has performed well. Under favorable conditions, SBA financing can provide a timely infusion of long-term debt, and the ongoing administration of the loan, with occasional modifications, can go smoothly.

The Cons of SBA Financing

Remember that SBA financing means dealing with the government. Despite the fact that there are many competent officials in the SBA, their concept of time differs from a businessperson's. Commercial bankers are well aware of the need to move promptly on a financing request, and sometimes even their credit systems can move with maddening slowness. The cardinal rule in dealing with SBA loans is to plan for a very, very slow process. A thirty-day turnaround from the time your application hits the bank is optimistic. If you must have the funds within forty-five days or you'll be in deep trouble, then expect to be in deep trouble.

Yes, there are cases in which the loan is processed and disbursed within two weeks. I know of one case that took six months. I recommend that you plan for a ninety-day process. If it turns out to be faster, you're ahead of the game, but if it takes that long, you have anticipated it. There are so many vagaries to the process that estimating the turnaround time is speculation, and don't let anyone tell you otherwise. Frequently, the entrepreneur applying for an SBA loan is running dangerously short of cash. The delays can endanger growth plans, sometimes even the business itself. The SBA will be oblivious to any such considerations.

I remember one owner who desperately needed the loan to support his expansion. Though his profitability was okay, his cash was dangerously short. While his case was at the SBA, there was a disastrous hurricane in Louisiana. SBA loan officers from around the country, including the one who was handling his case, were rushed south to handle the Disaster Relief Program. There was nothing he could do but hold on until the local SBA office went back to business again. The hurricane added thirty days to the processing time, which dragged on for over three months.

A further disadvantage to the SBA program is inflexibility. Any modification in the loan agreement has to be presented formally to the SBA for approval. Again, this means time. Since the SBA loan will be secured by all corporate assets at the time of the loan, plus any assets acquired thereafter, entrepreneurs have found their expansion programs blocked by the SBA lien. Perhaps a bank would be willing to extend a line of credit, but the SBA has a lien against all receivables. More than one unwary owner has purchased a piece of equipment with the intention of financing it, only to find that the SBA lien was in effect at the moment the equipment was acquired. Applications for release of collateral are not always acted on favorably by the SBA. On the other hand, if the bank has made the term loan on its own, adding a line of credit to a company's financing is an internal decision of the loan officer or officers who made the term loan in the first place. If it is a yes decision, the matter can be handled in a few days.

The procedural delays and actual difficulties of amending an SBA loan agreement can prove a serious detriment to an expanding small business. An intelligent owner must plan the process carefully to obtain additional financing on a timely basis. Many businesses which have strengthened their financial position sufficiently have refinanced the SBA loan with standard bank financing, to gain vital flexibility. On the other hand, an SBA loan can be a true blessing for the entrepreneur who can't get a bank term loan to finance opportunities for profitable expansion.

OTHER TYPES OF LOANS

Outside the system of standard bank loans—demand, line of credit, revolving line, term loan (with or without an SBA guarantee)—are the more specialized types of loans. These loans can be very helpful to a business owner whose business is suited for that type of financing. A computer retailer or an audio retailer, for example, can floor-plan inventory that is serial numbered and capable of being audited by the finance company. Since banks don't like to finance inventory, floor planning can be a valuable source of funds. However, a lumber supply company won't be able to floor-plan the sticks out in the yard.

As a business grows, financing becomes more a matter of piecing together the most advantageous types of financing. The bank and the trade are the most effective sources for funding basic growth. As other pieces are added to the puzzle, the owner should review alternative sources of funds. Substantial purchases of furniture and office equipment can be packaged for leasing. Equipment and vehicles can be financed by banks, by equipment finance companies, sometimes by the manufacturer, and through leasing companies. Banks require more equity in the deal; leases are more expensive. Incidentally, large banks frequently have their own leasing companies.

Companies with large amounts of accounts receivable frequently can get more financing dollars per outstanding receivables from commercial financing companies or from factors than from the bank. The interest expense will be greater, but the extra cash may be worth it. Commercial finance companies may also advance funds on a larger percentage of inventory, say up to fifty percent. There are some important issues to keep in mind when evaluating commercial financing:

- Commercial financing looks for volume. Some companies have minimum loans of a million dollars. An entrepreneur looking for

$50,000 to finance receivables is much more likely to find a bank than a commercial finance company to do the job.

- Commercial finance companies have less stringent ratio requirements than banks. A company's financial condition can warrant financing from this source, while the bank is saying no.
- Commercial financing is still financing. Financial statements will be reviewed and collateral will be evaluated. Excessive losses and insufficient equity will still disqualify the business, despite the lower standards.
- Not everybody's receivables qualify. Many commercial companies will not handle government contracts, for example. Though banks are more conservative, they will handle a broader range of companies and situations.
- Watch the cost. Heavy commercial financing means high interest expense. A company with a thin profit margin may find that the growth generated by commercial financing may be eating up the profits at the same time.

HOW MUCH SHOULD YOU BORROW?

Going from the boom 1980s to the bust 1990s has demonstrated the business cycle. Millionaires have become paupers. Once-proud businesses are on their knees.

Why? Scheduled debt payments that could be paid with ease when times are good go into default when times are bad. The 1980s financing that is now in default was predicated on cash flows that were to be generated from continuous expansion. Some financing even exceeded anticipated future debt capacity on the assumption that it could be refinanced or "rolled over" or syndicated.

You can get rich quick if you leverage to the hilt with other people's money. But can you stay rich? That depends on whether you get out in time or on how deep the downturn is when it comes.

For the more patient entrepreneur, measuring debt capacity takes recessions into consideration. You can establish prudent borrowing limits by forecasting profits and cash flow over several years, as shown in Figure 10-2. Plan for a recession in mid-stream. Can you make debt payments during the hypothetical recession? How deep can the recession go—ten, twenty, thirty percent—before you default on payments? Revise the forecasts as your business grows and eco-

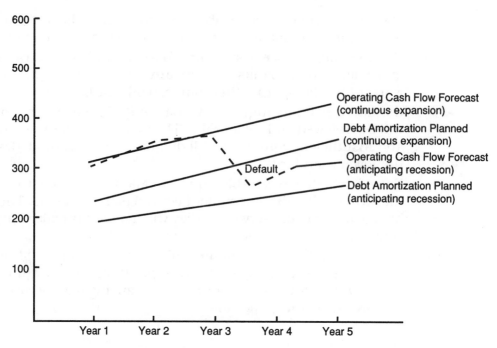

Figure 10-2   Planning debt around the business cycle.

nomic conditions change. The assessment of debt capacity is an ongoing process.

For recession-prone industries, the amount of repayment you can handle in a future recession establishes your present debt capacity. If you're to be in business for ten or more years, remember that most industries eventually suffer recessions.

SUMMARY

Though cash may be a constant problem, a business owner usually arranges financing at the bank only once or twice a year. Major financing of equipment may take place only every couple of years, but the degree of success the owner has with these infrequent transactions will have a major impact on day-to-day operations. This degree of success depends on how well the owner can make the banking system work to his or her advantage. Making the system work for a company requires insight into the differences among banks and into the differences among bankers. The owner must find the banker who will make the best financial member of his or her business team.

However, this is just the beginning of a successful financing program. As the business grows, the financing requirements become larger and more complicated. Instead of a $25,000 loan every few months, there must now be a $150,000 line of credit, a $200,000 term loan, and several equipment financing or leasing deals. To arrange more complicated loans, it is important to have the resources necessary to prepare a comprehensive business plan, not only to obtain the loan, but as a tool in managing the business.

The plan is an excellent vehicle for obtaining financing. It should be assembled in a presentation consistent with the loan officer's psychology in analyzing a loan request. At the same time, a carefully prepared cash-flow plan is the basis for evaluating the amount and type of financing needed for the planning period. Before going to the bank, it is important to understand, in terms of the debt-to-worth ratio, the available collateral, and the cash-flow plan, approximately what the company's borrowing capacity is.

Armed with these tools and having developed a long-term relationship with a banker who understands the business, the chances are excellent that the entrepreneur will be able to arrange the kind of financing that leads to success. However, the continued success of the marketing and sales program will bring growth, and growth will bring changes. What was good financing last year may not be sufficient this year. Therefore, the financing program requires continued monitoring, best done in the form of a periodic business plan, with profit plans and cash flows, to determine whether or not the growth has created new financing needs. It is important to keep the bank up to date with important developments, to allow the loan officer to provide the right kind of help at the right time.

Keeping the bank informed is not limited to favorable developments. Over the years, even the best of businesses experience financial problems, and experienced loan officers expect this. Keeping the banker fully informed helps to ensure that the owner can get help not only for positive developments, but for some problems as well. The ability to maintain a strong, creative banking relationship is a critical characteristic of the successful entrepreneur.

11

Deal with Trouble Early

GOD HELP US!

The controller, the operations vice president, and I sat down at George Thompson's conference table to wait for him to finish his telephone conference. We had just completed an intensive analysis of Software Systems, Inc., which showed a cash shortage of $1.5 million over the next three months. When the bank had called to ask for my help, the loan officer had said the situation was serious, but it turned out to be even worse than anticipated.

As George wrapped up his conversation to get to our meeting, none of us said anything. We didn't even look at each other. I was just doing my job, of course, but when I work with small companies I want them to survive. I care. I'm sure the other two were thinking about that and about where they would be working in a month or two. They probably wondered, as well, what fate had in store for their boss, who couldn't walk away so easily from the company he had built over fifteen years to a nationally recognized operation and for which he had personally guaranteed so much debt.

George hung up the phone and immediately moved over to the table to sit before the cash-flow plan, which we had spread out for him. He sat, wordless, as I reviewed the analysis, his eyes focusing on each figure as I pointed it out. I went over the bottom line of the cash flow, explaining how we had worked it out, explaining that his company was, in effect, $1.5 million short of cash at the very moment we sat there talking. I explained that we had prepared the estimates very carefully. His staff was certain that this represented the minimum requirement we faced.

George pushed back his chair, stood, and moved across the office to his window, where he looked out on the winter day. Having stood there earlier, I knew that he looked down eight floors at the scurrying pedestrians of a Washington, D.C. street—lawyers, bankers, secretaries, consultants, association executives—purposeful in their movements to and from meetings where the business side of the nation's capital was being conducted. As he looked directly across the street into the office windows of one of the country's most successful big businesses, he could see executives sitting at their desks. Not long ago they could have looked across the street into his office to see their mirror image. But now as he looked down the eight floors, it wasn't to see the height he had scaled, but an impending plunge into oblivion. Faintly his words echoed back from the window glass . . .

"God help us."

It Can Happen to You

I wish I had a pill I could give entrepreneurs to help keep their businesses sound. Many have failed, are failing, will fail. Anyone who starts and manages their own business must realize that they may fail . . . not only at the outset, but at any time during their history. Circumstances change over time. George Thompson's business was fifteen years old. I have seen some businesses fail simply because there wasn't enough sales potential to sustain the expense of running the business, even on the most frugal basis. I have seen more businesses fail because the owner made mistakes. There was no economic reason why the business could not have succeeded. An honest, gut-felt realization—not a lip service, theoretical understanding—that it could happen to you is a prerequisite of the survival personality.

Why So Many Failures?

Let's take another look at the entrepreneur. In the crisis situations I have experienced over the last fifteen years, some factors were almost always present. Knowing these might be like a mental pill you could take, if you really accepted them at the gut level. Do any of these factors apply to your business? If they do, look out!

- IMPATIENCE WITH ACCOUNTING. A willingness to go for extended periods not knowing where your business stands from a profit or loss standpoint. A lack of effort on your part to ensure that the statements are a reliable presentation of the accounting data. Superficial knowledge of the strengths and weaknesses of the internal accounting staff. Unquestioning dependence on the outside CPA. The assumption that somebody else will call your attention to the problem—the CPA, your own controller, your lawyer, your banker, your operations manger.
- NOT KNOWING HOW TO READ FINANCIAL STATEMENTS. Not understanding how the direct costs, gross profits, selling and marketing expenses, and general and administrative expenses all tie together to produce a profit or cause a loss. Confusion about the assets and liabilities. A sense that the balance sheet is some kind of black magic which bankers and accountants say hocus-pocus over. A deep determination to go out and grab sales growth wherever you can get it, which will make financial matters take care of themselves.
- A FEELING THAT THINGS WILL ALWAYS WORK OUT. Maybe sales are down, maybe everyone is warning you that the company is slipping badly, but you are sure, in your gut, that sales will bounce back. You think this in spite of the fact that sales never seem to be up to your expectations, but next time. . . .
- THE COMPANY HAS GROWN DRAMATICALLY. There seems a bewildering array of management tasks you never dreamed of before. You don't like the work. You never seem to get everything done. You're uncertain what the priorities should be. You're always putting out fires. Nothing in your experience seems to be a reliable guide to what to do.
- YOU FEEL IRRITABLE, ANGRY. At the same time you're tired. You never seem to be able to get anything done. You're having trouble at home as well as the office. You have a hard time keeping your attention on the work at hand.

- PERHAPS YOU ARE COMPELLED, INSTEAD, TO FOLLOW UP ON MANY DETAILS. No matter what anyone says about priorities, you have to do it that way. Everything is secondary to this goal. At the same time, you feel nervous and anxious at the strangest times. What you feel compelled to do is the only way out. But no matter how many details you straighten out, you can feel control slipping away.
- MAYBE YOU'VE HAD SOME PROBLEMS WITH YOUR BUSINESS, BUT IT WAS JUST BAD LUCK. Perhaps it was someone else's fault. The point is, nobody can tell you what to do. Your banker, your CPA, consultants, your managers . . . you haven't made mistakes, you haven't done things wrong. There's nothing to be learned from rehashing what happened, because you know what to do. What happened yesterday isn't the problem now.

Financial Trouble Is a Treacherous Disease

The treachery of deep financial trouble is that it starts with a symptom identical to that of some ordinary operating problems. Cash is short. Cash can be short because of rapid growth, or because of seasonal fluctuations; in fact, being cash-short is a daily way of life for many small businesses. But as payables become more and more past due, as it becomes increasingly difficult to make withholding deposits to the IRS, as the bank loans are renewed for the third or fourth time, the situation takes a different course. Creditors become increasingly strict, until goods can be had only for cash. Intense pressure builds from a multitude of suppliers for payment against past due. Some become nasty, belligerent. Now the company is past due with the IRS, not just a single deposit, but perhaps a couple of hundred thousand. The bank has called a meeting to inform you that they will not renew the loan. You have no hope of paying them.

Closer scrutiny shows that you have lost many times what you had thought. By year-end, the losses are so great that your business has a deficit net worth of several hundred thousand. What began as a cash shortage is now a runaway hemorrhage. Sales have dropped due to the shortage of cash, which has compounded the losses to astronomical proportions. Everyone wants their money now! You miss the next payroll—wholesale staff resignations threaten the very ability to operate from day to day. Perhaps it took a year to get here. Perhaps it took two years. Perhaps this insidious disease developed over several years. But now it has become an insane rush into bankruptcy. What took so many years for you to build has blown apart, once trouble came out in the open, in a matter of months, even weeks. Survival, now, can be measured in terms of only a day at a time.

ONCE IN DEEP TROUBLE—WHAT DO YOU DO?

Step One: Find Out Where You Are

In every deep-trouble situation I have been asked to work with, the owner wasn't sure where the company stood. Cash was lethally tight, but how much additional cash was needed to survive? The company was losing money, but at what rate? What monthly sales were needed just to break even? There was a mountain of past due accounts payable, but how much and how old? Mistakes and operating problems were contributing heavily to the problems, but which ones needed to be tackled first? When your business is dying, you have only so much time. The way you set priorities will have a lot to do with whether you make it or not.

Usually the problem had been building for at least a year. I found most situations to be much worse, even after all the trouble, than the owner realized. In about half the cases, it was too late to save the company, no matter how hard we tried. In every case, I believe the company could have been saved if we had started to work on it a year sooner.

A stunning fact in each company was the degree to which the owner's ignorance of where the company stood joined with the owner's innate optimism to produce decision after decision based on feelings that were drastically divorced from marketing, financial, and organizational realities. Some people reading these words right now are probably going to have this happen to them.

The bankruptcy of a business is abrupt, final, and deeply painful. It is an economic death.

Finding out where a deeply troubled company stands is hard; it is difficult to fix the degree of trouble. This is usually due to inadequacy and confusion in the accounting departments of these companies. Unfortunately, accounting problems can't be resolved overnight. Messed up systems and procedures block quick accounting action. It takes time to catch up on postings that are seriously in arrears. The situation is compounded by confused, inadequately trained personnel.

It takes a person with experience in the intensive care ward to come into a situation of panic, despair, and confusion and make a reliable estimate of where things stand. This reliable estimate is essential to working the company out of trouble, if such is possible. It is the basis literally for slashing the operation down to a new size. It is the basis for establishing a survival schedule out of the cash/payables confrontation. It is the basis for arranging additional financing with the bank or other sources, if possible. The reliable estimate is an assessment of the degree of trouble, which determines the severity of the salvage program.

When doctors diagnose cancer, the stage of the disease is critical to the treatment. If the patient is seventy-five percent gone, drastic measures are taken, even if they are dangerous to the patient, because there isn't much choice. Chances are the patient is going to die, but a certain percentage may survive if heroic measures are used. On the other hand, if the patient is five percent gone, the treatment is different, because there is plenty of time to bring the disease under control, and protecting the patient is part of the proper treatment.

How to estimate the degree of trouble

Gaining control requires the same analytical tools in trouble as when the company is in good shape. It's just that you have to do it with bombs going off over your head. There isn't much time, so you have to strike fast and effectively.

1. *What's the marketing situation?* Are sales running down because of the economy? Has a new competitor taken some of your market share? Has your sales force fallen apart, possibly through bad sales management? The issue is to size up, quickly, whether your financial trouble is a marketing problem; if it is, is this problem one you have to accept (home builder in a deep recession), or is fixing the marketing problem part of the rescue plan for the company?

2. *What is your most realistic sales projection for the next three months?* Extend this projection, as realistically as you can, to complete a twelve-month period. This estimate is the core of the survival program. It is vital not to overestimate potential sales.

Your company is losing money. The only way to stop that is to bring expenses in line with sales volume. If you overestimate the volume, you will underestimate the expense reductions. Result . . . more losses.

3. *Make a tough profit plan, using the sales projection as the basis.* The plan will show a substantial loss. You must cut expenses drastically to make a profit on the sales you've got. BE DECISIVE. IF IN DOUBT. OVERCUT. The worst mistake is to plan for reductions insufficient to make a profit.

4. *Prepare an honest, realistic cash-flow plan.* Make sure you are not optimistic about collections on accounts receivable. Don't kid yourself about when you have to pay creditors. You have to look unflinchingly at the reality of your situation. If you don't, you're pulling the lid of the coffin down on your own head.

What to do when you have no time

If the situation is so bad you don't have time to think about marketing and sales; if you can't wait for enough accounting information to make a meaningful profit plan, then go straight to the cash flow. Manage for survival, first, by working with a hard-nosed cash-flow plan which tells you what you have to do. You have only so much cash now, plus what is coming in over the next thirty to sixty days. Work out deals with your creditors on what you can pay; with the bank the best payment schedule you can make; with employees what you can do with payroll; with the IRS the best long-range payout you can make. Use the plan as a tool for bargaining with people. Unless your situation is so totally hopeless that it doesn't matter to people what happens to your company, creditors will try to be realistic about what they can get if they feel they are being told the truth. Keep track of plan versus actual. Using the weekly cash budget I mentioned in chapter 4 is very effective for surviving this kind of crisis. A monthly cash flow is academic. You have to survive the week before you can survive the month. Then start doing what is needed to get financial statements, as a first step in getting control of profits. Be sure your marketing/sales operation is as powerful as you can make it.

Step Two: Take Immediate, Decisive Action

Cut expenses immediately. Be decisive. Be fast. Err on the side of too much rather than too little. Even in the face of disaster, I have seen entrepreneurs hold back from cutting costs. "I can't operate with fewer people. I can't get the sales without the advertising. If I don't develop that new product, I won't have any future."

I have one rule for business owners to use for crisis decisions. Imagine you have a disease. With this disease, if you don't cut the payroll (or whatever), you will die. If you do cut the payroll, you will live. Which will you do? If you're in a crisis situation right now, ask yourself this question. You can see why knowing where you stand is so important—if you undercut, you will still die. But overcutting can kill the patient, too. You can't have sales without any salespeople. You can't produce financial information without a bookkeeper. You can't execute a contract without direct labor. If you don't know where you stand, you don't know where to hit the tree with your ax.

It's not pleasant to cut payroll. I have been the hatchet man many times, and I do not like it. But if the company is certain to die, you have no choice. If you do nothing, everyone will lose their jobs. If you act decisively, you may save sixty percent of them. In cutting, you have to let the weak performers go and save the strong performers. This will salvage the company, and it will give those who have worked hard a fair shake while being honest with those who didn't work as hard. Frequently, troubled companies have gotten into crises because too many marginal employees were tolerated. In these situations cleaning house means facing up to decisions that should have been made a long time ago. The irony is that the employees who are let go are likely to find other jobs and be in better shape a lot sooner than you will be.

Sometimes a problem manager has been a significant part of the company's difficulty: a big salary without results, incompetent management of a division, the sales force, the controller's job. When things are going well, maybe you can wrestle with the dilemma of whether or not to fire good old Jack. But if you're in a financial crisis, can him. Right now.

Leave no expense account unexamined. Assume there is no such thing as a fixed expense. Yes, fixed it may be, but perhaps there is a contract you can get out of if the creditor realizes there's no hope of payment. Equipment can be repossessed.

Let go of your cherished projects for the time being. That new product won't make a nickel in sales if your company is in the graveyard. You may have to operate your company in an insane way for a while—people working two or three jobs, projects on indefinite hold, inordinate time spent trying to keep the doors open. No business can move ahead in those circumstances, but you will have to do the impossible for long enough to pull yourself out.

Common Problem Areas

Frequently, small companies lose money because general and administrative expenses are excessive. If the gross profit percentage is satisfactory, either in terms of industry averages or from what you hear about a good gross profit for your kind of business, and if sales volume is increasing, then the reason for your losses can be found in G&A. Sometimes there are too many high-priced overhead people. Sometimes there are too many layers of management, whatever the individual salary level. The objective is to chop the G&A down to less than the gross profit dollars, with enough margin for a reasonable profit. The obstacles to solving a G&A expense problem are the fixed costs associated with leases and contracts and the interest on loans.

Sometimes losses are incurred in companies that would be profitable except for a division that's such a loser that the company loses money as a whole. Many times the losses on the division are not clearly understood because the income statement is not divisionalized. With figures shown only for the company total, how do you know? The problem is magnified when the loss division happens to be the owner's pet project. The same logic applies to a losing store or stores in a chain; to losing contracts for a builder or research firm; to losing product lines for a manufacturer. The problems won't be resolved until the financial statements and job cost reports show profitability by the management units of the company—division, store, contract, product.

A classic cause of financial trouble is rapid growth combined with lack of profitability. A company does not have to lose money to grow. But with inadequate management reports and controls, a too often repeated scenario will find the company growing at the top line only. The owner sees success in the sales increase, without sufficient monitoring of the bottom line. Without profitability, growth is funded entirely by debt. When the trade credit rubber band stretches too far and the bank says, "no more," the owner discovers that there isn't enough cash to meet obligations and that there is no immediate avenue to profitability because of the low margin on sales and the high costs of administration. Remember the printer whose business grew to $3 million plus in sales, only to find that the gross profit was zero?

Trouble can come from outside factors, as well. Home builders, retailers, and manufacturers all know the effects of a major recession. The entrepreneur who gets caught off guard by a sudden drop in sales can go under just like that. In cyclical industries flexibility is vital. The owner knows sales will drop in some years, due to the economic cycle. Consequently, he or she must be able to reduce overhead, cut back on direct expenses, and operate free from heavy fixed debt obligations. Survival comes from the ability to contract. Builders with excessive speculative homes in inventory, retailers who have overexpanded store locations, manufacturers with heavy equipment financing obligations, all will pay the price. The trick is to expand while keeping the levels of fixed expenses and fixed debt obligations at a point which can be maintained at, say, twenty-five percent less in sales than the current year. Perhaps the contractions capability is fifteen percent; perhaps it is thirty-five percent—the degree depends on the industry and the company's susceptibility to cyclical reductions in the level of sales.

Another outside factor is competition. Many entrepreneurs have gone under because a creative and well-financed competitor took market share away from them. The combination of tough competition with an economic downturn is particularly devastating. Knowing competition, both potential and actual, is critical. Knowing the company's strengths and weaknesses in comparison to this competition is crucial.

Finally, companies can have serious problems due to improper financing. Ed Simpson is a classic example. Substantial loans that must be repaid too quickly or a line of credit that's financing long-term investments will strip cash from daily operations.

The resulting shortages can make it difficult to get product, which can reduce sales, ultimately resulting in substantial operating losses. If the problem repeats itself year after year, a company can literally go down the tubes from bad financing. However, the problem can be resolved by good financial planning, which can, properly presented, prompt the bank to restructure the company's loans or which can prompt a new bank to provide better financing.

Step Three: Follow Up Relentlessly on All Priorities

The truth is that you have made some bad mistakes for your business to have gone to the brink like this. You must recognize what those mistakes are and then admit them to yourself. Take full responsibility for them. This is not a moral issue, nor does its importance stem from the military principle that the commander always takes responsibility. The issue is intensely practical: Unless you recognize the mistakes which led to the trouble, you will continue to make the same mistakes. Think of a tennis player who doesn't know how to hit a backhand. No matter how hard the player tries, every time the ball comes to the backhand it is hit off the court. Only when the player recognizes the mistakes can the changes be made in the swing to keep the ball in play. You have to change some of the ways you manage, right away, to keep the problems you create from putting the company under at the very time you are cutting costs and putting every ounce of your energy into survival.

To survive you must think in terms of management control. Your priorities, every hour of every day, are sales, cost control, and cash flow. You can't assume anything. Follow up on all important tasks you have assigned. Is your sales manger making things happen with each salesperson? Is each salesperson going for the bucks with good organization and intensity? No matter what kind of sales program you have, it must be executed with a high degree of competence, because survival can't be achieved by cost cutting alone. You must get sales.

Don't let up on the accounting department. It is imperative that you get profit and loss information as soon as possible after the close of the month. This is the only way you'll know if you've turned the company around. It's like hitting that backhand. If you stroke the ball and it goes off to the left, then you have to hit the ball more to the right. The next time the ball comes to your backhand, you make adjustments for the mistake you made last time. By the same token, if the income statement shows a loss, even after the cuts, you have to cut some more. Of course, there are many more issues, just as there are in hitting a backhand. But taking all the relevant considerations into account, you must respond immediately. No financial statements means no response. In a financial crisis, you are allowed no mistakes, and you have limited time. If you miss a backhand, you lose the point. If you don't turn your company around from a profit to a loss, right away, you're out of the game.

Follow cash-flow-versus-actual. Cash is so volatile that a potentially fatal problem, such as a sudden slowdown in collections on accounts receivable, can develop even while the profit situation has been improved. Though there can be no hope of staying out of bankruptcy if you continue operating at a loss, the moment of life or death for your company will be decided by cash flow. Therefore, every day you must have complete control of your cash-flow situation. Most entrepreneurs in deep trouble don't need any coaching on the ways and means of keeping creditors at bay; it's obvious that working with the creditors and the bank is the first task of survival.

GETTING HELP: TIMING IS CRITICAL

Troubled companies have to get additional cash to survive. Even when operations have been turned around form a loss to a profit, there will be a gap between the cash that eventually comes from monthly profitability and the large amounts that must be paid against past due obligations. Frequently the cash shortage, itself, can prevent a company from achieving profits, despite expense cuts, because of product shortages and employee defections.

If timing is a critical factor in all phases of business, it is like breath itself in a life-or-death situation. The survival time can shrink from a matter of months to a matter of weeks virtually to a matter of hours. A chance missed because it wasn't anticipated, or a chance missed due to a lack of attention, or an opportunity pursued too late can mean the difference between making it or not. I often draw Figure 11-1 when organizing a survival action plan for a client in trouble.

Early in trouble the owner can pursue several options to pull out of the situation. As time passes and the performance of the business

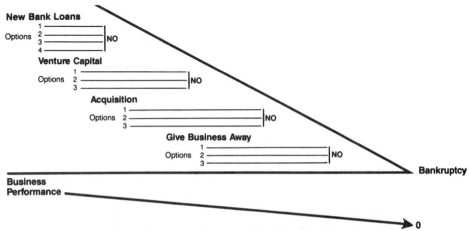

Figure 11-1   Range of options in deep trouble.

continues to decline, the number of options decreases. As the company moves closer to failure, the options become increasingly unattractive as well as increasingly scarce. As the figure indicates, it is essential to pursue several options concurrently. Sequencing bailout options end to end is tantamount to disaster, because it takes time to find out whether a bank will grant a loan or whether venture capital can be raised. Raising money for a troubled company takes an inordinate amount of time. Each analyst will sift through the plans and statements, weighing the possibility of a turnaround against the risk of total failure. The trick is to begin with the most viable option first, presumably bank financing, by applying to several banks simultaneously. While the banks are considering the presentations, the owner must explore venture capital—if it is an option—with the intent of finding out whether the proposal is acceptable as soon as possible after learning about the bank requests. If a bank accepts the request, then the venture capital requests can be withdrawn. If the banks refuse, the owner is already under way with the second set of options.

Similarly, the third option, possibly an acquisition of the company by a stronger company, should begin while venture capital proposals are being evaluated. If the answer is no to venture capital, the owner still has a chance for an acquisition. The possibility of letting someone take over the company in exchange for their assumption of the liabilities should also be explored. Maybe the owner will wind up giving the company away, but that is the last step before declaring bankruptcy. Believe me, there are companies in such bad shape they can't be given away. Owners shouldn't turn up their noses at this option—it can take someone off the hook for liabilities which have been personally guaranteed, possibly a personal liability for past due withholding taxes. The owner can ask for an option on stock which could be earned back based on the performance of the company after the acquisition.

HOW TO RAISE MONEY WHEN YOU ARE IN TROUBLE

When you are in trouble, you should take the same approach to getting a loan as when things are going well—essentially an application of the techniques we discussed in chapter 10 except that every aspect of the presentation has to be done even more thoroughly. The preparation of a business plan is mandatory. Your chances of getting a loan under these circumstances rest on the quality of your business plan and how convincingly you have presented it. A yes decision can be obtained only if you persuade the loan officer that you have turned your company around from a loss operation to a profit operation. The business plan is a hard-hitting presentation of the work you have done to estimate the degree of trouble you are in, to develop your turnaround action plan, and to establish the follow-up controls to make the turnaround stick. Several factors should be highlighted in your presentation:

- You should identify your mistakes and admit to them. The loan officer needs to feel that you won't repeat the gaffes which got you where you are now.
- You must outline how you can achieve profitability through specific expense reductions and the solution of specific operating problems.
- A before and after schedule can be used to show expenses before reductions and expenses after reductions, with the after column detailing how all the changes accumulate to a profit for the immediate future.
- We must show by use of a cash-flow plan how the financial obligations of your company, including all past due accounts, can be met according to the required payment schedules.
- You should lay out a system of plan-versus-actual controls that will enable you to monitor results and to make any changes necessary to ensure profits.
- Be alert to cash-flow problems created by the wrong kind of financing. The cash-flow plan must show the benefits of restructuring the existing financing, especially in terms of improved cash flow and enhanced profitability.

Getting a loan when you are in trouble is the hardest job in business. The task is doubly difficult when you approach a strange bank with your request. Yet you won't make it without help. You will have to try several banks or finance companies. This is why a strong, long-term relationship with a bank is so crucial. Working with people whose trust you have earned, despite your present trouble, is the best chance you have. This chance will be further improved if you can produce evidence—an income statement—which shows that the turnaround is working. If the wrong financing is at the root of the problem, often a new bank offers the best chance for help, because it can see the present financing more objectively.

VENTURE CAPITAL OR BEING ACQUIRED

Getting venture capital when you are in trouble is a long shot. The circumstances have to be right:

- The climate for small-company equities comes and goes. The climate for a particular industry comes and goes. Your chances are particularly dim if you are looking at a bad market.
- Your company must be a type which is interesting to a venture financing source (i.e., one that has a chance of being sold or going public within three or four years).
- There must be a compelling story concerning the immediate market demand for your products and services. Big sales growth can be attained if the venture capital is put in as soon as the turnaround is achieved.
- There must be a good chance that a turnaround from loss to profit can be achieved quickly.
- The venture capital sources can get a big chunk of the ownership for a steal. This is the worst time to raise equity capital, but if you're trying to survive, what can you do?

Being acquired by another company is more likely than raising venture capital. Your business would be most attractive to a company that desires to get into your market. They may have allied products or services but not immediate entry to the customer segment you serve. Despite your bad financial condition, it may still be cheaper for them to acquire you than to start up an operation in a new market. Or you may offer a different type of diversification—they are a manufacturer, you are a distributor; they are a government contractor, you are totally private sector; they are a service operation, you are a manufacturer. Perhaps the other company can see how your business can be turned around quickly, which could provide them a high rate of return on the low purchase price you must accept in your present circumstances. On the other hand, you have a special skill—marketing, technical, operations—which the other company is willing to acquire your company to obtain.

A Matter of Time, Energy, and Resources

Both venture capital and an acquisition take time. Remember, the people with money are not in a hurry, you are. After the initial contact, the process will move slowly. Since you are in financial distress, the other parties will be cautious. They will have to investigate your operation to evaluate the marketability of your goods or services, the competence of your personnel. They will have to make a definitive assessment of your financial condition to ensure that the full extent of your liabilities are known to them. The appointments to make these evaluations will be strung out over a matter of weeks and months. Assuming you passed successfully through these investigations, an initial offer will be made. You are not in a bargaining position, but you may want to make a counter proposal. There will be a few exchanges involving these issues. Then lawyers will have to draw up the necessary agreements. Inventories, in the case of an acquisition, will have to be taken. The entire process can take several months.

To get very far with either venture capital or an acquisition, you must have a persuasive business plan. Most troubled companies will be rejected out of hand. If what you are offering holds some attractions, there may be several expressions of interest. This is the deep pitfall of seeking outside capital or an acquisition when you are in trouble. These expressions of interest do not mean anything, one way or the other. It is only good business for the money party to take a look at something that has potential. An investor is prepared to walk away from the deal at any time, right up to the last minute. In the meantime, you are excited because the XYZ venture capital company is considering the deal or because ACE Technologies is sending a team down to evaluate a possible acquisition. Don't be excited. Talk is cheap. You'll know if the deal will go through only when they sign on the dotted line.

The process of holding conferences, taking part in evaluations of your own business, and negotiating hypothetical deals is tremendously distracting. It's a significant drain on the energies of an already overtaxed business owner. The process of trying to cut one of these deals can, in itself, help push your company over the brink.

Always keep in mind that every possible deal is likely to be a wild goose chase. Don't take your eye off your business operation for a single minute. You have to accept the double burden of constant attention to your business while conducting a series of difficult negotiations. This time-consuming factor of raising capital or searching for an acquisition is why it is so crucial to stage your survival scenarios according to Figure 11-1. If you start pursuing your capital-raising efforts sequentially, rather than concurrently, you are courting disaster.

WHAT KEEPS BUSINESSES ALIVE?

Many times I have been shown balance sheets that look just as bankrupt as they could be, yet the company is still operating. How can that be? Some owners keep going just from the sheer will to survive—begging off one supplier, making a partial payment to another, spreading out a third by converting the payable to a note with monthly installments. A payout of several months can be negotiated with the IRS. As long as no one sues to get an attachment on the checking account, as long as the bank does not apply all the company's cash to the loan balance, which they can do when the loan is in default, a company can keep going. Even in these cases, owners can survive if they can come up with the cash to keep enough people at bay.

Suppliers are spread out; they have different credit policies; they have a number of accounts to manage. The company may be just one of several problem accounts. So they haven't been paid in a while. If they know the owner is in honest financial trouble, what can they do about it? Even if they went to court, how could they be paid? This line of reasoning keeps some suppliers out of court for long periods of time, especially if the owner has had a good long-term relationship with them. Nobody wants to see a company fail. Perhaps the supplier's chance of getting paid is better if a turnaround takes place than if it goes to court. Of course, if the owner has made an enemy out of everyone, then it is a different story. In the meantime, the company has been forced to pay cash for most of its purchases, which means that many suppliers are still making money on the account.

WHEN SHOULD YOU THROW IN THE TOWEL?

Courage and sheer determination, at some point, can get you in more trouble rather than less. Your corporation can protect you from personal bankruptcy, as long as you are not personally liable for specific liabilities. One good decision point, in terms of going into bankruptcy or continuing to fight it out, is when you have to sign suppliers' notes or some other large note personally. This is especially true when you are faced with past due IRS withholding, for which you and the officers of the company will be personally liable. Devastating as it is to walk away from a corporate failure, it is much more so to go into personal bankruptcy as well.

Another decision point is when the immediate outlook for reaching profitable operations is just not there. After your company has been incurring losses for many months or years, if (because of falling sales or because of an excess of fixed expense) you still cannot operate at a profit for the foreseeable future, then you should fold the company before incurring additional debt and further risk to yourself. I have seen some businesses go on for months, even years, when I thought it wasn't possible. I also have seen owners encumber themselves with personal liabilities and then lose everything in the bankruptcies of their businesses and themselves.

CHARACTERISTICS OF COMPANIES THAT TURNED AROUND

There are three characteristics I have seen in companies able to pull through a serious financial crisis. First, the owner was able to cut expenses substantially. There was a reasonably low level of fixed expenses—rents, leases, contracted expenses, etc.—in proportion to total expenses. Second, there was market demand for the company's goods or services. Sales were there, as long as the company could deliver. Combined with the expense cuts, this kind of opportunity can be attractive for a bank, because a clear case can be made that the loan will make the difference.

Third, the surviving companies had a hidden asset. In many cases this was real estate, which is carried on the books at the cost of acquisition but which can have a verifiable market value substantially greater. Sometimes a company may have had equipment with a higher resale value than the book value at which it was carried on the financial statements. In either case, the hidden equity provided the bank with a margin of bona fide collateral to support the emergency loan. Frequently this collateral was in the personal assets of the owner. Though there may be a strong case for a business turn-around, a bank must have collateral to act as protection if a high-risk loan is to be made.

Companies that have entered a bad loss period from a position of substantial stockholders' equity have a better chance of survival. The equity may exist because of several previous years of profits or because the company began with a substantial equity investment. Whatever the case, a strong starting position can leave the owner with some equity after the losses have been incurred. There should still be some collateral available for the bank to lend against, which means, in the banker's eyes, that it is making a risk loan to a company that still has a margin of stockholders' capital in the business.

The scenario for bail-out financing with a bank or with a finance company is as follows:

- The lender can see why the company got into trouble and how the owner has corrected the problems.
- There is a clear case that the turnaround from loss to profit has been made.
- The market demand for the product or services is strong.
- There is collateral for the loan.

SUMMARY

Jump on trouble early. This will keep losses from destroying your financial balance. The loss of financial balance means liabilities in excess of your ability to pay. It means that cash is so short you cannot conduct an orderly operation, which translates into declining sales just at the wrong time.

Fixing trouble depends on your ability to find out what's wrong. You may have to fight through some accounting problems that you have let build up for several years. The starting point is to admit your mistakes, which will point the way to the operational problems you will have to solve.

You must define the degree of trouble you are in. You must act decisively to cut expenses and to eradicate your operational problems, to turn your company around from a loss to a profit quickly. You must follow up to ensure that the turnaround sticks.

Be alert to cash-flow problems caused by the wrong kind of financing. In looking for bail-out money, remember Figure 11-1. Don't stage your requests end to end, but run them concurrently. Timing is crucial, and raising money in distress takes more time than you have. A good business plan, persuasively presented, is mandatory.

Your company can survive for longer than you think possible, as long as you have the will to do so. But watch the personal guarantees. Throw in the towel before you expose yourself, your officers, and your employees to excessive risks.

Business failure is an economic death, but not a personal one. Determined people have come back to lead successful lives after a business failure, and so can you. But deal with trouble early, and don't let it happen to you in the first place.

12

Don't Waste Success

YOUR OWN BUSINESS IS YOUR BEST TAX SHELTER

The First Taste of Success

After years of blood, sweat, and tears, you've achieved success. Profits have soared well beyond $100,000. Your first reward is a huge tax bite taken by Uncle Sam and the state.

The U.S. tax system is brutal to the newly emerging business. Federal and state combined, your increased profits will be taxed at about forty percent. More significantly, these taxes will be a large percentage of owner's equity, since retained earnings from previous years have been low. A strong equity is needed to borrow from the banks.

The first big tax year is a double whammy. Tax must be paid on last year plus an equal amount of estimated tax for the current year. The government siphons off your capital just when you need every nickel to continue expansion.

Beware of the First Advice

A host of advisors offer urgent advice. There are advantages to what they recommend:

- Pay yourself a large bonus. Buy a big house with lots of interest and taxes, which are deductible. The value of your house will increase.
- Set up profit-sharing and pension plans. These shelter retirement money for you and your employees.
- Buy insurance policies which shelter future annuities.
- Build or buy your own building. The rent which you pay yourself is deductible, while the building will increase in value over the years.

Beware of accepting any of these recommendations too quickly. I don't dispute the advantages of traditional tax management practices. Many of my clients employ them. But as an entrepreneur you must tend to first things first. None of these practices contributes directly to the productivity of your business.

Each technique requires the commitment of cash. With houses and buildings, the commitment is irrevocable. Though profit-sharing and pension plans are discretionary, they create the expectation of a commitment in the minds of the employees. Success is here today and gone tomorrow. Flexibility is the cornerstone of finance for a small business, which can drop like a rock with the business cycle.

The Best Tax Shelter

Ask yourself, "How can I invest profits in my operations today to produce increased sales and profits tomorrow?" In effect, the federal and state governments will underwrite forty cents of each profit dollar that you convert into an operating expense. The benefit of increased profits will be taxed in the future.

Profitability Is Power

An extra margin of profit enables you to make moves that can produce new products, improved management, increased efficiency, and greater customer awareness of your company. Marginal profits mean that every penny must be turned for day-to-day survival. Expenses must be curtailed at all times. Nothing can be done to build for the future.

Spending profits must be done intelligently. An entrepreneur walks the high wire of economic conditions. There is no safety net. Investments can be commitments or they can be discretionary. To make a commitment you must be certain that current profitability can be sustained indefinitely. Discretionary investments can be cancelled next year if business turns down.

Paying yourself a big bonus simply transfers the tax problem from your business to yourself. Before you commit to that bigger house to get interest deductions, take a look at the commitments you can make to build your business. Look beyond the obvious investments in equipment. Look at management.

Can you build future power by bringing on a sales manager, or operations manager, or R&D director, or controller today? You can absorb the learning curve of a new manager this year, with the feds and state underwriting forty percent. You can capitalize on his or her performance next year.

Put effort into developing your management team. Sometimes big profits this year can evaporate next year because you didn't have the management to continue the growth. The lower profits can coincide with the larger interest payments on that big new house.

There Is Such a Thing as Too Much Profit

Sometimes big profits signal that the management job isn't being done. Several years ago I was called by a frantic client who had just realized he'd make over $700,000 profit for the year. The tax bite would be horrendous. By slowing production on some key jobs, he was able to defer shipments to the following year, which wasn't good for short-term cash flow, but it moved some profit ahead.

But there was a deeper issue. This owner was burning out his employees and himself. He had no operations manager, no controller, and he was short a senior design engineer. Many people wore two hats. His office was a constant bottleneck. All this for the privilege of paying higher taxes.

The company's performance fell off the next year because the entire staff was exhausted and because many critical management tasks went undone since there was no manager to do them. Older and wiser, the owner filled some key spots, which enabled the company to regain its momentum.

Building staff is a commitment, not a discretionary decision. Hiring a senior design engineer from Seattle this year doesn't make it easy to lay him or her off next year. Other possible commitments should be reviewed before you take money out of operations to reduce taxes. Do you need new equipment? Should your computer hardware and software system be upgraded? Are your facilities adequate?

There are a host of powerful discretionary uses for profits; moves you can make this year to produce benefits next year. But if next year turns down, you can reduce or discontinue the program. Always consider the following options first.

Marketing

You can expend the creative budget for a new advertising campaign this year with the media blitz next year. Collateral materials can be purchased before year-end. Start now on long-range business development, such as trade shows or sales trips for new account prospecting. Perhaps this is the year to experiment with a sales rep, if you don't have one, or in working with sales trainees. Leave no stone unturned in developing your marketing base for future sales.

Research and development

Today's profits are the ideal source of funding for new-product development. The expense is incurred now; the products will generate future sales. In fact, the products you work on this year may be just what you'll need three years from now to keep sales going.

Employee education

A carefully planned program for enhancing the management and technical skills of your personnel will pay dividends in future productivity. I have seen one seminar turn a struggling manager into an effective one.

Financial Planning Is Crucial to Tax Planning

The ability to tap profit power comes from good planning. By the end of the first quarter, you should be able to make a rough estimate of what your profits will be for the year. At the end of six months you should have a pretty good idea. This comes from making a realistic profit plan, and then comparing results to the actual.

A timely estimate of year-end profits enables the owner to make the commitments and the discretionary expenditures in time to use a portion of this year's profits for future years' gain. If you don't know how profitable you are until late in the year, all you can do is take a big bonus or make contributions to profit plans. You're deriving short-term benefits but not creating long-term productivity.

THE ULTIMATE GOAL IS TO CREATE VALUE

What Is Your Business Worth?

The financial outcome of operating a business successfully is the creation of value. The business is worth something, and that something is usually much more than the stockholders' equity shown on the balance sheet. Stockholders' equity is merely the initial stock investment plus the accumulated retained earnings (net income after tax, net of dividends, which an entrepreneur never pays because of double taxation) since the inception of the business.

The true financial value of a corporation is what it can be sold for. Of course that's the catch, too, because for that value to mean something, at some point it has to be converted to cash. An owner of thousands of shares in AT&T could convert them to cash by calling a broker with instructions to sell. After costs, he or she would receive a check, out of which taxes would have to be paid on capital gains. An owner can't do that with the business, obviously. Yet the full value of the company may be hundreds of thousands of dollars, perhaps millions.

How Do You Get the Value?

One way to realize this value is to sell the business to another corporation or to an individual or group of individuals. Like anything in life, an owner won't be able to have the cake and eat it too, because there will be capital gains taxes on the profit. Half of $3.7 million, say, is still a lot of money. Of course, an installment sale can be set up, to spread out the profit over several years. However, spreading out the payments makes the owner a creditor of the company which is buying him or her out. If the buyer is an AT&T or IBM, great, but more than one entrepreneur has lost a substantial part of the sales price when a less-than-solid buyer proved to be a bad credit risk. Selling out to people who are to run the company after the owner retires is especially hazardous. Will they be able to keep the profits up and cash flow well managed while the owner is in Florida depending on the annual payment from the old company to make retirement financially sound?

In acquiring a small business, astute management teams know that they are really acquiring the skills, drive, and determination of the owner. The owner has made the business what it is today, and the owner is the person with the best chance to further develop the potential in the immediate future. For this reason it makes sense to require the owner to stay on for at least five years after the acquisition, until the surviving company has developed the management capabilities to take over. A profitable sale may not let the owner off the hook; he or she may have to run the company successfully for several years before sailing around the world in the new boat.

Another way to convert ownership into cash is to go public. An owner is not selling shares in the offering, but after the offering has been subscribed there is a market in which the shares can be sold. It is unlikely that the owner could dump all the shares on the market at any one time, since trading in small-company equities is usually a modest affair. However, with a marketplace, the owner has the opportunity to convert shares to cash at a known value. Again, there is the cake and the eating. Going public creates an entirely different world for the sole owner. Now there is a real board of directors. Now there are stockholder relations to worry about. The company's performance will dramatically affect the market price of the stock, to everyone's advantage or disadvantage. Some entrepreneurs thrive in this environment, others are miserable. Some entrepreneurs find the value of their stock increasing in future years, others find the value declining, and with it, possibly millions in initial value. Besides, there are a limited number of small companies operating in the right kinds of markets and with the right kinds of products or services to attract this kind of attention from the investor community.

There is a choice between the extremes of taking the maximum out of the company to spend and to invest personally or of leaving the maximum in to build up the value of the business. Personal preference must be weighed against the best economic opportunities. If the company is a real money-maker, but not attractive to other companies or to other individuals, does it make sense to leave extra cash in the operation? It does if there are significant growth opportunities which will generate a return for the owner. In the absence of rapid growth, the chances of creating value with outside investments are probably greater. On the other hand, if it is a growing company which is highly attractive to potential buyers, then the owner is diluting the potential gain by raking off the maximum for personal use. The value of the company to investors is enhanced by the soundness of the financial position—as measured in the fullest sense by the company's profitability, liquidity, and financial position (debt-to-equity ratio or similar measures). The owner's ability to develop the full marketing potential is strengthened if the company has maximum resources with which to work.

RAISING VENTURE CAPITAL

Growth Creates a Need for Funds

Success creates needs for funds. Sometimes the opportunities which come from aggressive development of the product or service require more funds than can be generated from the combination of borrowing and retained earnings. In these situations, venture capital beckons. The owner must address a number of practical considerations when evaluating whether venture capital is the right thing to do:

- How close are the company's products to the market? Some entrepreneurs are trying to raise capital to support products that still require major development before going to market. It takes a very compelling idea to attract venture capital into a company with a large gap between the development of a new product and sales. An attractive new product which is already producing sales orders is a better bet to attract venture funds.
- Is the product or service potentially glamorous to venture capitalists? In many respects the venture capital market acts like a fashion business. Some products are in; some are out; the chance of getting interest from venture capital sources depends on whether these products appear to have the zing, both to attract equity money and to generate enough growth in sales and profits to create a substantial return on the investors' money within a few years.

- Is the window currently open for small-company equities? There are always small companies successfully raising equity, but some periods are active small-company markets while others are definite dry periods. During the active periods, money is chasing investment opportunities, sometimes beyond reason. Dry periods are very bleak for any but the most glamorous opportunities, especially if the company happens to be in the industry which fast money foolishly chased in recent years.
- Why are the funds needed? Raising venture capital puts outsiders inside the company, either as individual stockholders or as institutional investors, such as a small-business investment corporation. The entrepreneur will have to produce to keep the new owners happy. That means that the new money must be employed productively, with sales growth and profits the consequence. Some development time will be allowed for a glamorous, high-tech company, but even they must produce results before too many years have passed. I have seen many financial statements of companies which raised, say, $1.5 million, only to lose that much in the following couple of years, placing the owner back in the position of trying to build sales and profits on a shoestring budget. A secondary offering is more fun for everyone if it is made to add support for an explosive growth in sales and profits.

Some Realities of Raising Venture Capital

Timing is critical to a venture capital effort. The goal is to raise equity at the crest of a series of high-growth and increasingly profitable years. That kind of track record combined with a good-looking balance sheet will bring in the maximum amount of money for the minimum amount of ownership sold. Unlike debt, the cost of which is interest, the cost of venture capital is the percentage of ownership given up. Perhaps ten percent given up to get a partner seems academic early in the game, but if the company becomes worth $10 million sometime in the future, that ten percent will mean a million dollars more or less for the owner.

Many companies have run short of funds before their growth curve put them in a strong bargaining position for raising equity. If the owner must have cash to get the products or services to market, then a larger chunk of the company will have to change hands. When I asked a well-known venture capitalist how much ownership he would take for an investment, he said, "Anywhere from five to fifty percent depending on the deal." The smaller the investment being raised, the more expensive it is proportionately. The legal work, warrants, and other costs of a private or public placement are a much smaller percentage of a $2.5 million deal than they are of a $500,000 deal.

One of the most bewildering realities for the entrepreneur trying to raise venture capital is the vagueness of the venture capital market. Arranging bank financing takes place within a highly defined marketplace. The banks are clearly visible; the owner can pick among small, large, medium; and the procedures for making a loan application are well understood by the experienced person. In contrast, the venture capital market is scattered, varied, and confusing. There are investment banking firms which specialize in small-company equities, but they are not household names. There may not be one in the community, almost assuredly not if the business is located outside a major finance center. The Merryl Lynches won't listen to an equity deal unless it's in the millions.

The most visible venture capital sources are the small-business investment companies, which are scattered around the country. SBICs have been instrumental in helping many small companies grow by making packages of debt and equity available at just the right time. The debt portions of these packages are usually subordinated to bank borrowing, which helps the business arrange for additional loans. Frequently a little SBIC money can go a long way. However, SBICs have to make both a return on equity and interest income. SBICs raise money through bonds floated by the Treasury on behalf of the Small Business Administration, which means they must have current income to defray interest and other operating costs. That income has to come from the companies in their portfolio. For many owners the higher cost of SBIC financing is offset because the high visibility of SBICs enables entrepreneurs to find them and because the money is available when private placements and similar straight-equity deals are not.

It can take an inordinate amount of time to raise venture capital. There are always leads: investments bankers; brokers and money finders who work for a fee of from one to five percent of the dollars raised; SBICs; wealthy investors; rich foreigners; friends; that rich uncle in Texas the owner hasn't seen in fifteen years. One of my clients raised $2.5 million in a public offering. The funds hit the bank about a week before the company would have gone down the tubes. It was over a year from the time we began looking for venture capital to that successful offering. Presentations were made to other companies, SBICs, investment bankers, Arab oil millionaires, you name it. Each introduction to a party who had the ability to invest the capital and who expressed initial interest had to be followed up aggressively, because you can never tell at the outset which one will eventually work out. They all operate alike . . . there is an expression of interest; a desire to look at the plan; some time to think it over; perhaps a second or third visit to the company; then a last-minute loss of interest.

One of the most difficult venture capital jobs is trying to raise money from a larger company. For a well-organized small company, the elapsed time from the decision to go after a new product, to the development, to the implementation of the marketing plan, to the on-line selling effort can be a matter of months. A large company can take a year or years before a similar process is completed. A series of department heads and technical experts must receive presentations and make analyses. These investigations must be written up and presented to various committees. The committees must report their findings to the authorized executive who must make the final decision, frequently on the basis of policy (political?) issues that may be unrelated to the merits of the investment in question. By the time the larger company has decided, the smaller company has lost its marketing chance, has gone broke from the lack of funds, has given up the effort. Any entrepreneur negotiating with a larger company must anticipate the long life cycle of the large-company decision-making process.

A Persuasive Business Plan Is Mandatory

In raising venture capital, a persuasive business plan is an absolute necessity. Venture capital sources invariably ask to see the business plan before entering into any further discussions. This means that the decision to talk will be made on an evaluation of the plan, so it had better be a good one. The applicant should be aware that the venture capitalist sees literally hundreds of proposals for every one which becomes a deal. That means the plan will have to stand out to have a chance. A successful venture capital plan differs from a bank presentation in several key respects:

- The marketing section is crucial. The appeal of the product or service, which the company's growth hinges on and for which the capital is being requested, will determine whether or not the money will be raised. This product appeal must be backed up by a sound marketing plan which demonstrates the owner's ability to conceive of and organize a first-class effort.
- It is important to show that the management team has the experience and ability to achieve profitable and exceptional sales growth.
- The use of the proceeds must be spelled out. The soundness of the plan to employ the new money, including the appropriateness of the types of investments for venture capital, is crucial.
- A five-year projection of revenues and expenses is the primary financial exhibit, in addition to the financial statements and a summary of sales growth and profitability for recent years. The long-range forecast should demonstrate how the company can produce sales and profits that would make an equity investment worthwhile. Venture money needs to increase substantially in value within three to four years, though in reality this frequently doesn't happen.

HOW TO SELL YOUR COMPANY

First, Establish Your Price

Selling a business is a way of converting the value that has been created into cash. But how much is the business worth? There are three basic ways to value a company. Book value is the total stockholders' equity—common stock, surplus, and retained earnings—as taken from the balance sheet. It is an accounting number, the difference between the total of all liabilities and the total of all assets. The advantages of book value is that it is easily calculated, and it is a number which everyone can agree to, although even book value can be disputed if there are assets of questionable value, such as bad receivables, stale inventory, or intangible assets such as good will. On the other hand, book value has little relationship to a company's true value, either to the owner or to a potential investor, because there are far more important factors to consider than the static accounting equity, such as market potential, growth trends, rates of profitability, all of which will culminate in a potential return on the buyer's investment.

Liquidation value is an estimate of what a company would be worth if liquidated. How much would be collected on receivables? How much would inventory sell for? How much for fixed assets? Usually liquidation value is less than book value, because most assets won't liquidate for the amount carried on the balance sheet. On rare occasions a major asset may sell for more than book value, but the relationship of liquidation to the value of the company for acquisition is vague.

Calculating a market value for a company is the basis for negotiating a sale price in an acquisition. The owner may never show the calculations to the buyer because, ultimately, the price is a matter of horse trading over how low the owner will go versus how high the other party will go. In the give-and-take between the owner's price and theirs, it is of great benefit to have an economic analysis which establishes a market value. If the potential buyer's maximum is too far below the value established by the owner's valuation, then he or she should walk away from the deal, unless really desperate to sell. In that case, as always when a financial transaction is ill timed, the company will have to be sold cheap.

How to Establish Market Value Based on Future Performance

Table 12-1 shows a straightforward concept for establishing a market value. Estimating market value is a speculative process, but a rationale can be used to provide logic and consistency in arriving at some numbers. The value for Exotic Tech is established by looking at the five years following the point at which the acquisition is being discussed: 1993 through 1997. Sales are expected to grow by thirty-five percent annually. Direct costs are projected at sixty percent of sales, which makes the gross profit forty percent. Since selling and general and administrative expenses are projected at thirty percent of sales, the net income before tax is projected at ten percent of sales. All these percentages should be consistent with the company's recent experience, as adjusted by any known changes in operations. After application of federal and state taxes, the net income for each year is as shown.

TABLE 12-1 EXOTIC TECH, INC., VALUATION
FISCAL YEARS 1993–1997

	1993	1994	1995	1996	1997
Sales	5,000,000	6,750,000	9,112,500	12,301,875	16,607,531
Direct Costs	3,000,000	4,050,000	5,467,500	7,381,125	9,964,519
Gross Profit	2,000,000	2,700,000	3,645,000	4,920,750	6,643,013
Selling, Gen. & Admin.	1,500,000	2,025,000	2,733,750	3,690,563	4,982,259
Net Income before Tax	500,000	675,000	911,250	1,230,188	1,660,753
Income Tax	230,000	317,500	435,625	595,094	810,377
Net Income	270,000	357,500	475,625	635,094	850,377
Present Value Factor @ 10%	0.90909	0.82645	0.75131	0.68301	0.62092
Present Value Net Income	245,454	295,456	357,342	433,775	528,016
Average income			372,009		
Company Value @ 5×			1,860,043		
Company Value @ 10×			3,720,086		
Company Value @ 15×			5,580,130		

However, the $528,000 of net income in 1997 is not equal to the same amount of dollars today, since the potential buyer could invest that amount now and have more dollars by 1989. The present value factor reduces the value of future dollars to a present equivalent, assuming some annual percentage return the buyer could make on an investment. For this example I chose ten percent (you can get present value factors for different rates of return from your CPA). Now we have five net income figures expressed in current dollars. This gives the business the benefit of future earning power, but recognizes the position of the potential buyer by reducing future values to present values. The average of the five incomes is $372,000.

We need to multiply that net income by some number to derive a market value, because that's the way the market price of stock works—on a price-earnings ratio. If we use a multiple of five, the company is worth almost $1.9 million; if we use the multiple of fifteen, the company is worth almost $5.6 million. Obviously the multiple makes a big difference. The rationale for the multiple comes from what a company in the industry, with roughly the same chances for growth and profitability as the company being valued, would command. Ranges of multiples can be obtained from brokers, possibly some bankers or CPAs. If industry standards are unavailable, then the owner will just have to wing it. Some industries have rules of thumb which are always applied in the sale of a company, possibly based on sales volume or some other special factor.

Your Negotiations with Buyers Are Horse Trading

Whatever the case, the final value comes down to horse trading. How anxious is the owner to sell? How anxious are the investors to buy? How good a negotiator is the owner?

Once a value is agreed to, there are other factors to be negotiated. Does the owner want cash, or will he or she accept a down payment plus installments? Getting cash creates a horrendous tax problem because the seller gets all the capital gains in one year. Taking installment payments turns the owner into a creditor, which has the risks I mentioned earlier. If the buyer is financially strong, the risk is small; if it is a marginal company, the risk is great. However, the marginal company may not be able to pay cash for the full amount. If the seller has to give a substantial amount of credit, the loan should be secured. If the seller takes the stock which has been sold as collateral, he or she can reassume control of the company if there is a default on the notes or if the company falls below a minimum acceptable financial condition, as expressed by some key ratios. A good banker can help draw up a loan agreement which would give some sensible protection.

However, an important question remains. What is expected of the seller after the acquisition? Smart managers of larger companies which are acquiring a small business know they are buying the owner, not the company. If they let the owner go immediately after the sale, the company will fall to pieces in short order. After all, the owner is the one who held it together for all these years. It won't run so well without him or her, until the buyers can get organized and learn the business. For this reason, many acquiring companies will require an owner to sign an employment agreement for up to five years after the sale. The owner will have to decide how badly he or she wants out, as opposed to how important it is to get the cash from a good sale.

In some acquisitions the acquiring company will negotiate a lower down payment, based on Exotic Tech's multiple of five, for example, after which the owner can get a piece of the higher multiple if the company performs up to the projections during the five years after the acquisition. The owner of Exotic Tech would be offered $1.9

million for the sale but could earn the full $5.6 million by 1997, if the projections were achieved. Frequently this kind of "earn out" is the only way an owner can get the higher multiple, depending on the relative bargaining power of buyer versus seller.

HOW TO MAKE AN ACQUISITION

Again, Start with the Value to You

The methods of valuing a business to be acquired are the same as valuing one's own business; the roles are reversed. But the first question to ask is what purpose the acquisition will serve. Is it a diversification into another market? Are the skills of another entrepreneur being acquired? Is sales volume being added? Is the owner taking advantage of a deal which just fell into his or her lap? Whatever the case, there are some important points to keep in mind:

- The owner should keep the acquisition within an industry about which he or she has some ability to judge the market. Studies of major acquisitions have shown that companies did better when they acquired other companies which were in markets their management knew something about. Gross departures, say a sewing machine company acquiring an ice cream company, ended in trouble because top management had trouble understanding how the other industry worked.
- An equitable deal works out best in the long run, assuming the other owner is kept on board after the acquisition. The buyer will be relying on that person to produce results. If there is dissatisfaction with the deal after the fact, then the incentive for that person to produce will be damaged. Too sharp a deal cut at first can reduce the results afterward.
- Will the selling entrepreneur stay motivated as an employee? It's one thing to grow a company when it's yours, but will it mean the same when someone else is the boss?
- Don't pay too much for the chance to own another company. If the price goes too high, the chances are that there won't be a good return on the investment.

Acquisitions Need to Be Financed

Usually a buyer pays more for a company than its book value (total assets minus total liabilities). The total acquisition price, including this market value, must be financed in some way. During the 1980s, financing of market value, as opposed to financing assets, led to the junk-bond craze.

The presumption was that increases in cash flow from growth would provide adequate coverage for repaying principal and interest. Previously, debt was used primarily to finance asset values, exclusive of any market value considerations. Market value financing was the province of venture capital, which usually involved a mixture of debt and equity.

The 1990s are proving that future cash flows often are not sufficient to pay back large amounts of debt used to finance market values. Nevertheless, most acquisitions have to be leveraged buyouts, which means that the payback of the financing for the deal is to come from the cash flow of the company being acquired. Otherwise, a reasonable price for the seller could not be financed.

Beware of "hot money"

Financing an acquisition can be hazardous for two reasons. The first hazard comes from financing the market value paid to the seller. Since market value is not true collateral, it lies outside traditional bank financing. Enter venture capital financing, which is money looking for speculative, therefore high-yield, investments.

Venture capital funds are "hot money" in the sense that very high rates of return are sought over short time periods. Typically, venture capitalists structure deals to earn returns on investment of thirty percent or more over three to five years. Usually the funding of acquisitions involves principal and interest that is to be amortized according to a set schedule, with warrants or rights that increase the return to thirty percent.

Too often the acquiring company winds up working for the venture capitalist. By the time the buyer pays off the acquisition financing, with its thirty percent return, not much return is left for the buyer. Sometimes the amortization of the debt is so severe the buyer defaults.

At this point anything can happen. On the good side, more reasonable amortization schedules can be negotiated. However this is usually for a price (i.e., more ownership for the venture capitalist). The price for more venture money and for rescheduled amortization schedules under distress can transfer so much additional ownership to the venture capital source(s) that the buyer loses control of his or her company.

The second hazard comes from using the assets of both the acquired company and the buyer to finance the deal. Too often this acquisition financing exhausts the credit capacity of the surviving company. Subsequently, any cash-flow needs beyond what can be funded from operations are a serious problem. They can't be financed. If you hit good growth opportunities, you may have to pass them up for lack of financing. If you hit a slump, the bank may not be there to help out because all of your collateral was used to make the acquisition.

Productive versus unproductive money

Money used to finance market value is unproductive money. Productive money is used to purchase assets that create sales or reduce costs. Market value is a return to the seller. A productive asset or an increase in efficiency is not created by purchasing market value. In reality, buying market value is a drain on your corporate resources. It is made worthwhile by giving you the opportunity to add new markets to your existing position.

To negotiate the hazards of financing an acquisition, you must keep the price in line with the true earning power and cash flow of the company you acquire, in light of what you can do with it working from the resources of your own company. Be careful to keep the financing within what you can afford to pay. Make sure you leave enough credit capacity for the surviving company to meet working capital and growth needs subsequent to the acquisition. If you don't, you'll strangle.

Sometimes the financing hazard is addressed by having the seller hold notes for a substantial portion of the purchase price. Amortization of these notes is usually based on normal principal and interest schedules, without exorbitant rate-of-return requirements. The cash paid to the seller beyond the down payment is often based on an earn-out schedule, which requires the acquired operations to meet performance goals. If the performance isn't there, the seller doesn't get the money.

In the Final Analysis

A successful acquisition is a combination of marketing know-how, intelligent financial analysis, and good psychology. Many companies, large and small, have regretted the day they made an acquisition. On the other hand, sales can be picked up in a desirable new market at less cost than a start-up. If the owner understands why he or she is buying and why the other party is selling, if the price is right, if the owner can enter the deal with eyes wide open to the amount of time and risk involved for both the owner and the management team, then there is a business decision to make. Like any other major decision, the owner will find out how good it was after the fact.

SUMMARY

A successful business generates annual income for the owner as well as a value in itself. But the owner must capitalize on success when it happens. That high net income runs head-on into forty percent tax brackets, both corporate and personal. Thus, good financial planning on both accounts is necessary, to be prepared. How can an owner invest company dollars today to produce sales and profits next year? What trade-off does the entrepreneur want to make between maximizing the growth and net income of the business, as opposed to taking the maximum out for personal use? What kind of lifestyle does the owner want? How much personal income does the owner want to invest to create assets for retirement? How should those assets be sheltered from high tax brackets?

The degree of right or wrong in the answers to these questions depends on the goals of the owner. Someone who wants the biggest yacht in the marina may not be willing to build the maximum value in the company. As long as the owner realizes this trade-off of corporate value for lifestyle, it's his or her choice. If the owner is unaware of the loss of corporate value, he or she may live to regret the decisions of earlier years.

The value of a company should be converted to cash when it best suits the owner's advantage. A sale can be made to another company;

the owner can go public; there can be a sale to other individuals. Each of these alternatives has pros and cons. At the same time, there is a range of options to maximize the owner's personal income in the future, including qualified and nonqualified plans. The business can be its own tax shelter, to include the possibility of the owner owning the building and renting it back to the company.

In raising venture capital or making an acquisition, timing is the name of the game. If the move is made when the company is in a series of growing and profitable years, the cost of raising capital or acquiring another business will be much less, and the value made when selling out will be near the maximum. In raising venture capital, a good business plan is essential. This plan differs in some important respects from a good presentation for a bank loan.

The same kind of sensible management planning that brought success to the company can be applied to capitalizing on that success. In this way the owner can enjoy the fruits of his or her labors, not only for the present, but in future years.

13

_____

Manage Growth—Don't Let Growth Manage You

SUCCESS MEANS HANDLING THE STAGES OF GROWTH

We talk about marketing position; we talk about cash flow. We plan equipment purchases; we develop production schedules. These are simply the resources that people move around. There is a trap in thinking of these things as the business. A business is what people do. A financial statement is only numbers to approximate what people have done during an arbitrarily selected accounting period. Production schedules are an idea which someone has had about how they would like things to go, but a schedule by itself won't make things happen that way. The production schedule isn't the production line any more than the sales plan is the sales effort.

What makes things happen is a complex activity, even for a small business, made up of the owner, the managers, the employees, the customers, the competitors, the creditors, the governments (tax departments and regulators), and the public (say the company truck runs into somebody's car). The owner tries to orchestrate all this in a

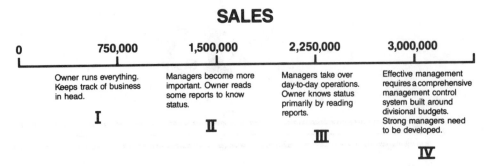

Figure 13-1   Stages of growth.

constantly changing situation, which is sometimes moving ahead, sometimes falling behind; sometimes coming into control, sometimes going out of control. To be successful the owner must be effective in managing others. In the process, the owner also must come to terms with himself or herself, at each of the major stages of the company's history.

These stages represent the most difficult problem with which an owner will have to contend—the stages of growth, a rough outline of which is shown in Figure 13-1. As the company passes through each stage, the owner must adopt new management approaches, not in a sudden shift to brand-new ideas, but in an evolutionary way. Those owners who can sense the need for change, who can visualize what the changes should be, who can then implement them without disrupting the company's daily efficiency, will move successfully from one stage to the next. Those owners who cannot deal with this kind of management change will find their companies stuck in a certain stage of growth, from which they will find it very difficult to move.

STAGE I: THE ONE-PERSON SHOW

At the beginning the owner is involved in almost everything— opening the mail, keeping the books, buying product, greeting customers, performing the work on contracts or jobs, supervising the employee or employees. The owner knows the sales volume, because he or she drops the receipts into the till or takes the deposit slips to the bank. If the owner isn't selling directly to the customers, he or she is standing right behind the person who does. The quality of the products or services delivered is assured because the owner makes it so personally. Employees are motivated because they are working side by side with the boss. The owner literally sees whether operations are profitable or not, because the money coming in and the money going out passes through his or her hands.

Early Problems

Early in the game the greatest pressure for the owner is dealing with the long hours and low personal income, both of which are necessary to start up from scratch. According to the statistics, this is a dangerous time: Fifty percent of businesses fail during their first year. From what I have seen, many of the businesses which have failed this quickly have had one of the following problems:

- The concept of the business was bad to begin with. Either the store location was poor or the demand for the service was too low or the only available contract was won by another firm.
- The owner was just not good at business. Even the most basic decisions about what to spend money on and what not to were bungled. There was no insight into how to promote the business or sell to potential customers.
- The owner started with so little capital that the business was never able to get going. Though this is an often cited cause of business failure, perhaps a practical side of undercapitalization is not fully understood. Inadequate funding frequently results because the would-be entrepreneur had limited personal assets to pledge for a bank loan. Some owners start their businesses with only a few thousand dollars, but the equity in their homes enables them to establish a bank line of credit to finance the early stages of the business. Another owner may start with the same few thousand, but without enough equity in a home or without a home to begin with; they will be unable to arrange enough financing to carry their business in the early days.

Dealing with the problems in Stage I, then, are a matter of personal effort. Did the owner begin with a viable business idea? Did the owner start off with enough business skill to survive the first year? Were expenses kept at reasonable levels? Did the owner have enough financial resources, both in start-up cash and in personal assets, to act as collateral for the initial bank loans? Was the owner willing to work long hours at the low pay necessary to make it through the lean times? Fifty percent of those who start businesses can answer these questions with a yes, while fifty percent would have to answer many of them with no.

How Long Does Stage I Last?

How long a business stays in Stage I depends on many factors. Some companies never leave. A one-person repair shop, for example, or a small dress shop may operate year after year without ever growing out of the first stage. At the other extreme, a tightly wound high-tech firm may go through three or four stages of growth in a couple of years. Some businesses languish in Stage I for several years only to explode into the next few stages very quickly.

The idea of stages of growth is just that—a widely held observation that the management requirements of a business change over time as the business grows. The actual process varies enormously. Some businesses develop millions in sales, especially in some kinds of distribution industries, with the owner still personally involved in every phase of operations while working with a small staff. A personal services firm may develop layers of management, with the owner acting as a manager of managers by the time sales reach a million.

Generally speaking, I have seen many small businesses begin to phase out of Stage I and into Stage II somewhere between $500,000 and $1 million in sales. When this will actually happen depends on the growth of the market, the owner's growth objectives, and the type of industry involved. Rather than sales volume or length of time, the real clue to the transition from the first stage to the next is how the owner feels about the business on a day-to-day basis.

If the owner feels overloaded with tasks; if the owner feels—based on the number of tasks left undone—that he or she will never get to some critical priorities; if the sales volume begins to slip because of what the owner hasn't been able to do; or if profits begin to dip for the same reasons, then the business has gotten to the point where the owner must change his or her basic approach to management. The ongoing job of management has gone beyond what one person can do efficiently. Another critical tipoff is when the owner begins to be surprised by the results—either sales are much less or much more than expected; profits are way off from what the owner anticipated; customers are complaining about things the owner is completely unaware of—all signs that the owner can no longer manage the business by the seat of the pants.

At the point of needing a manager, the one-person operator can experience some stress and anxieties. If another person is to have responsibilities, can they be trusted? Might they steal from the company? Can someone who isn't family be trusted? Would they apply the same standards to their job that the owner has? Employees don't seem willing to learn from their mistakes; they don't care as much about the quality of work; how can an employee be a good manager? On the other hand, some owners can be concerned about becoming too dependent on a good manager. What will happen if they leave? These psychological difficulties frequently are major stumbling blocks to an entrepreneur who is faced with the end of doing everything himself or herself and the beginning of having a manager.

STAGE II: MANAGERS APPEAR ON THE SCENE

The Problems That Begin Stage II

Where does the management process start to break down between Stages I and II? One of the most common problems is trouble with information. As a business grows, the owner discovers that the progress in sales and profits becomes harder to judge. Where once the amount of cash in the till at a certain time of year was a reliable measure, it doesn't hold up anymore. The same is true in the difference between receivables and payables. Without a glance at a financial statement, many owners used to know that they would be profitable as soon as sales exceeded a certain amount for the year. Now growth has distorted these tried-and-true measures, and the owner doesn't know where the business stands.

Like it or not, the owner will have to study financial statements more frequently. This may require a reorganization of the accounting department. Perhaps a full-charge bookkeeper is needed—a person who can keep a general ledger, draw off a trial balance, and prepare a financial statement. Many experienced bookkeepers can do this work; a formally trained accountant is not always required, but a full-charge bookkeeper may cost twice as much as the regular bookkeeper who can only post to accounts. Perhaps the need for better financial information will require adding assistants for an already existing full-charge bookkeeper. If an outside accounting service is being used, a better service may be required, or perhaps the time has come to move the books in house. The proliferation of accounting data in the company may require the purchase of a computer system, a big step in itself. Whatever the case, the owner must have more frequent, more timely, and better prepared information about the business. Owners whose businesses have grown into Stage II, but who persist in using gut feelings to measure their financial condition, are frequently the ones who wind up in bankruptcy.

A second problem area of growth is sales. Many owners bring in most of the sales themselves during the early years of the business. Their skill as salespeople creates success, along with some significant problems. Each salesperson, even the best, has some limit to the amount of sales they can generate, depending on the industry. Once an owner has reached this personal sales limit, the company has also reached its limit, unless some changes are made. An obvious step would be to add sales personnel. But though the owner may be a good salesperson, he or she may not be a good sales manager. In creating a sales force, can the owner make the switch from direct sales to sales management? With the owner off the street, will this mean that sales will go down as sales expenses go up? The new sales forces better produce in a hurry to make up the difference.

The simple if physically exhausting sales effort of Stage I is becoming the more complicated and more expensive effort of Stage II. Salespeople must be interviewed, hired, trained, planned for, supervised. Incentive programs need to be established, auto allowances set up, draws against commissions considered—you name it. As a consequence, some businesses remain stuck at the owner's personal sales limit, while others go beyond that limit, depending on the owner's ability to move from the direct sales effort to effective sales management.

A third problem area is operations. Many businesses are built around the owner's skills as an operator, whether it be in manufacturing, electronics design, graphic arts, air conditioning/heating installation, or computer systems design. The owner's reputation as a practitioner in the field draws the first customers. The owner's performance on the job creates the customer satisfaction that results in reorders and the word-of-mouth advertising about the hot new company everybody should try.

As the company grows, it will reach a limit defined by the amount of work the owner can personally do and the drawing power of the owner's reputation. Then the owner is caught in a two-pronged trap. If he or she is doing the work, then selling must take a back seat, because there will be no time to sell, or, if someone is hired to sell for the owner, that salesperson will have to operate without much supervision while the owner grinds out the work. Unsupervised small-company salespeople frequently turn out to be unproductive. By the same token, any increased volume will reach the owner's personal production capacity. If the business is to grow beyond that point, the owner will have to turn work over to some assistants, which some owners have trouble doing. Will the new workers be able to produce the same quality? Their work pace is so slow, it seems that the owner can produce more work in the time wasted in trying to supervise a bunch of other people.

The Stage II Barriers to Success

If the company is ever to reach Stage II, the owner will have to get out of the shop, to manage the efforts of other production workers, as well as to develop the added sales effort necessary to reach new sales levels. Here were come to another of the major psychological barriers to successful growth. Does the owner truly want to become more of a manager, less of a technician? Many an electronic engineer, microbiologist, top tradesman, or whatever has grown a company to the threshold of Stage II, only to find that becoming a business manager held limited appeal. There the company has remained, as perhaps it should have, with the owner continuing as a happy technician rather than a frustrated manager. Problems have come when the owner chases growth while trying to stay divorced from the management of the business. Hiring someone else to do the management usually doesn't work.

Some of the major stumbling blocks to a smooth transition from doing everything oneself to working with other people to get things done are as follows:

- Many owners misunderstand the true meaning of delegation. They will turn over a phase of operations to an individual, with the assumptions that this will take care of things. There is little, if any, follow-up. This is especially true of functions which are unfamiliar to the owner, such as accounting for a sales-oriented owner; sales for a technical owner; production for a financially oriented owner. Problems can fester and grow for months, even years, before they become so bad that the owner finds out about them. At this point, the company may have suffered some serious damage. In the process of delegating to managers, the owner must establish from the beginning how he or she will follow up on the progress of that phase of the company's operations.

• The mirror image of the lack of follow-up is the owner who has trouble letting go of the day-to-day management of many phases of the company. Managers are frustrated and ineffective when the owner steps in to make even the most minor decisions. The owner becomes the biggest bottleneck in the company, because everything must wait for his or her decision.

• Early in the phasing from Stage I to Stage II the owner is caught between the need to add managers to operate more effectively, and the need to keep the overhead down due to a thin profit margin. What is needed are carefully selected changes—a new manager here, later a new manager there, in those places where growth will be stimulated or efficiencies magnified. Once again financial planning is crucial. Laying out a profit plan, with estimated sales and carefully budgeted expenses, can give the owner a good picture of the effect of the new management before the decisions are made. The analysis can cut both ways. Jack Sheridan would have been wise to add management support early in the year when his company had ballooned in profitability. Conversely, many are the owners who added layers of management only to find that their company had no chance of being profitable with so much overhead.

STAGE III: THE OWNER STEPS OUT OF THE DAY-TO-DAY

The Owner Must Develop New Skills

Depending on the kind of business, growth beyond $2 million in sales purchases the owner out of day-to-day contact with many phases of the operation. There is simply too much going on. In Stage II the owner was still in touch with daily activity, even though managers were being developed—a half-in, half-out position. In Stage III the owner is completely out of contact with many activities. There may be some employees the owner won't even see during the course

of a day. The success of the company depends both on the performance of middle managers, who are now the ones in touch with daily
activities, and on the owner's ability to work effectively with these
managers.

The owner will learn the status of the company on a second-
hand basis, either from what the managers tell him or her or from
the financial and operating reports. In this stage some kind of management control book or a series of reports on the critical phases of
the company—sales, cost controls, cash flow, inventories, etc.—is of
great importance. Even more so, the owner's ability to engage managers in an ongoing dialogue about progress in their areas is crucial
to the company's growth and profitability. The effective owner often
uses a good reporting system as part of this dialogue.

Stage III is when communication problems become more apparent. These come in the form of misunderstandings between the
owner and managers. Misunderstandings also take place between
the managers. As a consequence, important things aren't getting
done, or they aren't getting done on time, or they aren't getting done
properly. Previously, an owner could step in personally to solve the
problem, but now the company is too big for that. The owner can't
step in here, because another problem is going on there. The owner
who still tries to solve the problems directly is like the juggler in the
circus who is balancing five plates on the ends of five sticks, running
madly back and forth trying to keep them all spinning. If an owner
gets involved in making decisions for the managers, the chances are
that the managers will not make decisions on their own. The owner
winds up managing the departments over the bodies that sit in the
department managers' chairs. If the owner is to get things done, he
or she must get them done through other people.

Effective work from the managers starts with the boss. If the
boss doesn't have his or her management act together, then the
managers won't have their management acts together either. It is
surprising how often the owner's management shortcomings set the
tone for everyone. Owners who procrastinate, for example, find their
managers procrastinating. "Smith never takes the initiative to get
something done!" Well, Smith figures that if he pushes something
ahead it will only sit on the boss's desk for a couple of weeks anyway,
so . . . .

One of the reasons why some owners procrastinate about dealing with management issues is a fear of confronting the managers.
Confrontations can be extremely uncomfortable. An owner may be

afraid of his or her own temper getting out of hand. Another owner can be afraid that a key manager may quit if pressed too hard on an issue. Ironically, in this stage of growth, the managers are subject to the same concerns about managing that the owner has been. Can they trust their employees to do the job? Will someone steal something out from under them? Managers can get so focused on getting the job done, much of the work being produced by themselves, that they lose sight of how to get the employees to produce. Managers aren't really managing programs, they are managing people. Many managers are unaware of ways to motivate their employees. They miss opportunities to gain from employee participation. They neglect ways of promoting an atmosphere for growth and advancement of those who work for them, missing chances for their own growth and advancement in the process.

Some Realities in Dealing with Managers

In managing managers, there are some realities which many entrepreneurs don't come to terms with. The result can be years of frustration, without a remedy. A complaint I hear time and again is, "How can people be so dumb? Sam should have made that call! It's as plain as the nose on your face. Yet he didn't do it. Why? How can I run a business if I have to do my managers' thinking for them?" This complaint addresses a nest of issues. To begin with, a manager is not sitting in the owner's chair. What seems perfectly clear to the owner may not be so clear to someone who sees only part of the picture. Sam doesn't realize that this call is going to trigger a whole series of events, which is what makes it so high on the boss's priority list. He may have put some other action ahead of it which made sense to him at the time, given his view of the company.

But let's assume that Sam did fully understand the priorities yet still didn't make the call. We have arrived at the knots of human behavior which make the world go around. Why do people do what they do or not do what they don't do? Entrepreneur after entrepreneur faces these questions as their businesses grow. Those who can get to the root of it continue to grow profitably, while those who can't get a handle on it begin to peak out at that point. The reason Sam didn't make that call is probably part of a complex web of factors that make up his relationship with the boss:

- I know one Sam who didn't make the call because if he'd failed to handle it well the boss would have bitten his head off at the neck. He knew the boss was going to be mad when he found out the call hadn't been made, but the chewing out he would get for not doing something was better than the danger of getting fired for actually doing something wrong.

- Another Sam didn't make the call because it was another task in the owner's push for rapid growth. Sam had a good thing going—a decent salary, a department he could handle without too much strain. But the owner's plan called for new systems, new personnel. He might have had to work much harder without getting a much greater salary. Perhaps he wouldn't be able to handle the new systems. Maybe one of the new people would be a hot-shot who would take his job away from him. Sam could handle a chewing out from an excitable owner better than he could handle the risks of new systems and a company reorganization. Besides, this kind of Sam can come up with a hundred rationalizations as to why he didn't call. "But boss, truck 32 broke down on Route 463. I had to get a back-up there or we'd have lost a whole day's deliveries." The fact is that Sam was following company policy. Technically he was correct, even if the priority, in this case, was the call. Many owners know all too well that discussing this with Sam only goes round and round, ending with, "Well boss, if you say so, I'll make the call next time." Only next time it will be something else that goes wrong.

- Sam was afraid to call because he didn't know how to handle the situation. Perhaps the owner would be surprised to know this, because Sam didn't seem nervous. Well . . . Sam didn't want to create that impression. After all, he's one of the key managers, and he wanted to appear in command of the situation. But when push came to shove, he put the unpleasant (to him) task off. Or perhaps Sam didn't know he was afraid. We've known for a long time that many of our motives are beneath our level of awareness. The owner didn't know Sam was afraid to make the call because Sam didn't know he was afraid.

- There are many, many other Sams. The fact is that Sam didn't call. There are many possibilities as to why not. Too often the entrepreneur will react with the complaint, "How can Sam be so dumb?" The truth is that Sam isn't so dumb. Something else is at work here.

No matter which Sam we're dealing with, the solution isn't to chew him out. Neither is it to suffer in frustration and anguish over Sam's faults. The solution is to recognize that Sam's failure to make that call is an indication of something. The way to find out what that is is to talk to Sam about it. Not in a seize-the-bull-by-the-horns, "Why the @#$!&* didn't you make that call, Sam?" I'm suggesting, instead, a talk which allows you to listen to what Sam says. He'll eventually tell you. Not directly. But you've known Sam for several years. You know the situation. You'll hear what's going on if you discipline yourself to listen. I opened a Chinese fortune cookie once and read, "If you talk, you repeat what you already know. If you listen, you learn." That was a pretty good cookie.

STAGE IV: BIG-TIME MANAGEMENT

When a business has grown beyond $3 million in sales, it is becoming a big operation. Inventories can exceed $750,000; receivables may exceed $450,000; there may be $500,000 in fixed assets; there are fifty to seventy-five employees. The bank line may exceed $500,000. The organization has probably changed two or three times. Now the owner has a staff of division managers rather than department heads. There is a controller rather than an accounting manager. Each worry has become a function. It's financing, rather than getting a bank loan. It's marketing, rather than getting the next sales buck. It's manufacturing, rather than the production shop. Management is still management, no matter what you call it, but size necessitates formalizing some procedures if operations are to continue on an efficient basis as the quantity of everything increases: people, assets, dollars.

Organization

The owner must keep an eye on some crucial areas if the rate of growth from $3 million on is to keep up and if operations are to be maintained at the same rate of profitability. The first area is the way the company is organized. A long-standing management concept links a company's strategy to its structure. Once the owner has established the strategy to achieve short-term and long-term growth, attention needs to be turned to the company's structure, because the way the company is organized can either facilitate the implementation of the owner's strategy or it can hamper it.

Jack Sheridan experienced this problem immediately after he tangled with his high-profit/tax-problem year. He had maintained a one-man control concept for many years, with the result that he had reporting to him a marketing manager, an accounting manager, a purchasing agent, three project managers, an assembly manager, a quality assurance manager, the graphics department manager, and the warehouse manager. By the time the company had reached $3 million, he had become a major log jam. There was a steady stream of managers in and out of his office, and he was constantly behind on several management tasks. His strategy was to maintain a controlled growth, with emphasis on financial control, quality control, and timely deliveries, to ensure the highest customer satisfaction and a high return on the stockholders' investment.

Jack's balance of control was thrown off because the company was growing faster than he had anticipated. The organization had gotten too big for one-man control. Schedules were not met, financial problems had developed, and quality assurance was becoming extremely difficult to execute. Jack was forced to reorganize around some key functions. He hired an experienced controller to assume all financial duties, including the purchasing functions. He hired a top operations manager, who took responsibility for the three project managers, the assembly manager, the graphics manager, and the warehouse. Now Jack could focus his efforts on working with a controller, a marketing manager, and an operations manager, instead of ten individual managers besieging him with a dizzying array of detailed problems. Jack's moves created the time and focus he needed to orchestrate operations within the guidelines of his corporate strategy, which he could redesign as growth continued.

Management Controls

A second area is management controls. As a business evolves to a larger and larger size, the owner is forced to become less involved in day-to-day activities. At the same time it becomes increasingly difficult to measure the progress of the corporation. A management control system, properly executed, is a blend of psychology and analysis. When the owner is actively involved in daily activity, his or her priorities are no mystery to the employees. They can see what the owner is paying attention to for themselves. But when the owner becomes distanced from daily operations and other managers take part in the communications of instructions and guidelines, the priorities can become ambiguous and the situation confusing.

In these circumstances people dig in to do the best they can, according to their personalities, aptitudes, and personal goals. Rare are the individuals who, on their own, can assess the owner's goals, translate them to the terms of their immediate function in the organization, draw up a plan of action, and implement it effectively. (If they have this ability, they are likely to own their own business or be on their way to achieving that goal.) The usual result is a group of employees who think they are doing the right thing, on the one hand, and a frustrated owner who asks, "What's wrong with the communication around here?" on the other.

During this entire process, the owner is communicating like mad. Managers are chewed out, met with, instructed. Memos are sent out from the owner's office to specify the guidelines and make instructions perfectly clear. Yet the right things still don't get done at the right time and with the right emphasis.

Quincy Thomas's solution

Quincy Thomas had just this problem. He used to send out memos made up of a few clear sentences describing exactly what was to be done. "They ought to understand plain English," he once said to me. He shook his head ruefully. "But they don't! Things still don't get done right."

Quincy struggled with the problem for several years, along with high blood pressure and constant frustration. He had a growing company with several operating divisions, but both the rate of growth and the rate of profits were well below the goals he set each year. He saw how the countless transactions done improperly each day added up to an overall level of inefficiency, but the company had become too large for him to step in and get it straightened out himself. He had to get it done through his division managers, and that was the rub. No matter how hard he came down on them, it was of no avail. The company sputtered along, as if he hadn't spoken at all. Yes, something he'd get mad about wouldn't be repeated, but as soon as that problem was straightened out, something else just as bad would come up.

"You'd think people would learn that if one thing is wrong, then other things like it would be wrong, too. But, no, they don't take a lesson from a 'for instance.' You have to get after them one problem at a time . . . they don't draw any conclusions." Quincy threw up his hands. "I can't keep after everybody about every little thing around here. The place is too damn big!"

The breakthrough in Quincy's company came when we were able to reorganize his accounting to set up each division as a profit center. Each division manager became financially responsible for his or her division, to include the revenues, direct costs/gross profit, division sales and marketing, and division administration. The division net profit became a clear measure of the overall performance under that manager's supervision.

To achieve this management focus, Quincy had to divulge financial information he had previously kept to himself. He realized that giving the division managers a complete picture of the financial performance of their division would greatly expand their understanding of priorities, in a way similar to his own. Instead of a constant battle over specific tasks and procedures, Quincy could now talk to the managers about sales versus the plan, gross profit versus the plan, expenses versus the budgets. A specific operating problem could be discussed within the context of the overall performance. Was the problem a significant threat to division performance? How could the problem be solved to enhance sales growth and profitability?

The system was set up with great care. Division managers were given responsibility only for those revenues and expenses over which they had some reasonable influence. Expenses incurred on behalf of other divisions were charged back to those divisions, while revenues received due to the efforts of another division were credited to that division. The managers were actively involved with the process, with the result that the system got under way with a spirit of fair play and with a good understanding of how it would work.

There were several immediate benefits. Communications between Quincy and his managers improved greatly. Discussions were focused more on the specifics of how to reach division goals than on wrangling about whether task A or B was done correctly or not. The tension between Quincy and his managers was reduced. The first year of the program, the company made a modest profit, but it was clear that the profit was achieved because of the management control system. Without it, Quincy might have taken a loss. In the second year of the program, the company experienced its greatest performance in sales growth and profitability.

A management control program is really a system which takes the place of the owner's presence on a day-to-day basis. If divisions are reporting results according to a certain format, then the managers will see many priorities in terms of the format if the system is set up properly. In Quincy's case, the system worked because both he and the managers were involved in setting it up. There was agreement on the priorities, on methods of measuring results, and on the levels of planned performance. Results were gathered quickly and accurately, so monthly evaluations of progress could be made by Quincy and his managers.

Management Development

The third area is management development. In many companies, the managers have been with the owner for years. The controller may have been the head bookkeeper; the sales manager may have been in customer service; the operations manager may have started as shop foreman. Each of them has grown tremendously since those years. An outsider wouldn't see the bookkeeper or shop foreman in them.

But the owner is dissatisfied with their performance. If the company is to grow, these managers must grow in their job performance. That's not happening. They're not showing initiative. They are not seeing opportunities. They are not reaching out for improvement in themselves or in their personnel. They don't show good basic organization, sensible use of time, and they are not demonstrating good leadership with their staffs. How does the owner change this?

The heart of the problem is that the managers have never had these kinds of responsibilities before. The old bookkeeper didn't have to do cash-flow plans or manage interdivisional budget systems. The customer service manager didn't have to manage a nationwide network of fourteen manufacturer's reps. The shop foreman had never managed four departments producing $3.5 million in sales. To be frank, the owner had never directed a business of this diversity, size, and scope either.

Nobody knows exactly what to do. If you don't know what to do, the safest bet is to keep going with what has worked for you in the past. The result is lost initiatives, lost opportunities, disorganization. No matter how mad the boss gets, people often find present discomfort preferable to the risk of the unknown if changes are made. The inner voice says, "Yeah, it's uncomfortable now, but at least I know what it's like. Maybe the change will bring something worse."

To get movement away from this kind of stagnation toward change is a true test of an owner's ability to grow, because the change has to begin at the top. The owner must be able to work with the managers in the following areas:

- HOW TO: Whether a manager seems self-confident or not, a job which is evolving from day to day requires some guidance in the tools and techniques that will work best at the new level of activity. As a foreman, the operations manager went out on the floor to get a problem solved; now he has to work through a production manager. That means meetings, in which the communications can go both ways. Many times the operations manager may get further listening than telling. The owner is the primary source of this guidance, but there are also seminars, books, and, possibly, consultants with a special expertise, such as inventory control, computers, and financial planning.

- TOOLS: The owner needs to provide the tools for the job—not only equipment and facilities, but people, changes in organization, and effective systems, such as Quincy's management control program. The owner must be alert to these needs to ensure that the managers get the right support at the right time, all within sound budgetary constraints.

- DIALOGUE: When you learn how to drive, you first weave from side to side. This weaving teaches you how to adjust your movements of the steering wheel, under the guidance of a knowledgeable instructor, to cut down the unnecessary movements until you can keep the car on the right side of the road and off the shoulder. In a much more complicated environment, the owner's dialogue with the managers accomplishes much the same purpose. Constructive criticism, which acknowledges good performance while pointing out areas which need improvement, can take place within a set of guidelines for performance which have been agreed on beforehand. A book could be written on how to do this, but a good dialogue comes from practical experience in dealing with people and a willingness to keep at it. Nobody ever said Quincy was particularly good at dealing with people, but once he had a good management control system that his managers could work with, his ability to enage them in constructive discussions greatly improved. It took years, but he finally succeeded.

HOW TO DETECT THE NEED FOR CHANGE

The indications that a business has grown into a new stage of operations can be detected by common sense. The trick is to recognize that some of the feelings about how things are going are really symptoms of the need for a new management approach. If the owner can get free from reactions that something is good or bad or that such-and-such is somebody's fault, he or she will be more able to analyze what is happening. The company is the way it is. Getting angry at managers because they do the wrong thing may be justifiable, but it may not be very helpful. The more effective method is to study what is happening for the purpose of identifying what kind of management problems there are. Given the stage of growth, what should the owner do to engage the problem, whether it be an ineffective manager, a breakdown in communication, or a chronic loss division?

Some of the common-sense indicators of these types of problems are as follows:

- SIGNS OF BREAKDOWN IN EFFICIENCY: Schedules are not being met. There are increases in quality assurance problems. There are an increasing number of financial problems—cash flow, profitability, collections, payables, etc. There is an increasing amount of trouble in getting good reports on how the business is doing. There are problems in executing marketing and sales problems the way they are planned.
- OWNER'S FRUSTRATION AND DISTRESS: The owner is dissatisfied, frustrated, and depressed about the business, without being able to pinpoint why. There is a growing gap between what has been planned to happen and what actually happens. There is an increasing number of management tasks which either the owner isn't getting done or the managers aren't getting done.
- MANAGER'S FRUSTRATION AND DISTRESS: A key danger sign is the loss of one or more critical managers by resignation. There can also be an increasing amount of interdepartmental bicker-

ing and a breakdown in cooperation among departments or divisions. Managers and employees can be walking around with long faces.

- COMMUNICATION BREAKDOWNS: There is confusion about company priorities. Much of what the owner says to managers seems to be misunderstood. There is insufficient discussion among managers about coordination. Many of the managers have little understanding of the financial results of their operations. Problems in communication are usually an indication of a management problem, not the root cause of the problem itself.

One of the greatest difficulties for the owners of rapidly growing companies is that they don't have the same sense of what to do about people as they do for the other aspects of their business. There may be a superb computer system, sound financial controls, an ingenious marketing strategy, but the means of supervising and motivating the employees may be very crude. The owner needs to step back from his or her sense of what is right about dealing with people to take a look at it from a different perspective. Things don't make success, people do. How can they be motivated? How does the owner work with a manager to help him or her become more effective? If something goes wrong chronically, what needs to be done to solve the problem? After months and years of throwing money at it, beating somebody on the head about it, isn't it time to take a different look at how to work and communicate with people? Those entrepreneurs who come to terms with these weaknesses in their management skills may not become expert psychologists, but they do change some habits which had been holding the company back from the growth they had so craved.

HOW TO GET GENERAL MANAGEMENT WITHOUT A GENERAL MANAGER

Explosive-Growth Phil

Phil guided his company from annual sales of $1.5 million to $16 million in just three years. The period was a constant mobilization of personnel, facilities, equipment, administrative systems, and financing. During the fourth year, Phil was totally exasperated about management. "I spend every day in meetings, reading reports and putting out fires! There's no time to plan for the future and get new business."

Every decision depended on Phil, but he couldn't attend to the issues fast enough. He became a log jam. Morale was suffering. Managers grumbled that forwarding a decision to Phil was like filing it away for a month. Phil wanted to keep growing, but new sales contracts were coming slowly.

"I need a general manager," he said. "But none of my managers seems qualified for the job. Yet I'm afraid to bring in an outsider for fear he won't work out."

The Perils of a General Manager

Phil's need for a general manager was real. So were his anxieties about the perils of appointing a general manager. If someone failed at that job, operations would be damaged severely. If the GM was only mediocre, the quality of operations would grind down to the lowest common denominator. Phil was between the rock and the hard place, because operations were already suffering under the status quo. The situation could only get worse.

If Phil appointed his best manager to the job out of desperation, a double penalty might be incurred. When your best manager fails at the general manager job, not only do you have operating problems to deal with, but you've probably ruined your best manager in the process. A respected manager has become a failure on the job. His self-esteem has been damaged; you probably have had some serious conflicts with him; and the other managers have lost confidence in his abilities. Moving him back to his old job is a demotion. He will probably resign, if you don't ask him to go, leaving you without your general manager and with one capable manager now gone forever.

Bringing in an outsider is equally hazardous. I have witnessed many, many situations where an outsider has made hash out of operations in a few months. It is very difficult to judge a person's abilities to be effective at this level of management from an interview or the study of a resume. As a small growing company, you probably can't afford to hire someone with a proven track record of excellence at general management, and some of them don't work out in a new company.

An outsider will face all of the jealousy and resentment of your in-house managers and staff, from day one. I have seen general managers fail because they were sabotaged by the resident management team. One owner tried three general managers before he gave up. Each one had serious weaknesses that the owner didn't detect, but the ultimate defeat was at the hands of the management team.

A group of competent managers can withhold support from a new GM in practically invisible ways. Yet the result is devastating. It takes an unusually competent, experienced senior manager to come in from the outside and pull the management team together, streamline operations, get along with you, and deal with growth all at the same time.

Evolve a Solution

A fixed, rigid solution (see Figure 13-2) to create general management in a rapidly growing company is asking for trouble. The situation is too explosive. Management is in the process of evolving from one stage to the next . . . it's a moving target. You can't keep an iron hand on every aspect of operations because the growth will bury you, as it did Phil. Either that, or the growth will slow to a trickle. Designating your best manager for the job can ruin both him or her and the operations at the same time. The results of hiring an outsider to be general manager of a small business are frequently dismal.

Figure 13-2 shows an alternative that I have seen work in several companies. Phil's company is a good example. I encouraged him not to try for the ultimate solution. Instead we assembled the key managers into a management group that met regularly to discuss management problems. The purpose was *not* to review schedules, agendas, and daily details. The purpose *was* to identify problems that existed between the operating divisions and to devise recommended solutions to those problems for Phil's approval. It was not to create management by committee but to create a forum where managers could voice their views of what needed to be done to operate more efficiently.

"If each of you does a 100 percent job of managing your division," we said, "the job will be only half done. Efficiency comes from catching problems that exist between the divisions and working out solutions to them. That's what develops a smooth operation throughout the company and prepares for the next stage of growth." Phil went on to say that he was assigning the management group with custody of day-to-day operations for the purpose of identifying the needs for action and recommending the initiatives (systems, pro-

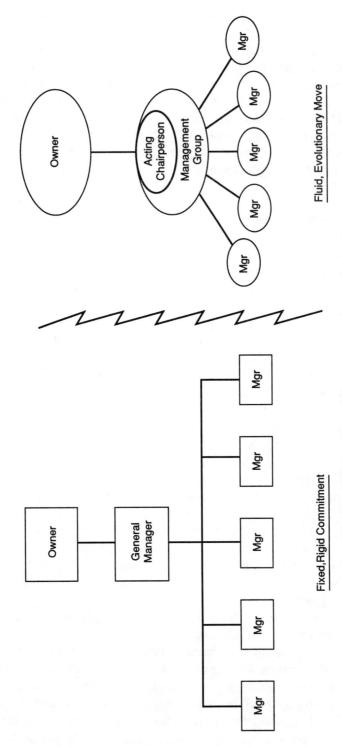

Fluid, Evolutionary Move

Fixed, Rigid Commitment

Figure 13-2 Approaches to general management.

cedures, communication requirements . . . the whole ball of wax) that would improve team work and cooperation between the divisions.

One of the managers was to act as chairperson of the group, responsible for the agenda, conducting the meetings, making sure that notes of each meeting were distributed, following up on action items, and reporting to Phil. The chairperson position rotated among all of the managers.

Phil was *not* to be chairperson. He could attend any meeting as he wished, but he was to act as consultant, not to dominate the meeting. When owners conduct or dominate a meeting, they only hear what they have to say. But for general management, it's what the managers are thinking that is most important. You only hear what they're thinking when your mouth is shut and they're talking.

Twofold Objectives

Establishing the management group pursues two objectives simultaneously:

* The group format introduces general management to the management team, including you. It focuses everyone's attention on problems between the divisions that are the obstacles to meeting corporate goals and creating overall efficiency.
* The rotating chairperson exposes each manager to the task of guiding the management group to get at the real issues and to come up with practical initiatives for improving the company's performance. Hopefully the person who can become the general manager will emerge to take the job.

After some struggle, some false starts, and some disappointment, Phil's management group began to show results. Two key managers were clearly uncooperative and unable to deliver results at the same level as the rest. They resigned from the company to be replaced by more effective people. The group produced some meaningful initiatives to solve some old problems. Operations began to go more smoothly, and Phil was able to plan the use of his time more effectively.

Furthermore, a very effective manager emerged during the meetings. After his turn as acting chairperson, Phil extended his chairpersonship indefinitely. He continued to be effective. Subsequently he was appointed to be general manager on a full-time basis, which was actively supported by the other managers.

Stay Involved

The success of the management group is strongly influenced by the owner. He or she must stay involved in the process, but in the right way. The group can drift aimlessly if it has no sense of direction from the boss. What are the key problem areas they should discuss at the outset? You can give them some critical issues to provide them with an initial focus.

What kind of product should they prepare for the owner? You should require them to present a definition of the problem, a summary of their analysis and a completely worked out solution as their recommendation for action. You should be able to approve or disapprove their plans based on what they present to you. You may have to kick it back to them for more work.

Don't procrastinate. Don't duck the decisions. If you do, then the management group will become ineffective. Managers lose interest when they think no action will ever come from the boss. By the same token, don't turn down every recommendation because it isn't exactly how you'd do it. If you always say no, the group's output will degenerate into oatmeal, because "the boss is going to do it his or her way, and why should we bother?"

Maintain Your Flexibility

Creating general management is a crucial stage of management growth. To keep growing you must obtain effective coordination of operations without having to be the coordinator yourself. Rather than rolling dice on a fixed, rigid decision—either appointing your best manager for the job or bringing in an outsider—consider trying an evolutionary approach. Set up the management group to begin delegating the general management process to your management team.

In the process, your aim would be to develop a general manager from your management team, but one step at a time: from rotating group chairperson to acting chairperson on an indefinite basis to general manager. Any manager who doesn't work out in steps one or two can step down from the group chairpersonship without prejudice. You never committed yourself to a permanent solution. He or she took the assignment on a temporary basis, just like all the other managers.

If you're not pleased with the group format, you can discontinue it to try another approach without major disruption. At no time was the process a rigid commitment. Rather, it was an experiment, a test, something that could be continued or discontinued at your discretion based on the results. You maintained maximum flexibility for deciding your course of action.

SUMMARY

Businesses go through stages of growth. Each stage requires the development of a new management approach, involving the owner's management style, the organization structure of the company, the development of managers, the development of management reporting and control systems, and the development of tools and techniques for an effective dialogue between the owner and the managers. The movement from one stage to another evolves, rather than happening in concrete chunks. Some companies grow so fast they go through more than one stage in a single year. Other companies take years to get from one stage to the next.

The owner's job is to be alert to the common-sense indicators that the company has grown into a stage requiring alterations in management. The process of adapting to new methods starts at the top. If the owner can't develop new techniques and approaches, it is unlikely that the management team will. In fact, usually the management team mirrors the owner's own problems in coming to terms with the new requirements. Owners who can make the changes will take their companies to further stages of growth, while owners who cannot make the transition tend to find their companies stuck at the growth stage where they, themselves, have peaked as managers.

The techniques for dealing with the need for management change are not mysterious. Owners can sense when the time has come for change by perceiving their own distress and frustration as a symptom or indicator that a business problem is at hand. Once the problem has been identified, what are the most practical ways of dealing with it, given the company's current stage of growth and the rate at which it is growing toward the next stage? Figure 13-1 is a rough guide to these stages and to the general requirements which will have to be met if the company is to operate successfully at each new level of activity.

Index